A Community in Conflict

FRANKFURT SOCIETY IN THE SEVENTEENTH AND EARLY EIGHTEENTH CENTURIES

FRANCOFURTI AD MOENUM, URBIS IMPERIALIS, ELECTIONI ROM:REGUM ATQ, IMPERATO

M O E N U

M O E N U

GERALD LYMAN SOLIDAY

A Community in Conflict

FRANKFURT SOCIETY IN
THE SEVENTEENTH AND EARLY
EIGHTEENTH CENTURIES

Published for
Brandeis University Press
by
The University Press of New England
Hanover, New Hampshire
1974

The University Press of New England

Frontispiece:
Frankfurt in the Seventeenth Century,
an engraving by
Matthäus Merian the Elder published in 1682.
(Courtesy of the Frankfurt Historical Museum)

For my mother and father

Preface

Of the various approaches to the study of early modern European societies, I have chosen to analyze the role of corporate social groups in the
public life of Frankfurt am Main, one of Europe's chief commercial centers in the seventeenth and eighteenth centuries. Several factors conditioned the choice. Local scholars had already traced the broad outlines
of Frankfurt's political, administrative, and economic development in
the period. Moreover, the city archive suffered heavy losses during
World War Two, and the destruction of one of Europe's finest series of
tax registers precluded a structural analysis of the society based on its
levels of wealth. Yet a twenty-six-year conflict between the citizens and
their aristocratic magistracy during the early eighteenth century offered
a good opportunity to integrate the city's social and constitutional history, if the researcher were willing to fit fragmentary and sometimes
scattered evidence together. What remained feasible was precisely what
interested me most. I decided to use Frankfurt's constitutional conflict
to examine the social structure of the community and, in particular, to
gauge the effects of internal division on the city's traditional social
organization.

Other approaches to the study of Frankfurt society could be equally
valid and useful. For an investigation of family life and individual occupational and social mobility in Frankfurt, I plan in the future to use
the remarkably informative parish records kept by the city government.
Such a project has not been undertaken for a city of Frankfurt's size,
and it is possible there only because, for purposes of vital registration,
the community was considered a single parish. Should the research succeed as I hope, its emphasis on mobility and on individuals and families
would complement the present book. I stress the word "complement,"
for the two approaches do not work at cross purposes. The social experience of individuals and families cannot be understood outside of
its institutional context, which in Frankfurt was a corporative social
structure.

The monograph is based on a thesis written originally for Professor
Franklin Ford at Harvard University. A Kennedy Traveling Fellowship
from Harvard and a stipend from the German Academic Exchange
Service (DAAD) enabled me to undertake most of the necessary archival
research in 1966–1967. The following year a Killam Memorial Fellowship at Dalhousie University gave me free time for writing as well as
funds for microfilming previously unused sources. In the summer of
1969 a grant-in-aid from the American Council of Learned Societies and

supplementary funds from Brandeis University allowed me to return
for additional work in the Frankfurt City Archive. I am most grateful to
all these institutions for the financial support which enabled me to undertake the project. I am also indebted, of course, to the libraries and
archives which gave me access to their holdings: the Widener Library
at Harvard, the Frankfurt City and University Library, the Bavarian
State Archive in Würzburg, the Haus- Hof- und Staatsarchiv in Vienna,
and, above all, the Frankfurt City Archive. Dr. Dietrich Andernacht
and his entire staff in the Stadtarchiv have shown me such professional
helpfulness and personal friendliness that my work with them has always been both productive and enjoyable. Many colleagues and friends
have read and commented on parts or all of the book at various stages
of its preparation. Although I cannot mention each one here, I can re-
peat my sincerest thanks to them all. A few have placed me so deeply in
their debt, however, that I wish to acknowledge in print the valuable
suggestions of Rudolph Binion, William H. Beik, Allan Kulikoff, Nancy
Roelker, and Mack Walker. While I bear full responsibility for the
book, I am also keenly aware of the contributions others inevitably make
to any scholarly enterprise. As the book now goes to press, I recall with
pleasure and gratitude several experiences important for its inception
and completion: Professor Ford's seminar on seventeenth-century cities,
which awakened my interest in local history; a most pleasant year in the
Frankfurt archive and my subsequent contacts there through Dr. Joachim Fischer; the generous hospitality of the department of history at
Dalhousie University; and the intellectual stimulation and personal
encouragement provided by my colleagues and our students at Brandeis.
As is only right, the last is really first. My wife, Donna, helped with many
of the burdensome tasks in the archive and at the typewriter, but her
main contribution, like that of our daughters, Elizabeth and Karin,
has been her unfailing patience and good cheer.

Marburg/Lahn   G.L.S.
August 1973

Contents

Illustrations

Charts and Tables

Abbreviations

AFGK	*Archiv für Frankfurts Geschichte und Kunst*
Bgb	Bürgerbuch: the register of citizens
Bgmb	Bürgermeisterbuch: the council's own (manuscript) collection of its decisions
CLF	Corpus Legum Francofurtensium: a collection of original printed ordinances in the Frankfurt City Archive
Dietz, *FftHG*	Alexander Dietz, *Frankfurter Handelsgeschichte*
FftRH	*Franckfurtische Religions-Handlungen*
HHSA Wien	Haus-, Hof- und Staatsarchiv in Vienna
RHR	Reichshofrat
Trb	Traubuch: a marriage register
Ugb	Untergewölbe: a class of manuscripts in the Frankfurt City Archive
VSWG	*Vierteljahrschrift für Sozial- und Wirtschaftsgeschichte*
ZRG GA	*Zeitschrift der Savigny Stiftung für Rechtsgeschichte: Germanistische Abteilung*

COINAGE

1 Gulden (fl.) : 24 Schillinge (Sch.)
1 Gulden (fl.) : 60 Kreuzer (kr. or xr.)
1 Reichstaler (Rtlr.) : 1½ Gulden (fl.)

NOTE: Documents without indication of archive are from the Frankfurt City Archive. The original (often inconsistent) orthography in documents has not been changed to modern spelling.

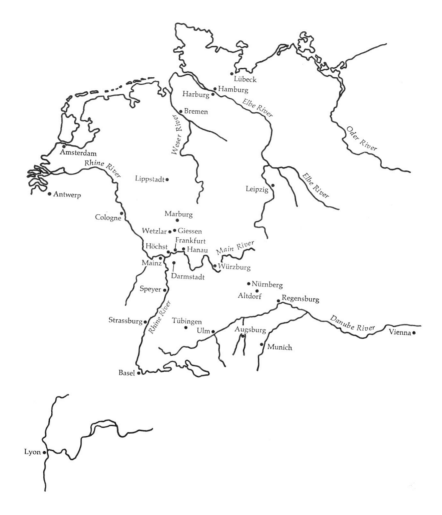

Central European Cities Mentioned in the Text.

Introduction

... a place of good Trade
and well seated for it.
Edward Brown (1677)

Die Handlung ist die Seele der Stadt
Frankfurt; sie allein hält sie empor
und giebt ihr einen Rang unter den
vornehmsten Städten der Welt ...
Johann Moritz (1786)

In 1706 the proudest chronicler of Frankfurt's history, the patrician
scholar Achilles Augustus Lersner, described his home as a "widely cele-
brated free imperial, electoral, and commercial city."[1] The learned
aristocrat emphasized both the political and economic significance of his
native land. Frankfurt's special status as an imperial city (subject to the
emperor himself and to no other German prince) and as the site of the
Kaiser's election and coronation was the source of great local pride. For
most informed and traveled Europeans, however, Frankfurt's reputation
rested on its importance as a center of international trade and finance.
This view was summed up in the dictum repeated in almost every con-
temporary description of the city: "the soul of Frankfurt is commerce."

Its geographic location on major water and land routes prepared
Frankfurt for this role as a center for European-wide trade. The city is
situated on the Main River, the principal east-west waterway draining
the streams of central and southern Germany into the Rhine. During
most of the medieval period, shipping on the two rivers was safer and
easier than overland transport. But this situation changed between the
mid-fourteenth and mid-sixteenth centuries, as tolls on the Rhine became heavier and heavier and as protection from robbery on land routes
improved.[2] Frankfurt's real advantage over Mainz, the city which com-
manded shipping between the Main and the Rhine, was its location
some twenty miles eastward—directly on the north-south land routes
which largely avoided the highlands on both sides of the Rhine north

1. Achilles Augustus Lersner, *Der weit-berühmten freyen reichs- wahl- und
handels-stadt Franckfurt am Mayn Chronica, oder Ordentliche Beschreibung der
Stadt Franckfurt* 2v (Frankfurt, 1706–1734).

2. An interesting discussion of trade routes and transportation appears in Alexander
Dietz, *Frankfurter Handelsgeschichte* (Frankfurt, 1910–1925), III, 287–360, esp. 287–
292. I shall cite this standard work as Dietz, *FftHG*.

of the archepiscopal city. Frankfurt was thus in the extremely fortunate position of having access to the two rivers and being at the same time the city where the major east-west and north-south roads of Central Europe converged. Some twenty-six trade routes linked early modern Frankfurt with most of the principal commercial cities of continental Europe.[3]

In Lersner's own lifetime the city experienced its third and most impressive period of commercial greatness. The first had begun in the early fourteenth century, when Frankfurt became more than the focus of a regional economy centered on the lower Main and middle Rhine valleys. With the decline of the Champagne fairs and the eastward shift of major trade routes, the city's two annual fairs gained European prominence by handling the business that came along the north-south axis between Italy and Flanders and from such eastern lands as Prussia, Poland, Austria, and Hungary. Italian silks, the draperies of Flanders and Brabant, as well as local Frankfurt and Hessian woolens and linens made the city one of the most important cloth centers of the fourteenth century. Decline had followed during the next century, however, as those cloths suffered stiff English competition and robber barons made the trade routes dangerous.[4] The city's impact on the general European economy was not strong again until the late sixteenth century. The fairs continued to attract merchants from widely scattered points, but Frankfurt was overshadowed in Central Europe by the industrial and commercial preeminence of Augsburg and Nürnberg until the Thirty Years War.

In the last years of the sixteenth century, Protestant refugees from the Spanish Netherlands laid the foundations for Frankfurt's seventeenth- and eighteenth-century commercial fame. The immigrants, especially those from Antwerp, invigorated both industry and commerce and gave Frankfurt a second period of great prosperity from the 1580's until about 1630.[5] The newcomers' industrial innovations left no lasting mark on the city's handicrafts, but their commercial connections in the Netherlands were vital to Frankfurt's future position in European trade and finance. As the center of world trade shifted from Antwerp to Amsterdam, Frankfurt became an integral part of that city's commercial network—a "little Amsterdam" in southern Germany. At the same time, it attained importance as a financial center. Here not only the Netherlanders but also the growing Jewish community within the city played

3. Ibid., 316–332.

4. Probably the most convenient short summary of Frankfurt's role in the European economy of the fourteenth century is that by C. Verlinden in *The Cambridge Economic History of Europe*, III (Cambridge, 1963), 142–143.

5. On the city's economy during the sixteenth, seventeenth, and early eighteenth centuries, I rely throughout on Dietz, *FftHG*, esp. II and IV, i.

a significant role. Jews expelled from Nürnberg, Ulm, Augsburg, Mainz, and Cologne gathered in Frankfurt's ghetto, and their trading and moneylending activities soon extended throughout Central Europe.

During the Thirty Years War Frankfurt entered a period of depression, relative to its earlier prosperity or its future commercial importance in the late seventeenth century. Compared with most German areas, however, the city did fairly well in the three decades after 1630. It felt no effects of the war until the 1630's, when Swedish occupation brought pestilence, famine, and heavy financial exactions. The loss of population was not as high as in most cities, though, and the fairs did continue feebly throughout the worst years of the war. The city was fortunate enough to avoid much direct conflict or physical damage. At the beginning of the war, moreover, Frankfurt became an important recruitment and military outfitting center, and this business continued to be very profitable throughout the seventeenth century. Frankfurt also began toward the end of the war to market some of the French wares that were becoming fashionable everywhere.

The city thus fared better during the war and recovered more rapidly than other commercial centers in Germany. Strassburg and Cologne, even Augsburg and Nürnberg were left behind, while Frankfurt emerged as the commercial and financial leader in the western and southern parts of the Holy Roman Empire. Only Hamburg and Leipzig showed more impressive growth than Frankfurt over the seventeenth century. Hamburg became the major seaport for Central Europe, and Leipzig's fairs probably edged ahead of Frankfurt's at the beginning of the eighteenth century. Yet Frankfurt's fame and importance as a center of European trade were never greater than during the century after the 1670's.

In the last decades of the seventeenth century, then, Frankfurt entered the third great economic boom of its history. Once again the impulse for the city's commercial development came from outside: important merchants from the Swiss cities, the Palatinate, eastern France, Italy, and the Netherlands established themselves or family branches in the city. Their firms maintained and expanded Frankfurt's role as the major exchange center between Austria, Switzerland, the Lyonnais, and Burgundy to the south and Amsterdam, Hamburg, and Bremen in the north. The city's economic strength lay almost exclusively in facilitating the exchange of items produced elsewhere. Frankfurt became best known for its commission business, which handled the goods of foreign firms in the great fairs, and its banking interests, which made the city one of Europe's most important financial centers. The many trade routes that converged on the city brought enormous wealth and thousands of visitors to Frankfurt each spring and fall. The fairs were an economic windfall to all Frankfurters, but the wholesale merchants dominated them. Their sale of colonial products, precious gems and metals, wines, silks, English serges, and fashionable French cloths and clothing (at least until the embargoes on French goods during the wars against Louis XIV) reaped high profits. The old dictum that "commerce is the soul of Frankfurt" referred to their exchanges, and nothing symbolized their success or importance more clearly than the great trade fairs.

The inhabitants of the city itself—those left after the fairs were over— are the subject of this study. Seventeenth-century Frankfurt was a more complex community than its reputation as a city of commerce and high finance suggests. Although trade dominated the economy, merchants did not control the social and political organization of the city. The entrepreneurial attitudes usually associated with a free market like the fair did not pervade the economic thinking or activities of most Frankfurters. Although the importance of a social group cannot be measured by its numbers alone, we gain a necessary perspective from the fact that little more than 10 percent of the city's active population was engaged full time in commerce. And this commercial population was probably more one of retailers than of wholesalers with distant business connections. The majority of Frankfurt's burghers were organized in corporate handicraft associations. These artisans relied on careful regulation of industrial activity to guarantee themselves a minimum standard of living, and the degree to which their expectations corresponded to or clashed with the merchants' economic notions will be an important theme in this examination of Frankfurt society in the seventeenth and early eighteenth centuries. But we shall find the merchants themselves far from united on issues of public economic policy. Their divisions along religious lines and according to their legal status as full citizens or resident aliens suggests the complexity of a group usually defined only in terms of its economic interests.

The merchants of Frankfurt lived in a heterogeneous community. Since no major European city of the period sustained itself without heavy immigration, there was always an initial division between the native born and the newcomers. The admission of outsiders took different forms: some became regular citizens, and others were permitted to reside in the city under special conditions. The relations between Frankfurt burghers and the outsiders were not always harmonious, and, in fact, the late seventeenth and early eighteenth centuries witnessed increasingly sharp antagonisms between the two groups. The immigrants represented several nationalities—Germans, Netherlanders, Italians, and Frenchmen—but such cultural diversity presented fewer problems than religious differences.

Frankfurt was predominantly Lutheran, yet it housed a small number of Catholics and somewhat larger groups of Calvinists and Jews. The Jews were a group unto themselves; they lived in a ghetto and had no regular social contact with the Christian population. All indications are that most Frankfurters despised the Jewish religion and feared the Jews as economic competitors. As a source of special revenue, however, the Jewish community enjoyed the toleration and protection of both the emperor and the Frankfurt city council. According to a popular saying, the Catholics had the churches, the Calvinists had the money, and the Lutherans had power in Frankfurt. We know very little about the Roman Catholics in the city; the adage reflected the Lutherans' resentment that Charles V had forced them to surrender Frankfurt's largest churches to Catholicism, while they worshiped in smaller, more crowded sanctuaries. The Lutherans monopolized positions in the city government and usually excluded immigrant Catholics and Calvinists from full citizenship. A further discouragement of Reformed immigration was the prohibition of free public worship for Calvinists in Frankfurt. Informal arrangements for their services were sometimes tolerated, however, and business opportunities were so good that their numbers increased considerably over the early modern period. Many of the big merchants from Switzerland, France, and the Netherlands who made Frankfurt such an important commercial center in the seventeenth and eighteenth centuries were Calvinists. They were usually accepted in the city as denizens (resident aliens) with fewer privileges than burgher merchants, yet they made great fortunes that were the envy of their competitors. Their fight for citizenship and for public worship met with firm opposition from the Lutheran citizenry led by burgher merchants and the urban aristocracy.

Frankfurt's government was in the hands of an oligarchy which had little direct connection with commerce. Power was concentrated in the city council, which selected its own members from the local aristocracy. Numbered among the city's rulers were men from three groups: the Alt-Limpurg Society of patrician families which had withdrawn from commerce and lived as rentiers since the mid-sixteenth century; the Frauenstein Society, which combined in its ranks both wholesale merchants and some holders of doctors' degrees; and the Graduate Society, which included most of the lawyers and physicians with university degrees. During the seventeenth and early eighteenth centuries, the Limpurger and Frauensteiner—together never more than forty-five families, just under one percent of the city's population—enjoyed joint control of the council. They chose Graduates and some merchants from the body of "common" citizens to rule with them, but the educated and commercial elites both felt inadequately represented in city government. Because of their personal status as imperial nobles and their increasing power and prestige, the Graduates were not as alienated from their aristocratic colleagues as were the merchants. Only those few merchants who happened to be co-opted into the Frauenstein Society or directly into the council participated in decision-making for the entire community. In contrast to Hamburg or Bremen, where no patriciates had entrenched themselves and where the city councils and commercial people were closely allied, Frankfurt witnessed a growing alienation between the aristocrats who controlled city government and the burgher and denizen merchants on whose economic initiative the city's prosperity came to depend.[6]

Social, economic, religious, and political tensions among these different groups in Frankfurt intensified throughout the second half of the seventeenth century. Similar tensions had existed previously and had caused armed conflicts—insurrections which had few lasting effects on the political and social structure of the city. The antagonisms of the late seventeenth century, however, welded together an articulate party of citizens who successfully challenged the power of the city's aristocratic lodges in the first years of the eighteenth century. That party was strong enough to sustain a twenty-six-year legal battle against the aristocrats which greatly modified the city's conservative constitution. The result was a kind of equilibrium between the urban aristocracy and the leading elements of the citizenry—an equilibrium that was maintained until the end of the old Empire.[7]

Constitutional conflicts were not unusual in German imperial cities during the early modern period,[8] but the struggle between the magis-

6. This is not to say that Hamburg and Bremen experienced no quarrels between their city councils and merchants; in fact, both did. The point here is that the sharp cleavage between aristocrats and merchants so evident in Frankfurt was not found in the two northern cities, where even immigrant merchants seem to have enjoyed access to the seats of power. On Bremen, see Ruth Prange, *Die bremische Kaufmannschaft des 16. und 17. Jahrhunderts in sozialgeschichtlicher Betrachtung* (Bremen, 1963), 69, 112–114, 180. Helmut Böhme's *Frankfurt und Hamburg* (Frankfurt, 1968) deals briefly with early modern developments as a background for his comparisons of the two cities in the nineteenth century. Although his remarks on the earlier period are sometimes misinformed, his general interpretations are always stimulating; see 46–47 for his comments on the cleavage between the political and mercantile elites in Frankfurt and his assertion that no such division occurred in Hamburg.

7. Paul Darmstaedter, *Das Grossherzogtum Frankfurt* (Frankfurt, 1901), 18–19. Böhme denies that the result was a balance of forces, and I shall address myself to his position later.

8. Most of the disputes involved citizen opposition to heavy taxation or to a council's foreign policy; often they entailed charges of inept administration, corruption, nepotism, or misuse of judicial powers. The solutions to these conflicts were usually negotiated compromises, but increasingly in the seventeenth and early eighteenth centuries the emperor intervened to provide settlements. See Otto Brunner, "Souveränitätsproblem und Sozialstruktur in den deutschen Reichsstädten der früheren

tracy and the *Bürgerschaft* in Frankfurt was a particularly important one. The city's prominence as the official seat for the election of the emperor, the usual place of his coronation, a favorite site for political conferences, and a great commercial center meant that many outsiders took notice of events there. As an imperial city, Frankfurt was a direct vassal of the emperor and independent of any territorial prince. The degree of political freedom allowed the city or the corresponding extent of imperial control over the city's affairs was still an open question after 1648. Although the city council maintained a fairly autonomous position during much of the seventeenth century, the emperor intervened to assert his authority and to provide a settlement of internal conflicts in the early eighteenth century. This vigorous action showed that Frankfurt's peculiar relationship to the Kaiser was more than a constitutional formality, a lesson which imperial officials hoped would impress other cities as well. The clear connections between politics in Frankfurt and the general attempt by imperial reformers to extend the Kaiser's authority in the free cities figure prominently in my analysis, but I shall concentrate on the significant constitutional decisions that came out of the conflict, the economic and social problems they point to as important issues during the previous century, and especially the groups most interested in attaining particular solutions to each problem.

Frankfurt's constitutional conflict provides an excellent opportunity for a social historian to analyze group behavior, attitudes, and stratification in an important early modern community. A society experiencing strong tensions and then open strife usually reveals more of its structure than one enjoying relative calm. Its strains and antagonisms show how its constituent social groups related to one another. The struggle between the council and the citizenry gave almost every group in Frankfurt a chance to air its grievances, and the open discussion of economic, social, and political problems that had accumulated since the Thirty Years War offers rich material for an attempt to analyze each group's place in the community. Paul Hohenemser, an eminent Frankfurt librarian and a fine political historian, has already written a political and administrative account of the conflict.[9] But he did not explore the economic and social grievances which brought diverse groups into a common party of

Neuzeit," *Vierteljahrschrift für Sozial- und Wirtschaftsgeschichte* 50 (1963), 331–332; Hans Erich Feine, "Zur Verfassungsentwicklung des Heil. Röm. Reiches seit dem Westfälischen Frieden," *Zeitschrift der Savigny-Stiftung für Rechtsgeschichte: Germanistische Abteilung* (cited hereafter as *ZRG GA*) 32 (1932), 101–104, presents a list of some interventions and a discussion of their relationship to the general imperial reform movement at the end of the seventeenth century.

9. Paul Hohenemser, *Der Frankfurter Verfassungsstreit 1705–1732 und die kaiserlichen Kommissionen* (Frankfurt, 1920).

opposition to the council. The problems brought to light during the legal battle from 1705 to 1732 provide insight into the economic position, social status, and political goals of most groups residing in Frankfurt over the seventeenth and early eighteenth centuries. True, an important segment of the population had nothing to do with the fight against the council, and I have learned little about the laboring men outside handicraft corporations, the people on poor relief, or the floating population that worried the city government from time to time. But most residents formed groups active, to greater or lesser degrees, in the public controversy. They left behind them some record of their economic problems, their relationships with other groups, their expectations about city government, their notion of social order and rank, and their visions of the community in which they lived. From these collective self-portraits I have attempted to depict the structure of Frankfurt society.

This study of Frankfurt should serve, in turn, to elucidate more general problems of European social history. The particular task of local history is to put large analytical questions to controlled tests. By imposing spatial limitations on the data to be considered, we make large issues manageable topics of empirical research and give historical generalizations a degree of precision otherwise difficult to attain. A detailed analysis of group interaction in seventeenth-century Frankfurt can throw light on at least three general questions: what analytical categories are most appropriate to the study of social groups in the early modern period? What was the effect of conflict on corporate social organization? To what extent was this society changing toward more modern economic and social relationships?

The first issue concerns the language and concepts used to analyze social behavior in early modern Europe. The attention of historians has been drawn to the problem most recently by the debate between Boris Porchnev and Roland Mousnier over French popular uprisings in the first half of the seventeenth century.[10] Professor Mousnier's strong ob-

10. The controversy is most ably reviewed by J. H. M. Salmon, "Venality of Office and Popular Sedition in Seventeenth-Century France," *Past & Present* 37 (1969), 21–43; see also Daniel Ligou's review of the 1963 French edition of Porchnev's book in the *Revue d'histoire économique et sociale* 42 (1964), 378–385. Mousnier began with an attack on Porchnev in 1958 and has subsequently worked to refine his own views on social stratification; the most recent summary of his position has now appeared in English in *Peasant Uprisings in Seventeenth-Century France, Russia, and China* (New York, 1970), 3–31. In 1966 Professor Mousnier sponsored an international conference to consider different types of stratification (into castes, orders or status groups, and classes) as they applied to European social history, and the papers were collected in *Problèmes de stratification sociale: Actes du Colloque International (1966)*, ed. R. Mousnier (Paris, 1968).

jections to Porchnev's class analysis of the revolts in France have led him to emphasize contemporaneous social terms and noneconomic criteria for social stratification. The dispute has not only stimulated further research on specific uprisings but has encouraged a general reconsideration of the relative importance of economic and noneconomic factors in premodern social organization. Were early modern European societies stratified along class lines or according to less apparent, largely noneconomic criteria? How can we attempt for purposes of historical analysis to differentiate the motives of human behavior which are, in reality, always closely interrelated? For this purpose the categories suggested by Max Weber in his essay on "Class, Status, and Party" are still fruitful analytical tools.[11] The value of Weber's terminology lies in its clarity and flexibility; it allows for fairly precise distinctions among economic, social-psychological, and power-political aspects of group behavior. Social station in early modern Europe was generally determined less by economic position or "class" than by the traditional "status" that reflected "the estime, honor, or dignity attached by the society to social functions which have no particular connection with the production of material goods."[12] We must study the residents of Frankfurt in terms of the noneconomic status which dominated their own conceptions about their roles in the community and which, since group status was usually assigned in public legislation, also provided the legal termini for their economic and political action. But this perspective is not sufficient. The demographic and economic changes in Frankfurt from 1630 to 1740 conditioned the social possibilities open to the city's residents, and their class positions must also be examined as closely as the relatively sparse economic information will permit. Hence, though I agree with Professor Mousnier that the general principle of stratification in seventeenth-century European societies was status and not class, I want to stress the coexistence of the two kinds of gradation within individual social structures.[13] I shall examine the official social hierarchy defined in Frankfurt's police ordinances and show that a group's status was subject to change over the period of a century. But Weber's distinctions go further and encourage an examination of all groups in "multidimensional" terms,[14] and I shall try to gauge the relative importance of status and

11. Max Weber, "Class, Status, Party," *From Max Weber: Essays in Sociology*, tr. and ed. H. H. Gerth and C. Wright Mills (New York, 1946), 180–195.

12. Roland Mousnier, *Problèmes de stratification sociale: Deux cahiers de la noblesse pour les états généraux de 1649–1651* (Paris, 1965), 15.

13. Compare Stanislaw Ossowski, *Class Structure in the Social Consciousness* (New York, 1963), chapters 3 and 4, for a discussion of the interpenetration of different schemes of social gradation or ranking.

14. More recent and elaborate formulations of the "multidimensional approach" to the study of social stratification—most of which seem to derive from or be subsumed

class for each group in the city. Then we shall have a concrete basis for evaluating status considerations in a great European commercial center, where we might expect a group's class or market situation to be more significant.

The effect of conflict on the corporate community of Frankfurt citizens is an issue closely linked with the question of change and continuity in their society. How did economic or political changes bring conflict to the city, and to what extent did conflict act as an agent of change? Did the clash between the magistracy and its burgher opponents mean a sharp break in the communal traditions of Frankfurt? In a trenchant analysis published in 1963, Otto Brunner sketched the broad corporatist framework within which German urban communities were still organized and which continued to shape the burgher mentality in the early modern period.[15] Emphasis on tensions and conflicts in Frankfurt must not obscure a fundamental social fact—the persistence, despite internal cleavages, of this corporate or communitarian tradition in the imperial cities. How was such continuity possible in a period of rapid population growth, increasingly stiff economic competition, and open political and social strife? The answer can be found only in a close examination of the different kinds of conflict in Frankfurt. But the effects of conflict are also conditioned by the nature of the society in which they occur. Frankfurt's traditionally corporatist social structure gave internal conflicts particular directions which they might not have taken in another, less conservative setting. The complicated interaction between conflict and community tradition will thus become the most important theme of this study.

---

in the three basic categories used by Weber—are admirably summarized in Bernard Barber, "Social Stratification," *International Encyclopedia of the Social Sciences* (New York, 1968), XV, 288–295.

15. Brunner, "Souveränitätsproblem und Sozialstruktur," passim; while my focus is different from Brunner's, my debt to his insightful essay is great.

PART ONE

THE POLITY AND
THE SOCIETY

Es scheint also die Meynung dererjenigen
die beste zu seyn, die da behaupten, dass
die Regierungsform der Stadt Frankfurt
eine gemässigte Aristocratie, oder aus
Aristocratie und Democratie zusammengesetzt
sey.
Johann Moritz (1785)

Chapter 1

The Constitutional Conflict, 1705–1732

For almost twenty-seven years the burghers of Frankfurt and their city council were locked in the constitutional struggle that provides the framework for my analysis of Frankfurt society in the seventeenth and early eighteenth centuries. A brief survey of the conflict itself is necessary, therefore, as background to the examination of the city's residents which will follow in subsequent chapters. From the start we must realize that, despite the bitterness of the fight, the citizens never demanded an elimination of aristocratic power or any radical changes in Frankfurt's social structure. They were determined, though, to share power with the council and make city government responsive to the needs and wishes of the citizenry.

I. The Burgher Appeal for Imperial Intervention

On 25 October 1705 Count Friedrich Ernst von Solms und Tecklenburg, president of the *Reichskammergericht* and a close friend of Joseph I, came to Frankfurt to receive the city's oath of fealty on behalf of the new emperor, whose wartime responsibilities made it impossible for him to attend the ceremony personally. That same day several officers of the burgher militia obtained an audience with the count and secured his promise to take grievances to the emperor himself. Delighted with their initial success, the burgher officers decided to submit a formal request for confirmation of the city's privileges; in particular, the burgher leaders wanted the renewal and reinstitution both of the Citizens Agreement negotiated by an imperial commission between the council and its burghers in 1612/13 and of the *Stättigkeit* of 1616, the code of regulations for the Jewish community in Frankfurt.[1] This request aroused the immediate opposition of the city council for two reasons. First, the council, not the militia officers, represented the entire citizenry to its liege lord, and only the magistracy could request the customary renewal of Frankfurt's privileges from each new emperor. Besides resenting the encroachment on their prerogative, the council members objected to the militia officers' assertion that the Citizens Agreement of 1612/13 was the fundamental basis of the city's constitution. Although that Agreement has established important limitations on the council's power, the magistrates had ignored them and had exercised virtually unlimited authority over the inhabitants of the imperial city. By 1705, however, the council faced an opposition determined to seek the emperor's help in restoring basic checks on the aristocratic groups which had governed Frankfurt for nearly a century.[2]

To place the officers' move in historical perspective, we must look back at least to the events of the Fettmilch Uprising in the early seventeenth century. Frankfurt's patrician families organized in the Alt-Limpurg Society had successfully warded off challenges to their control of the city government during the fourteenth century and again in 1525, so that the city vied with Nürnberg for the distinction of having the most conservative constitution in the Empire. In the years 1612–1616, however, the patricians faced yet another serious attempt by their fellow citizens to share civic power. We cannot examine the details of the insurrection itself, but the major outlines of the struggle will indicate its significance for future events.[3] The burghers initially demanded the

1. Hohenemser, *Verfassungsstreit*, 2–6.
2. Ibid., 10, 15–16, 19.
3. The best accounts of the Fettmilch Uprising are those of Georg Ludwig Kriegk, *Geschichte von Frankfurt am Main in ausgewählten Darstellungen* (Frankfurt, 1871), 237–417, and B. J. Römer-Büchner, *Die Entwicklung der Stadtverfassung und die Bürgervereine der Stadt Frankfurt am Main* (Frankfurt, 1855), 104–120. On the social and economic background of the uprising, see Friedrich Bothe, "Zur wirtschaftlichen und sozialen Lage der Frankfurter Bevölkerung im 16. und zu Beginn des 17. Jahrhundert," in his *Beiträge zur Wirtschafts- und Sozialgeschichte der Reichsstadt Frankfurt* (Leipzig, 1906), 50–98. Bothe also published the most important documents of the period in *Frankfurts wirtschaftlich-soziale Entwicklung vor dem dreissigjährigen Kriege und der Fettmilchaufstand (1612–1616)* (Frankfurt, 1920), but the manuscript that was to have been his masterpiece—a thoroughgoing analysis of the period —was apparently lost in World War Two.

official publication of their privileges by the council, a limitation on the number of Jews permitted in the Frankfurt ghetto, and an end to Jewish usury. The threat of violence against the council by armed and angry citizens led to the appointment of an imperial commission which was to mediate a settlement between the two groups. By 24 December 1612 (new style 3 January 1613) the Citizens Agreement had been reached, and its seventy-one articles touched almost every aspect of public life.[4] Most important were the limitation on the number of patricians in the council (both a maximum limit of fourteen Limpurger and a guarantee against nepotism were included) and the establishment of two burgher committees to participate in governing the city. A Committee of Seven chosen from among the citizens was to see that burgher privileges were not violated by the magistracy, while a Committee of Nine was to oversee the city's finances. New blood was also infused into the council itself by the selection of eighteen burghers (all aristocrats, either university graduates or from the Frauenstein Society) to sit with the patricians, until the customary number of forty-three councilmen was restored and additional members could be co-opted according to the rules set up in the Agreement.[5]

These reforms did not satisfy a radical segment of the citizenry led by one Vincent Fettmilch, however, and the rebellion continued. Demanding suppression of Jewish userers and even tighter control over taxation and financial affairs, Fettmilch's group exerted increasing pressure on the council until the patricians resigned in May 1614. While moderates like the eighteen burghers who had been elected to the council hoped for an end to the movement, Fettmilch and his adherents continued to agitate for complete expulsion of the Jews. Finally, in August 1614, a group of artisans and their journeymen plundered the ghetto, and although Fettmilch did prevent wholesale butchery, he ordered the Jews to leave Frankfurt. But the uprising had gone too far: its radical leaders were placed under imperial ban, and Fettmilch himself was soon arrested by moderate burghers who feared armed intervention by the emperor. During the reaction which followed, the imperial commission not only restored the full council but also ordered the abolition of the guilds which had been the instruments of burgher political expression.[6] Although the Stättigkeit of 1616 regulated Jewish moneylending and retail activities to protect burghers, the Jews were returned to the ghetto under special imperial protection. The leaders of the uprising were ceremoni-

4. The best copy of the Citizens Agreement (*Bürgervertrag*) appears in Bothe, *Entwicklung vor dem 30jK*, 492–511.
5. On the council reforms, see below, 99–100.
6. See the Transfix appended to the Citizens Agreement in 1616 printed in Bothe, *Entwicklung vor dem 30jK*, 674–679.

ously hanged in 1616, and the aristocrats in the city council simply ignored the limitations on their power which had been instituted in 1612/13. The burgher committees were abolished, and the council ruled Frankfurt as it pleased during the rest of the century.

Although the constitutional conflict of the early eighteenth century was comparable to the Fettmilch Uprising in several respects, the differences between the two burgher movements were more important than the similarities. The aims of the two movements were so close that the militia officers could look to the constitutional documents of the early seventeenth century as their own models; in fact, like most early modern "revolutionaries," the burgher militiamen saw their task as restorative. If the old, fundamental laws of 1612/13 and the regulations on the Jewish community were enforced, the council's arbitrary rule would end and burghers would be protected from illegal Jewish competition. While the general goals of the two burgher movements seem to have been precisely the same, the intervening century had changed the substantive problems that troubled Frankfurt's citizens. A fight against the Jews, for example, figured prominently in each situation, but economic changes during the seventeenth century meant that a struggle against Jewish retailing superseded the older one against their moneylending. There were, however, more obvious and important differences between the two opposition movements. The early eighteenth-century conflict succeeded where the Fettmilch Uprising had failed to obtain permanent bodies to give nonaristocratic elements of the citizenry a voice in city government. That success may be attributed to at least three basic factors, each of which marked a departure from the earlier opposition movement. First, the character of burgher leadership (which I shall analyze in Chapter 5) changed significantly, so that the most memorable names associated with the constitutional conflict were those of wholesale merchants like Notebohm and Hoppe, not of artisans like Fettmilch, Gerngross, or Schopp. The burgher officer corps provided exceptionally intelligent leadership, and its strategy of fighting the aristocratic council in legal battle rather than in another insurrection showed how much burgher leaders had learned from Fettmilch's unhappy experience.[7] A final difference between Fettmilch's movement and that of the early eighteenth century lay in their respective relationships to imperial authority. Although a special imperial commission acted as mediator in 1612/13, imperial authorities then had to halt the radical developments of 1613 and 1614. While the emperor became the enemy of burgher

7. Cf. Römer-Büchner, Stadtverfassung, 130. A burgher pamphlet entitled Historische Nachrichten . . . (n.p., 1715) emphasized the peaceful approach of the militia leaders and refuted the council's argument that its citizenry was "ein von uralten Zeiten her zur Rebellion geneigtes Volk."

efforts under Fettmilch, the officer corps was to find imperial support the decisive factor in its victory over the council in the constitutional conflict.

The first task of the officers after 1705 was to secure active imperial intervention and the appointment of a special commission to investigate the situation in Frankfurt. They elected an executive committee to direct burgher efforts and then sent representatives to Vienna to make personal pleas to Joseph I and members of the *Reichshofrat* for a commission to consist, as in the early seventeenth century, of the Elector of Mainz and the Landgrave of Hesse-Darmstadt. The magistracy countered these moves by selecting its own Secret Deputation to combat local opposition and by working through its agents in Vienna for a rejection of the burgher petition. The council argued that a small group of agitators without broad support among the citizenry sought to interfere in matters that concerned only the properly constituted authorities of the city; the emperor had to put a quick end to such disrespect for authority, the possible dangers of which were patent. After the councilmen launched investigations and began to harass some of their antagonists, they succeeded in frightening most burghers into submission, until only a hard core of embittered opponents remained to work for imperial intervention. The magistracy enjoyed several advantages over its intransigent foes when it came to imperial diplomacy: it had greater savoir faire in working through the channels of imperial government, experienced jurists to act as its advisers, and greater financial resources with which to effect favorable decisions.[8] In May 1706 the emperor ordered the officers representing the burgher case in Vienna to return to Frankfurt and leave the business of requesting confirmation of the city's privileges to the council.[9] A further decree of April 1707 declared the request for confirmation of the Citizens Agreement and the Jewish Stättigkeit highly unusual and unnecessary; burghers should seek redress of specific grievances from the magistracy, not an imperial commission.[10] However disappointing these decisions must have been for the few officers who held out against the council, the undaunted Captain Wilhelm Fritsch refused to admit defeat. A quarrel over the appointment of militia officers in the city's eighth quarter kept burgher resentment against the council strong, while Fritsch sought to change the emperor's mind about intervening in Frankfurt. He soon found allies in high places.

Although the initiative for an investigating commission came from burgher leaders themselves, a group of imperial reformers led by Vice-Chancellor Friedrich Karl von Schönborn was decisive in winning the

8. Hohenemser, *Verfassungsstreit*, 17.
9. Ibid., 63.
10. Ibid., 91–92.

appointment. Captain Fritsch argued his case very well by appealing to imperial interests: the Citizens Agreement had been negotiated and then confirmed by the emperor. How could Joseph tolerate arbitrary changes made by the council without any consultation with officials in Vienna, the two original commissioners, or the entire citizenry of Frankfurt? The fact that Mainz and Hesse-Darmstadt had acted as guarantors of the Agreement in 1612/13 provided a ready justification for the elector's recurrent interest in Frankfurt's affairs, and Archbishop Lothar Franz von Schönborn, the uncle of the imperial vice-chancellor, seems to have given the first positive response to the burgher plea for outside intervention.[11] The idea was soon taken up by several members of the Schönborn family, not simply because of possible advantages Mainz might reap from participation but because they shared the view that the Empire should be revitalized as a political entity separate from Habsburg territorial ambitions. Central to the realization of this idea of the Empire was the strengthening of the ties between the emperor and the smaller *Reichsstände*, especially the ecclesiastical territories and the imperial cities traditionally dependent on imperial institutions for their own security and influence.[12] The example of Johann Philip von Schönborn, who had served as Elector of Mainz (hence imperial chancellor) in the middle of the seventeenth century, informed a family tradition which identified the interest of the lesser imperial nobility with that of general imperial reform. Lothar Franz and his older brother, Melchior Friedrich, kept the family's ambition alive in the following generation, and the latter's sons—the most notable was Friedrich Karl—formed the third and last generation of imperial reformers in the Schönborn family.[13]

Both Lothar Franz, the Archbishop of Mainz from 1695 to 1729, and his nephew and appointee in Vienna, Vice-Chancellor Friedrich Karl, appreciated the opportunity presented by the conflict between Frankfurt's council and citizens. One of the most important cities of the Empire could be made to feel the strength of its special bonds with the im-

11. Ibid., 37. The vice-chancellor indicated that his uncle was interested in heading a commission as early as January 1706. The only biography of the elector himself is Karl Wild, *Lothar Franz von Schönborn: Bischof von Bamberg und Erzbischof von Mainz 1693–1729* (Heidelberg, 1904), but it stresses his activity as a territorial prince and is not a satisfactory analysis of Lothar Franz's imperial politics.

12. See the excellent review of Hohenemser's book by Hans Erich Feine in *ZRG GA* 44 (1924), 449–455, as well as the summary of his book on the imperial bishoprics after 1648 which he published as "Einwirkungen des absoluten Staatsgedankens auf das deutsche Kaisertum im 17. und 18. Jahrhundert, insbesondere bei der Besetzung der Reichsbistümer," *ZRG GA* 42 (1921), 474–481.

13. See Max Domarus, *Würzburger Kirchenfürsten aus dem Hause Schönborn* (Wiesentheid, 1951), passim, on the family tradition; the outstanding work on the most talented and appealing figure in the family is Hugo Hantsch, *Reichsvizekanzler Friedrich Karl Graf von Schönborn, 1674–1746* (Augsburg, 1929).

1. The Oath of Fealty Ceremony in 1705, the event which marked the beginning of the constitutional conflict in Frankfurt.

(Courtesy of the Frankfurt Historical Museum)

perial government. The emperor's authority could be reasserted to give direction to the political life of an important group of *Reichsbürger*. The Schönborns' thoughts on the possibilities presented by the situation in Frankfurt were shared by the Franconian nobleman Georg Ludwig von Völkern, who had served as imperial resident in the city since 1695. The vice-chancellor received four Frankfurt militia officers in 1708 and agreed to have Völkern submit an impartial report on their quarrel with the council.[14] The emperor's representative responded in early 1709 with two reports which supported burgher charges of misconduct and arbitrary rule by the magistracy. Völkern reminded the emperor of the strong sense of independence which the council has expressed over the preceding decades[15] and urged that Joseph I join the burghers in opposing the Frankfurt aristocrats. While the object of the council's two opponents might be different, a sure result would be the strengthening of imperial power against the particularistic tendencies of the city government. These reports, Captain Fritsch's frequent repetition of burgher grievances, and the council's very impolitic interception of dispatches between Vienna and Frankfurt in 1710 finally convinced Joseph I—a reformer eager to extend his authority but preoccupied with more important problems than the quarrel in Frankfurt—of the necessity for an imperial investigating commission in March 1711.[16] Joseph's sudden death the following May, however, left many doubts about how soon the decision might be confirmed by his successor and then implemented. But the Schönborns' influence with Charles VI was even stronger than with Joseph, and, only eleven months after the new emperor's election, he established two commissions to sit in Frankfurt.[17]

The commissions appointed in 1712 worked in conjunction with the Reichshofrat for almost twenty years to reform Frankfurt's constitution. The commissioners were to investigate the grievances presented by burghers and send their reports and recommendations to the court in Vienna, which would then make final decisions. In practice the investigators made many of the less important decisions themselves, and their advice to the high court usually formed the substance of its legal judgments. The work itself was divided initially between a political and a financial commission, but in 1718 a third body had to be appointed to investigate the city's charitable foundations (*milde Stiftungen*). The Archbishop of Mainz and the Landgrave of Hesse-Darmstadt were

14. Hohenemser, *Verfassungsstreit*, 136; on Völkern, ibid., 137–142. His two reports to Vienna (dated 17 January and 2 February 1709) are reprinted ibid., 372–392.

15. Cf. Chapter 4, 113–115.

16. Hohenemser, *Verfassungsstreit*, 146–147.

17. Ibid., 149–153. On the Schönborns' greater influence with Charles VI, see Wild, *Lothar Franz von Schönborn*, 133–139.

named the two political commissioners, and each prince sent two sub-delegates to act in his name in Frankfurt. The investigations of the political commission were concentrated in the years 1713 to 1715 and were managed efficiently by Lothar Franz's subdelegate, his nephew Count Rudolf Franz Erwein von Schönborn. Melchior Friedrich von Schönborn (brother of Lothar Franz and father of both Franz Erwein and Friedrich Karl) was appointed financial commissioner directly from Vienna; upon the old gentleman's death in 1717, however, Franz Erwein took over the painstaking work of investigating the city's finances and then reorganizing its entire administrative machinery. The third commission, established in 1718 and headed by Count Solms, moved very slowly, because the count was usually busy with the work of the Reichskammergericht in Wetzlar. When he died in 1723, Franz Erwein also assumed the duties of reforming Frankfurt's charitable foundations.[18] Thus most of the responsibilities of all three commissions fell to the brother of the vice-chancellor, and Count Rudolf Franz Erwein even accepted an appointment as imperial inspector to oversee implementation of Reichshofrat decisions in Frankfurt. Certainly he did not expect in 1712 that his efforts to resolve the constitutional dispute would last almost twenty years. Anyone who examines the events of those two important decades in Frankfurt's history is bound, I think, to be highly impressed by the remarkable energy, strong sense of duty, and eminent fair-mindedness that characterized Count von Schönborn's prodigious activity as commissioner.[19] His only detractors were the councilmen, who opposed all his moves. Schönborn's sympathies lay clearly with the burgher party, and he played a large role in changing the city's conservative constitution in its favor.

II. The Constitutional Reforms

The major disagreement between the council and the "common" burghers concerned their own political relationship. The council believed that Frankfurt's privileges had been granted to the magistrates who exercised lordship in the feudal hierarchy over all other citizens. The burghers, on the other hand, argued that the city's corporate privileges applied to the entire citizenry and that the magistracy enjoyed only the special mandate to administer the city in behalf of all burghers.[20] From

18. On the various commission appointments, see Hohenemser, *Verfassungsstreit*, 153, 162–163, 219, 243, 332–334.

19. For a well-balanced biography with several important judgments on the count's work in Frankfurt, see Max Domarus, *Rudolf Franz Erwein von Schönborn* (Wiesentheid, 1954), especially 221–237.

20. The clashing views were most convincingly summarized in section 5 of the *Historische Nachrichten*; cf. Hohenemser, *Verfassungsstreit*, 112–113.

this clash of principles emerged all further disagreements, chiefly the dispute over the Citizens Agreement. Although the council did not feel bound by the Agreement after the Fettmilch Uprising was defeated, burgher leaders considered the compact the only valid constitutional basis for the regulation of public matters in Frankfurt. Restoration and implementation of the Agreement together with enforcement of the Stättigkeit was the principal goal of burgher efforts before the imperial commissions. As we shall see in Chapter 7, however, a direct appeal by the Jews to the Reichshofrat eliminated the issue of illegal Jewish retailing from the commission hearings, and the immediate economic grievance behind the burgher officers' determination to seek imperial intervention in 1705 was never satisfactorily redressed.

The investigations of both the political and the finance commissions were thus centered on burgher grievances concerning the council's failure to govern Frankfurt according to the Citizens Agreement. The subdelegates for Mainz and Hesse-Darmstadt held their most important sessions between March 1713 and June 1714. To remove any possible doubt (expressed earlier by the council) about their ability to speak for the citizenry, the militia officers first presented the signatures of four fifths of their fellow burghers in support of their leadership and general demands. Next, some forty-six different occupational groups aired their grievances, and the burgher deputies (who now made up an executive committee of the militia officer corps) presented a long brief containing 527 specific charges against the council.[21] These moves were designed to show the commissioners how deep burgher disaffection had become and to involve a broad spectrum of citizens in the action against the magistracy. After an unsuccessful attempt to negotiate a compromise between an intransigent council and its aggressive burghers, the political commission lost its patience with the aristocrats, ordered the consolidation of burgher charges into a more manageable brief, and proceeded with its detailed investigations. The city's artisan population was organized into handicraft associations (*Handwerke*), each of which had particular complaints against the magistracy's appointment of their supervisors and its unwillingness to stamp out competition from outside the Handwerke. The artisans wanted much tighter regulation of local handicraft industry and the right to nominate their own leaders for appointment by the council. Neither of these demands was derived from the Citizens Agreement, but they tied the economic dissatisfaction of the majority of Frankfurt's population to the general program advocated by burgher leaders.

The most important attack of the burgher deputies was on aristocratic control of the city government. The monopoly exercised by the Alt-

21. Ibid., 397–398, 174–180.

Limpurg and Frauenstein Societies over the council's two higher benches not only violated the intention of the Citizens Agreement and prevented other elements of the citizenry from participating in the government, it also resulted in nepotism, mismanagement of public funds, and outright corruption from the top to the bottom of the city administration. Posts in the bureaucracy were awarded according to the highest bribes; financial records were neither clear nor accurate; both regular and extraordinary taxes were increased over the seventeenth century without any consultation with the citizenry (i.e., with the Council of Nine) and, what was equally shocking to honorable burghers, without making the slightest dent in Frankfurt's heavy debts. These were only the most important charges heard by the younger Count Schönborn's commission in 1713 and 1714.

The recommendations submitted by the political commissioners to the Reichshofrat in their two reports of May 1715 corresponded closely with the position of burgher leaders.[22] First, the commissioners suggested that Frankfurt's constitution provided a mixed form of government, not an unlimited aristocracy; all the city's privileges had been granted jointly to the council and the citizenry. Since the Citizens Agreement of 1612/13 incorporated all previous privileges, it was the major constitutional document for Frankfurt and could be altered only by the emperor himself. The Agreement had included fundamental limitations on the power of the council, and the commissioners urged that burgher grievances resulting from council violations of the constitution be redressed. The key solution lay in breaking the strong hold of the aristocratic societies over the co-optation of new council members and the appointment of officeholders. This could be accomplished by limiting the number of councilmen from each society; by broadening the rules against close family relationships among council members, their syndics or legal advisers, and other bureaucrats; and by establishing a more impersonal method of choosing both councilmen and officeholders. The commissioners also urged that the artisans in each Handwerk nominate three candidates from which the council could appoint their craft supervisors. Although the Transfix of 1616 had abolished the guilds, the council could not use it to justify dissolution of the burgher Committee of Nine on the grounds that the committee had been named by guild leaders. Nor did the Transfix absolve the magistracy from its obligation to consult the citizenry about tax increases. The commissioners advised that the Nine be reestablished to check all financial records and to approve any future changes in taxation.

On only one important issue were Mainz and Hesse-Darmstadt unable to agree in their recommendations to Vienna: the question of the admis-

22. Both reports are summarized ibid., 185–218.

sion of outsiders to the Frankfurt citizenry.[23] The council argued that it enjoyed complete freedom in deciding who might be granted citizenship rights and who was to be rejected, but some burghers—particularly wealthy Calvinist merchants—appealed to Article 7 of the Citizens Agreement, which had limited council authority to exclude outsiders who married burghers. Only poor immigrants who might become a burden to public relief agencies were to be denied citizenship—not honorable and wealthy outsiders. But, as we shall see in Chapter 8, Lutheran merchants had exerted pressure for a Denizen Ordinance in 1708 which made the attainment of citizenship more difficult even for their rich wholesale competitors, most of whom were Calvinists. Economic and religious problems combined to make the issue of granting citizenship to denizens a difficult one as the constitutional conflict progressed, and even imperial officials were divided on how to settle it. In 1715 Mainz and Hesse-Darmstadt submitted separate reports that reflected the disagreement within the Frankfurt citizenry as well as their own religious prejudices. The Hessian Landgrave was a Lutheran and defended the right of Frankfurt's Lutheran council to make confessional discriminations among applicants for citizenship, while the Catholic Count Schönborn and his uncle the archbishop argued for strict adherence to the Citizens Agreement, which allowed exclusion only on the basis of insufficient wealth.

Like the investigations of the political commissioners, the hearings of the finance commission under the older Schönborn, Melchior Friedrich, opened in 1713, but by 1715 it was clear that the old count's painstaking work had scarcely begun.[24] His chief task was to check the city's financial records to see if burgher charges of mismanagement and corruption were valid, so Schönborn was to investigate not only the ledgers of the city treasury but also the accounts of individual offices. The complicated problems of taxation and the alienation of city property also fell to the finance commission, and we can easily understand why this work went slowly. It did not take Count Schönborn long, however, to agree with his son's conclusion that the burgher Committee of Nine had been illegally abolished in 1616. The initial samples of treasury records and annual office reports used by the commission to check the city's accounting practices revealed so many irregularities that the count favored reestablishment of the citizens' committee to serve as a check on the council's offices. Burgher leaders were delighted with this victory, but they asked for even more extensive limitations on city officials. In order to put an end to inaccurate records and the arbitrary charging of incidental fees, the burghers proposed major administrative reforms: the twenty-five offices

23. Ibid., 212–218. The issue will be analyzed in detail in Chapter 8.
24. Hohenemser, *Verfassungsstreit*, 218–231.

which collected indirect taxes should be farmed out to citizens, while a system of burgher supervisors (*Gegenschreiber*) should approve and countersign the records of all other bureaucratic agencies.[25] The council opposed the suggestion bitterly, but the burgher deputies pointed out that similar systems were working quite successfully in Wetzlar, Lübeck, and Hamburg. The proposal went far beyond anything envisaged in the Citizens Agreement, but burgher leaders assured the commissioner that their joint control of city administration with the council would net the budget a surplus of 100,000 fl. during its first year of operation. Furthermore, eight of the most important leaders were willing to put up their own money as collateral to back the promise.[26] Count Schönborn was highly impressed with the determination of the burgher Ausschuss, and he sent two preliminary reports to Vienna in 1715 urging the emperor to reestablish the Committee of Nine and to inaugurate the system of joint burgher-council control of the city bureaucracy.

The imperial resolution which Charles VI issued on 15 October 1716 dealt, on burgher request, with the recommendations of the finance commission and left political reforms for later consideration, at a time when the Reichshofrat could act on full financial reports from Count Schönborn. Burgher leaders apparently felt that the political changes already suggested would be of little benefit, unless thorough administrative reforms preceded them.[27] The resolution itself officially acknowledged the Citizens Agreement as the foundation upon which Frankfurt's constitution was based, then it reinstituted the Committee of Nine and ordered its members (whom the burgher officers nominated and the council appointed) to assist the imperial commission with continued investigations of the city's accounts. The emperor insisted that the council consult the Nine for approval of the budget and any new taxes it wished to levy, just as the Agreement of 1612/13 stipulated, but he also went beyond the Agreement when he authorized a trial period of one year for the burgher administrative reforms.[28] The Reichshofrat, in which the vice-chancellor's influence was strong, had urged Charles VI to

25. Table 23, 103, lists the city offices and divides them into those which were eventually farmed out and those which received supervisors; the work of the various offices is discussed in Chapter 4, 102–104, and specific burgher complaints against the old administration are dealt with in 109–113.

26. Table 31, 134, lists the eight burgher leaders and the sums they contributed as collateral.

27. Hohenemser, *Verfassungsstreit*, 232.

28. The resolution of 1716 is printed in a collection of the major documents related to the constitutional conflict edited by Christoph Sigismund Müller, *Vollständige Sammlung der Kaiserlichen in Sachen Frankfurt contra Frankfurt ergangenen Resolutionen und anderer dahin einschlagender Stadt-Verwaltungs-Grund-Gezzen* (Frankfurt, 1776–1779), I, 15–18. I shall cite Müller's collection as *Frankfurt contra Frankfurt*.

approve these reforms, because the emperor himself was responsible for the constitutions issued to citizens and administered by councils in the imperial cities. Thus the resolution was the occasion for a strong assertion of imperial authority in the cities, while it marked at the same time a major constitutional victory for Frankfurt citizens.[29]

In accord with the resolution of 1716, the work of the finance commission continued. The Committee of Nine was established in January 1717 and began its painstaking investigation of the council's financial policies during the previous century. The elder Schönborn died the following May, but his son Rudolf Franz Erwein took over supervision of the inquiry into the dark history of city finance. He also helped solve several problems involved in the introduction of burgher administrators into the bureaucracy in August of that year. The most dramatic development of the long period of real drudgery which followed was the budgetary surplus of 165,840 fl. produced by the burghers in 1718. Although the council disputed that impressive figure with the smaller one of 58,000 fl., there could be little doubt about the success of the administrative experiment. The system of having burgher supervisors in the city offices was continued, and Schönborn's report to Vienna in December 1720 was a strong endorsement of the citizens' joint control of the bureaucracy.[30] From the experience burghers gained in the individual city offices and the evidence accumulated by the Committee of Nine during the years 1717 to 1723 came several new reform proposals. The adoption of regular salaries for all governmental personnel would end the corruption that had plagued the council's administration during the seventeenth century. A schedule of fixed charges should replace the system of arbitrary service and incidental fees previously necessary for the maintenance of the officeholders. Finally, the incorporation of several smaller offices into larger ones would make a more efficient and less costly administration. These suggestions were more and more welcome, as the investigations of the Nine revealed an incredibly bad picture for the council and its officials; for instance, their financial records were so poor that neither tax arrears nor the city's debt could be determined accurately.[31] Since the magistracy's dismal record contrasted sharply with burgher achievements after 1717, the imperial government granted the citizens most of their requests when the decisions came in 1725.

The nine imperial resolutions of 1725 were Frankfurt's most important constitutional documents of the eighteenth century; together with the Improved Visitation Ordinance issued in 1726, they instituted the

29. Hohenemser, *Verfassungsstreit*, 232–237, summarizes the reports (22 June and 10 July 1716) of the RHR; he prints them fully ibid., 399–422.

30. Ibid., 242–250.

31. Ibid., 256–267.

governmental changes that gave Frankfurt its later reputation as one of the best administered cities in the Empire. The resolutions not only restored the Citizens Agreement but altered many of its provisions to reduce further the power of the magistracy vis-à-vis the citizenry.[32] The emperor weakened the hold of the aristocratic Limpurg and Frauenstein Societies over the council by establishing maximum numbers of members each could have in the two upper benches and by extending the restrictions on council membership for relatives. A complicated system of nominating and electing council members and officeholders by lot was designed to make bribery or exercise of special influence on new appointments impossible. But to ensure strict adherence to all these stipulations, the emperor created a special burgher Committee of Three to oversee all the elections of city officials. Following Count Schönborn's recommendation, Vienna granted artisans the right to present the candidates from whom the magistrates would select craft supervisors. Otherwise the resolutions were silent on industrial organization in Frankfurt. The position of the burgher deputies supporting the constitutional arguments of Calvinist merchants on the admission of outsiders to the citizenry also won imperial approval; the council had to accept immigrants who married into burgher families, as long as they posed no problem of poor relief. Charles VI also made permanent the burgher administrative system introduced in 1717, set up a salary scale reaching from the two burghermasters to the lowest city employees, abolished all incidental fees previously assessed by the city offices, and promised the imminent publication of a list of fixed service charges. The Improved Visitation Ordinance fulfilled that promise a few months later; city offices underwent considerable reorganization and received specific instructions about their fees.[33] To oversee the implementation of the resolutions and the Visitation Ordinance, the emperor appointed Count Schonborn as his special inspector in Frankfurt. Although the Reichshofrat wanted the inspectorate to be a permanent post, Charles VI followed the count's suggestion that its duration be limited to the period necessary to ascertain that the reforms had been put into practice.[34]

Although the jubilant citizens thought that the constitutional conflict was over at last, the disappointed aristocrats were determined to prolong it. The council's hope to have some decisions reversed; a bitter quarrel between Lutheran and Calvinist burghers over the economic

32. The resolutions are summarized ibid., 303–308, and are printed in Müller, *Frankfurt contra Frankfurt*, I, 8–120.

33. The *Verbesserte Visitations-Ordnung* is printed ibid., II, 16–228; it was actually issued in Vienna on 31 December 1725, but it was nonetheless generally referred to as the ordinance of 1726, the year of its publication in Frankfurt.

34. Hohenemser, *Verfassungsstreit*, 302.

privileges of denizens and the admission of outsiders to the citizen body; and Count Schönborn's instructions to continue his investigations of the smaller city offices, the salary scales set up in 1725, and the charitable foundations—all helped to continue the conflict another six years, until the emperor issued three final resolutions in 1732.[35] Council leaders went to Vienna in 1726 to gain more lenient regulations on family relationships permitted in the council's upper benches, higher salaries for councilmen, and changes in the new administrative system. They had little success, however, until the citizenry became embroiled in the divisive issues of denizen competition with burgher wholesalers and the admission of Calvinists to the citizenry. As burgher leaders in Frankfurt came to oppose openly the more liberal views of both Count Schönborn and their own representatives in Vienna (Captain Dietrich Notebohm) toward the outsiders, the council moved to take advantage of the confusion in its opponents' ranks. At the same time, Count Schönborn's investigations led to further administrative reforms, especially in the city's charitable foundations, and his consideration of the question of salaries supported an increase for most officials.

Yet the count was disappointed with the first imperial resolution of 1732, which raised salaries even higher than he proposed and also allowed the aristocrats to exceed their maximum number of council members, if other qualified burghers could not be found. The second resolution also favored the wishes of the burghers over Schönborn's recommendations on the issue of admitting denizens. While the two decisions should not be interpreted as a loss of confidence in Count Schönborn himself, they were indicative of the council's increased influence in Vienna in the early 1730's. Just then the imperial reform movement directed from Vienna seemed to have burned out: Lothar Franz von Schönborn, Archbishop of Mainz and one of the most powerful supporters of the vision of a revitalized Empire, had died in 1729, and the vice-chancellor's effectiveness in Vienna had been weakened by his accession to the archepiscopal sees of Bamberg and Würzburg.[36] Emperor Charles himself had already entered that second, less vigorous period of his rule, during which he was engrossed in the diplomatic problems involved in gaining acceptance of the Pragmatic Sanction by the European powers. Although the Schönborns' vision of the Empire had failed and

35. On the last six years of the conflict, see ibid., 309–371; the three resolutions of 1732 are printed in Müller, *Frankfurt contra Frankfurt*, III, 8–36.

36. Domarus, *Rudolf Franz Erwein von Schönborn*, 232–234, emphasizes the disappointment of the commissioner with the final resolutions and attributes council gains to decreased Schönborn influence in the RHR after 1729–30; Domarus's reference to burgher discontent in 1732 is a good balance to Hohenemser's rosy picture of burgher victory at the end of the conflict, but the discontent probably was not caused by the second and third resolutions, only by the first.

the Frankfurt council had seized the right moment to win some concessions in Vienna, the first imperial resolution of 1732 still did not mark a setback of any consequence to the burgher party. The second and third resolutions represented, in fact, major victories for the citizens. The Lutheran majority obtained a favorable decision which made Calvinist penetration into the burgher community difficult, while the third resolution capped the administrative reforms enacted between 1716 and 1726 with a final burgher Committee of Fifty-One to oversee the city bureaucracy and act as a general executive for the entire citizenry. With the creation of this committee, Frankfurt citizens finally gained three consultative bodies in the early eighteenth century comparable to those won in so many cities several centuries earlier.

III. The Significance of the Conflict

The point of departure for evaluating the significance of the constitutional conflicts which occurred in various German cities during the seventeenth and eighteenth centuries must be, as Otto Brunner has indicated, an analysis of the relationship between the city council and its citizenry.[37] Certainly the essential achievement of the long struggle in Frankfurt from 1705 to 1732 was the final establishment of effective limitations on the previously unrestricted power of the council and the aristocratic families which had always controlled it. New regulations for the election of councilmen and the creation of burgher committees to participate in the financial administration of the city provided the social and institutional foundations for a balance of power between the magistrates (whose social composition was to be slightly broadened) and the citizens (whose interests were to be represented by the three consultative bodies) that lasted into the nineteenth century.

In his recent book on Frankfurt and Hamburg, Helmut Böhme has denied that the constitutional settlement of the early eighteenth century established such a balance of political forces in Frankfurt.[38] His view seems to rest on two arguments. First he asserts that the burgher committees created by the reforms represented only merchants and not other citizens (in contrast to the militia officer corps or Hamburg's burgher *Konvent*, both of which represented, formally at least, urban districts rather than specific social groups).[39] Then he argues that internal

37. Brunner, "Souveränitätsproblem," 338.
38. *Frankfurt und Hamburg*, 102–103, 106–107.
39. In a book comparing developments chiefly in the nineteenth century, Böhme could not be expected to analyze the membership of the burgher committees in detail. He is, of course, quite right about the Committee of Nine; it was always dominated

disputes continued throughout Frankfurt's eighteenth-century history. But the persistence of quarrels among the city's governmental bodies does not in itself demonstrate political disequilibrium, as Böhme implies. Instead it indicates that important elements within the citizenry had gained regular channels through which they could readily affect public policy. Nothing could serve as better proof of the previous social and political imbalance in Frankfurt than the absence of concerted opposition to aristocratic policies from 1616 to 1705. This lack of debate and open dispute was not the case in Frankfurt during the eighteenth century. Furthermore, the fact that only a small segment of the citizenry was actively involved in the agencies which served as a check on the council does not make Frankfurt exceptional, as Böhme's own discussion of Hamburg's constitution shows. All early modern cities were ruled oligarchically, and I think Böhme would agree, in the end, that Hamburg saw fewer internal disputes than Frankfurt not because its constitution was better balanced but because its governing elite was less diversified in the eighteenth century. Hamburg was controlled more completely by commercial interests, while Frankfurt had three competing elements—mercantile, artisanal, and aristocratic—within its political tradition.

Formation of the committees or assemblies outside city councils which were supposed to share governmental responsibility occurred much earlier in Strassburg and Hamburg than in Frankfurt. Despite the comparative lateness of Frankfurt's constitutional reforms, however, burgher political thought and social attitudes were shaped in the traditionalistic molds that had characterized earlier urban movements.[40] The burgher party exhibited none of the liberal or democratic impulses often associated with the major seventeenth- or eighteenth-century revolutions, and, in fact, the term "revolution" has no relevance either to

---

by big merchants and bankers. But some artisans and retailers did enter the Fifty-One, and Böhme is incorrect in assuming—without the slightest documentary support—that Calvinist and Catholic merchants controlled the larger "Burgher Committee." Had those minorities enjoyed power in the Committee of Fifty-One, that body would have been a most unusual constitutional phenomenon and certainly would not have represented the interests of most Frankfurt citizens. In fact, Lutheran merchants along with some wealthy artisans and retailers manned the committee, and although their power never matched that of the council itself, they were capable of serving as a constitutional check on the magistrates. See Chapter 5, especially 136–137, for my analysis of the social composition of the burgher committees.

40. On earlier movements, see the essay by Erich Maschke, "Verfassung und soziale Kräfte in der deutschen Stadt des späten Mittelalters, vornehmlich in Oberdeutschland," *Vierteljahrschrift für Sozial- und Wirtschaftgeschichte* 46 (1959), 289–349, 433–476.

events or to the burgher mentality in Frankfurt during that period.[41] No one questioned the traditional, hierarchical social structure of the city or the special political role played by Frankfurt's aristocrats. Only their claim to exclusive control was resented by a burgher elite which sought to share power with them. Moreover, most citizens were antagonized not by an authoritarian social and political framework per se, but by specific abuses which resulted from the council's failure to satisfy their traditional notions about the responsibilities of the *Obrigkeit* to the entire community. Although the burgher committees acted as a check against illegitimate demands or poor administration by the magistracy, the citizens never had any intention to remove legislative initiative or judicial authority from the council. Accordingly, the changes of the early eighteenth century did not alter the oligarchic political and social structure of the city. The oligarchy itself was enlarged somewhat, and the basic relation between the council and the citizenry was expressed in the notion of the "mixed" or "half aristocratic, half democratic" constitution that was current in the writings of the German legists.[42] The aristocracy remained the leading element in this constitution, while important burgher interests gained an effective voice in Frankfurt government.

But what groups benefited directly from the reforms? University graduates and merchants were to be given special consideration for posts in the magistracy. What was their exact relationship to the old aristocracy which had previously governed alone? Did they provide the leadership for the burgher party which fought the council, or were the leaders the "simple artisans" of whom Paul Hohenemser wrote in his political his

41. Cf. Brunner, "Souveränitätsproblem," 336.

42. See Johann Anton Moritz, *Versuch einer Einleitung in die Staatsverfassung derer oberrheinischen Reichsstädte: Reichsstadt Frankfurt* (the only two volumes published cover Frankfurt, and I shall cite the work hereafter simply as *Reichsstadt Frankfurt*) (Frankfurt, 1785–1786), I, 318–322, for a survey of legists' opinions on Frankfurt's constitution. Professor Brunner's article concerns itself essentially with a *begriffskritische* analysis of the already anachronistic use of the concept of a "mixed" constitution to describe the governments of the imperial cities in the early eighteenth century. He shows that the tension-ridden political relationship [*Herrschaftsverhältnis*] between a council and its citizenry became even more problematic when citizens attained active participation in a city's financial administration. Disputes over specific policies naturally led to the question of principle: who had the power of final decision, who exercised sovereignty? The solution worked out by German legists made use of the current conception of sovereignty, but they extended it, contrary to its real meaning, to two bearers—the council and the citizenry. Thus, argues Brunner, the notion of sovereignty was transformed back into the traditional reciprocal relationship, with the anachronistic difference that the term then referred to state power rather than the *Jura et libertates* of medieval times.

tory of the conflict? A review of the general issues and results of the legal struggle in Frankfurt leads directly to such questions about specific social groups. In this way the constitutional conflict becomes a framework for the study of group relationships in the city. I shall examine, for example, the extent to which craftsmen and retailers were involved in the reform movement, for they made up the large majority of Frankfurt citizens. What concrete issues alienated them from the council, and on what bases were they prepared to cooperate with their social superiors, either aristocrats or merchants? Perhaps most fascinating were the relationships between burghers and the aliens who lived in the city, for they reveal the economic interests and social attitudes that worked to make Frankfurt an anachronism—a major commercial city of Central Europe and, at the same time, a closed community of privileged citizens. The long period of conflict in Frankfurt brought even subtle social relationships into clearer focus. It is therefore especially well suited to my purpose—to study this complex community by close examination of its composite parts.

Chapter 2

The City's Inhabitants

I. General Population Movements

A population curve for Frankfurt in the early modern period (Chart I) reflects general Central European developments fairly closely. An increase of population in the sixteenth century, especially in the last third, continued into the early seventeenth century. The period of the Thirty Years War then saw a sudden decline, only to be followed by rapid population increase in the decades after 1650. While the Empire as a whole may have taken a hundred years to recover its loss, Frankfurt had probably regained its prewar population level by 1675. Steady growth continued into the mid-eighteenth century, and the slump of the 1760's and 1770's was only a minor dip in a population curve that rose in the nineteenth century into what the early modernist considers astronomic figures. By comparison, population changes of the sixteenth and seventeenth centuries may seem minor. The changes in this period did not occur on the same scale as those of the nineteenth century, but their rapidity and sharpness represented major shocks to the social stability of an early modern community. Many of the economic frustrations and political problems of seventeenth- and eighteenth-century Frankfurt can be understood as results of the city's first experiences with sizable population changes.

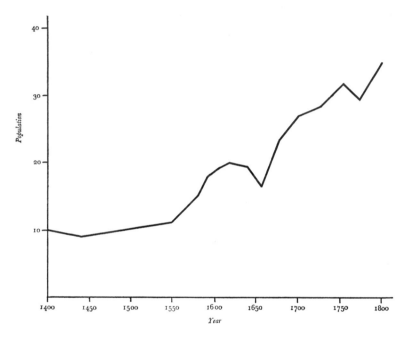

CHART I.
Population Curve, 1400–1800
(in thousands)

34

Hans Mauersberg's recently published estimates of Frankfurt's total population (Chart I) make early modern developments clear.[1] A decline of 10 percent from ten to nine thousand in the early fifteenth century was followed by a long period of recovery and population increase. To trace fluctuations before the 1530's is impossible because of inadequate source material, so we can see only a fairly steady increase of about 28 percent from 1440 to 1550. With this apparent stability the next hundred years provide a sharp contrast: a 76-percent increase in population from 1550 to about 1620 (reaching a height of 20,200), a faltering in the 1620's and 1630's, and then a decline of 16 percent down to 17,000 inhabitants in 1655. The sharp increase of the late sixteenth century can be attributed not only to a simultaneous rise in births and decline in the number of deaths (Chart II) but also to mass immigration, especially from the Netherlands. This large influx of religious refugees transformed the city's economy and created the social conflicts, religious antagonisms, and political discontent that produced the Fettmilch Uprising of 1612–1616.[2] Political confusion was soon followed by plagues, food shortages, population dislocation, and the general insecurity of the Thirty Years War. While Frankfurt suffered very little from warfare itself (there was a quiet occupation by the Swedes from 1631 to 1635),

1. Chart I is based on the estimates of Hans Mauersberg, *Wirtschafts- und Sozialgeschichte zentraleuropaischer Städte in neuerer Zeit* (Göttingen, 1960), 48–55. Mauersberg accepts the work of Karl Bücher, *Die Bevölkerung von Frankfurt am Main im XIV. und XV. Jahrhundert* (Tübingen, 1886), and Friedrich Bothe, *Beiträge zur Wirtschafts- und Sozialgeschichte der Reichsstadt Frankfurt* (Leipzig, 1906), 50–73, for the period before 1616. Both men used tax records and other lists of citizens to estimate total population for particular dates—1400, 1440, 1567, and 1616. For the period between 1616 and the first official census of 1811, Mauersberg estimates the population by using yearly baptism totals conveniently published for the period after 1635 in Heinrich Bleicher, *Statistische Beschreibung der Stadt Frankfurt am Main und ihrer Bevölkerung* (Frankfurt, 1895), 237. While adjustments must always be made for outside groups not accounted for in the church records kept by the city after the 1530's, the basic problem is to arrive at reasonably accurate figures for the overwhelmingly Lutheran population. Here Mauersberg rejects the static ratio of 40 births per thousand inhabitants used by Alexander Dietz, *Frankfurter Bürgerbuch* (Frankfurt, 1897), 186–193, to estimate population totals for each decade from 1533 to 1700. Instead he begins with Bothe's ratio of 1:39 for the early seventeenth century and gradually decreases it to 1:31 as his samples approach the nineteenth century. This more sophisticated use of baptismal data brings Mauersberg close to the figures presented by Werner Gley, "Grundriss und Wachstum der Stadt Frankfurt am Main," *Festschrift zur Hundertjahrfeier des Vereins für Geographie und Statistik zu Frankfurt am Main*, ed. Wolfgang Hartke (Frankfurt, 1936), 72–74, 98.

2. See Dietz, *FftHG*, II, 11–97, and passim, for a general discussion of the immigration as well as lists of the most important commercial figures involved. The outstanding analysis of the period before 1616, however, is that of Friedrich Bothe, *Beiträge*, 50–98.

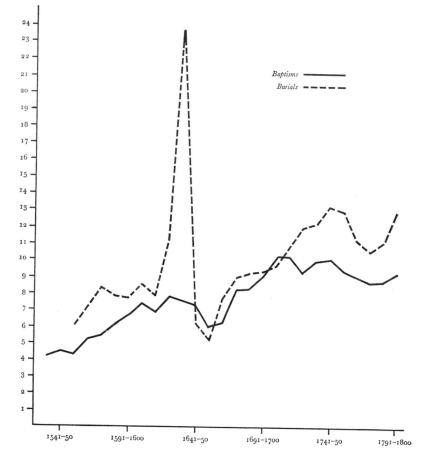

CHART II.
Baptism and Burial Averages
(by decades and in hundreds)

disease sent the number of deaths to remarkable heights between 1622 and 1646 (Chart II).[3] The total loss of population would have been far greater, had it not been compensated for by heavy immigration.[4] Of the 2726 persons who became citizens in Frankfurt between 1631 and 1650, 68 percent were immigrants.[5] For this reason Frankfurt did not suffer a terrible loss comparable to that of Augsburg (67 percent) in the war period, and, in fact, its population decline of 16 percent was only about half the 33-percent average estimated by Günther Franz for most German cities.[6]

The fifty years after the war saw rapid recovery from this demographic slump by 1675 (an increase of 35 percent brought the population to 24,000 by that date) and impressive growth (at a rate of 20 percent) in the final quarter of the century. If we ignore the destabilizing factors of war and recovery, Frankfurt experienced only a 36-percent increase in population from 1620 to 1700. But for purposes of understanding social relations in the seventeenth-century community, the fluctuations of wartime decline and then a remarkable population increase of 62 percent from 1655 to 1700 seem most significant. Though the city did not show as much vitality as Hamburg, its growth during the second half of the seventeenth century enabled Frankfurt to reach 27,500 inhabitants in 1700 and to outdistance the population of Munich.[7] By comparison with this boom of the last half of the seventeenth century, the increase of 19 percent in the first six decades of the eighteenth appears somewhat anticlimactic. Yet a sizable increase did continue, and Frankfurt was able to keep pace with the dynamic capital of Bavaria throughout the last century of the Empire's history.[8] Without doubt, however, the decades from 1655 to the constitutional conflict in 1705 remain a more impressive period in Frankfurt's population development. Changes

3. *Hessisches Städtebuch*, ed. Erich Keyser (Stuttgart, 1957), 132; see also Wilhelm Hanauer, "Geschichte der Sterblichkeit und der öffentlichen Gesundheitspflege in Frankfurt am Main," *Deutsche Vierteljahrschrift für öffentliche Gesundheitspflege* 40 (1908), 658–659, for a list of the major plagues and subsistence crises of the early modern period. Chart II itself is based on averages for each decade found in or calculated from Bleicher, *Statistische Beschreibung*, 237; Dietz, *Bürgerbuch*, 187–193; and Hanauer, "Sterblichkeit," 656–657.

4. Gley, "Grundriss und Wachstum," 72, disputes Dietz's pessimistic figures for the war period (decline to 12,000 in 1637) because of heavy immigration of Dutch refugees who moved on from Aachen and Cologne to Frankfurt in the 1620's and 1630's.

5. My calculations from the appropriate Bürgerbücher; see Tables 3 and 4.

6. Günther Franz, *Der Dreissigjährige Krieg und das deutsche Volk* (3rd ed.; Stuttgart, 1961), 46–47. Franz's figure for Augsburg appears too high, and I use that given by Wolfgang Zorn, *Augsburg* (Augsburg, 1955), 217.

7. Mauersberg, 76.

8. Ibid., 77.

in the relative numbers of births and deaths may help clarify the expansion during the late seventeenth century, but they cannot fully explain it. In only three decades of the entire early modern period was there an excess of births over deaths: 1641–1660 and 1701–1710.[9] Although these decades fell, as it were, at either end of the boom period, Chart II shows clearly that the birth and mortality curves were not nearly so far apart from 1655 to 1700 as was the case between 1560 and 1640 or later in the eighteenth century. And the ratio of baptisms per hundred deaths was high in the last three decades of the seventeenth century: 95, 95, and 99.[10] Yet such a narrowing of the margin between baptisms and burials cannot account for a population increase of 62 percent. Immigration provides the key explanation, just as it did in the seven decades before the Thirty Years War. Since the number of inhabitants increased roughly from 17,000 to 27,500 in the years from 1655 to 1700—a period that saw an excess of 1056 deaths over births instead of a natural population increase—net migration amounted to about 11,550. Allowing for deaths, total immigration was probably as high as three times that figure. Over the second half of the century, immigrants comprised more than 50 percent of the citizens granted full legal privileges.[11]

But not all immigrants, not even the majority, became privileged burghers. They were permitted to attach themselves to the community as denizens (*Beisassen*); they might be Jews accepted into the local ghetto; or they could be part of the floating population simply called aliens (*Fremde*), about whom we know next to nothing. Although statistical information on the outsiders is usually difficult to find, there are many indications that all these groups expanded their numbers at high rates in the seventeenth century. Because of the strict regulations under which the Jews lived, we have precise statistics to show that the ghetto increased its population from about 1800 in 1651 to something over 3000 in 1709.[12] This growth rate of 67 percent for the Jewish community was not much greater than that for the entire city, yet the increase in this hated minority group was especially noticeable. Jewish infringement on burgher economic privileges was, as pointed out earlier, the major issue for most citizens at the beginning of the constitutional con-

9. Bleicher, *Statistische Beschreibung*, 238; Hanauer, "Sterblichkeit," 664; Roger Mols, *Introduction à la démographie historique des villes d'Europe du XIVᵉ au XVIIIᵉ siècle* (Louvain, 1954–1956), III, 225.

10. Mols, III, 225.

11. My calculations from the Bürgerbücher; see Table 4.

12. Isidor Kracauer, "Beiträge zur Geschichte der Frankfurter Juden im Dreissigjährigen Krieg," *Zeitschrift für die Geschichte der Juden in Deutschland* 3 (1889), 131–132, as well as his "Geschichte der Judengasse in Frankfurt am Main," *Festschrift zur Jahrhundertfeier der Realschule der israelitischen Gemeinde (Philanthropin) zu Frankfurt am Main 1804–1904* (Frankfurt, 1904), 322.

flict. My brief discussion of the conflict also indicated how important a political issue the denizens became in the early eighteenth century. The fees collected from denizens and other outsiders by the city's Office of Inquisition increased from 420 fl. in 1615 to 7809 fl. in 1717.[13] Since the fees varied according to the wealth of the denizens, however, the Inquisition accounts do not allow a calculation of the total number of people involved. But they do give an impression of the tremendous influx that must have taken place over the century.

Perhaps more helpful for our purposes is an indication of the approximate size of the major groups living in the city at the beginning of the eighteenth century. The total number of inhabitants was about 27,500, and we know that 3000 people belonged to the Jewish community. We are left with 24,500 residents, divided between burgher and denizen households. There are two methods by which we can estimate the ratio between the two groups. Hans Mauersberg believes that there was one denizen for every three citizens in Frankfurt by the 1720's.[14] If we apply that ratio here, we get roughly 6100 persons living in denizen households and 18,400 in burgher homes. On the other hand, we can also work with fairly reliable figures for the number of denizen and burgher households—1212 and 2840 respectively—in 1713–1714.[15] Using a multiplier of six (on the assumption that the average size of households was about the same for Christians as that found for Jews), we have approximately 7350 persons in denizen households and 17,150 in burgher homes. Such estimates are always based on uncertainties, but at least they provide a reasonable order of magnitude. During the first years of the constitutional conflict, then, Frankfurt's residents included 3000 Jews (11 percent), between 6100 and 7350 people (22 to 27 percent) in denizen households,

13. Ugb B76 G1 and G2: "Extract der Inquisitions Rechnungen, 1609–1717." The regular fees netted the city as much as 11,867 fl. in 1711. To these fees were added increasingly frequent extraordinary taxes, so that in some years the city collected almost twice as much as the normal fees (e.g., in 1719 normal fees came to 8509 fl., but total levies came to 15,640 fl. 3 kr.). See also Mauersberg, 136, who quotes burgher complaints about the increase of outsiders in the late seventeenth century. On the system of coinage in Frankfurt, see Gottlieb Schnapper-Arndt, *Studien zur Geschichte der Lebenshaltung in Frankfurt a. M. während des 17. und 18. Jahrhunderts*, ed. Karl Bräuer (Frankfurt, 1915), II, 411.

14. Mauersberg, 138.

15. On the number of denizen households, see below, 56. In 1713, some 2270 burghers signed a statement of support for the officer corps in its fight against the council; Hohenemser, *Verfassungsstreit*, 397–398, says that they made up about four fifths of the entire citizen body. Hence there were probably about 2480 burgher households. I should note here the attempt by Dietz, *Bürgerbuch*, 190–193, to estimate the relative numbers of Jews and denizens over the seventeenth century; his figures for total population and for Jews are almost certainly too low, but that for denizens at the end of the century is not far from the estimate made here for the early eighteenth.

and from 17,150 to 18,400 (62 to 67 percent) within burgher households. From citizenship records we know that half of the burghers were immigrants, and we may assume that over half the Jews and no less than two thirds of the denizens were also from outside. At least 15,200 (or about 55 percent) of the city's residents in 1700 were immigrants.

II. The Burghers

Of the five groups which came under Frankfurt's jurisdiction—burghers, denizens, Jews, the transient Fremde, and the dependent villagers living outside the city walls—the most important was the body of citizens who enjoyed legal privileges recognized and guaranteed by the emperor. The others were merely attached to the periphery of the community whose real core was its own *Bürger*. Compared with the outsider, the burgher was a man of more secure legal position and greater privileges. Only citizens could own property inside the city walls or in its adjacent territory, though some exceptions might be made for resident noblemen who did not fall under the council's jurisdiction. Seats in the council itself and all important offices in the city government were reserved for burghers, and only they could attain membership in aristocratic societies or in handicraft corporations. They received special considerations in the collection of taxes and tolls and could pursue any type of economic activity—subject, of course, to regulation by the city council.[16] Burgher appeals to their rights as citizens during the constitutional conflict were always appeals to this privileged status in the community.

Citizenship could be acquired in three ways: by inheritance, by marriage into a family enjoying burgher privileges, or by a special grant of those privileges from the city council. The first method was, of course, the easiest and least expensive. Fees were always lowest for natives, and the legitimate children of citizens could not be denied *Bürgerrecht* on their appearance at the city hall to take the necessary steps. A man became a burgher when he took his oath of allegiance to the emperor and city, paid a fee, and was registered in the official book of citizens (*Bürgerbuch*). He gained the privileges of citizenship and accepted, at the same time, its obligations: to remain loyal to the emperor, to obey the city government, to pay taxes, and to defend the city against possible enemies. A burgher's son was required to assume formal citizenship no later than one month after his marriage, if he had not done so previ-

16. Johann Anton Moritz, *Reichsstadt Frankfurt* (Frankfurt, 1785–86), I, 206–7, outlines the privileges of all citizens; see also Otto Ruppersberg, "Der Aufbau der reichsstädtischen Behörden," *Die Stadt Goethes: Frankfurt am Main im XVIII. Jahrhundert*, ed. Heinrich Voelker (Frankfurt, 1932), 62.

ously.[17] The daughters of a burgher family, on the other hand, received a kind of latent citizenship automatically. They did not pay a fee or take the oath; in fact, it was not necessary for burgher daughters or widows to be registered in the Bürgerbuch unless they became independent heads of households.[18] Even without registration, however, they ordinarily bestowed the right to become citizens on their husbands. In contrast, women who were not from burgher families had to pay fees and be registered when they were admitted as citizens.[19] Almost all such women acquired citizenship as the wives of native or immigrant burghers, though, and the fee was simply paid to the city without any formal oath.

Granting citizenship as a result of marriage into a burgher family became, as I have already pointed out, a major issue in the constitutional conflict. The issue did not revolve around women's coming into Frankfurt as wives of burghers, but, on the contrary, it concerned men who attained citizenship by marrying burgher widows and daughters. This method seems to have been a sure way for most outsiders to gain full legal privileges, at least until the practice was questioned by the council's opponents in the early eighteenth century. Such a marriage was beneficial to any immigrant who wished to become a citizen. It apparently eliminated the need to petition the council for a special grant of citizenship, and it often reduced the fees by half. Furthermore, marriage into the community was almost the only way for Calvinists or Catholics —whom the council regularly refused—to receive the privilege.[20] Of the 11,476 immigrants (male and female) who became Frankfurt citizens between 1600 and 1735, 7607 or 66.3 percent married into the *Bürgerschaft*. Table 1 gives a statistical breakdown of this immigrant group and its marriage patterns.[21]

The table shows that at no time in these 136 years was the proportion of immigrants who attained citizenship by marriage lower than 60 percent of the entire immigrant group. We should note also that the rate

17. Bürgermeisterbuch (hereafter, Bgmb) 1617–18, 158v, for the ordinance of 29 January 1618 on burgher sons' assuming citizenship soon after marriage.

18. Count von Schönborn's suggestion in his final statement to the Reichshofrat (HHSA Wien: RHR Decisa 2205, 226r–266v) that Captain Notebohm was quite correct in asking that burgher daughters also be forced to pay 1 fl. and register with the chancellery at the time of marriage apparently came to nothing.

19. Bgmb 1623–24, 39v–40r, 42v: ordinances of 24 and 31 July 1623.

20. Dietz, *FftHG*, IV, i, 157.

21. Table 1 is based on hand and machine computations of information gathered from the Bürgerbücher from 1600 to 1735. Since fees for outsiders were higher and were carefully watched, the records on immigrants are probably very accurate. The reader should note that the last column of percentage figures gives the proportion of males marrying into Frankfurt to male immigrants only, while the other percentages are proportions of all immigrant citizens.

TABLE I
Immigrant Citizens, 1600–1735

Period	Total Immigrants	Total Marrying into Community		Male Immigrants		Males Marrying into Community	
1600–30	3088	1959	63.4%	2653	85.9%	1586	59.8%
1631–50	1863	1345	72.2	1131	60.7	757	66.9
1651–75	1868	1285	68.8	1063	56.9	720	67.7
1676–1704	2278	1586	69.6	1407	61.8	975	69.3
1705–35	2379	1432	60.2	1610	67.7	792	49.2
1600–1735	11,476	7607	66.3	7864	68.5	4830	61.4

was near 70 percent for most of the seventeenth century and that efforts to reduce the number of outsiders who obtained citizenship by marriage had some success in the period of the constitutional conflict. But the number of men who married into the community was the major concern of the native burghers who wished to exclude outsiders from easy access to their privileges. If we look only at immigrant men, the success of burgher efforts during the conflict seems more striking—the number of male immigrants who attained citizenship by means of marriage declined by almost 19 percent for the years 1705–1735. Yet this was a limited success; there can be no doubt that marrying into the citizenry was the chief means by which outsiders gained the legal privileges of citizenship throughout the seventeenth and early eighteenth centuries.

The third method of attaining citizenship was to petition the city council to grant the privilege. Immigrants who gained a council grant often paid twice as much as those who married into the community and many times more than native sons. Such newcomers were accepted, however, only if they met the criteria established by the council. Although no formal statement of these criteria seems to have been laid down, examination of the Bürgerbücher gives a good impression of what standards were set for burghers. The citizen had, of course, to be "honorable"—legitimate by birth, upright in conduct, and capable of economic independence. The first two considerations touched the heart of the burgher ethos; when evaluating an applicant's moral fitness for citizenship, however, the city council did not take them as seriously as the artisans who refused membership in their handicraft corporations to anyone who was in some way dishonorable.[22] The wealthy faced little difficulty

22. Bürgerbuch (hereafter, Bgb) 1634–56, 144v, shows that the council admitted to citizenship on 24 January 1646 a shoemaker from Durlach whose wife had conceived a child before their marriage. He was not permitted to join the corporation and thus to train apprentices, but he could make shoes on his own. A look at the records on

in obtaining citizenship, because they brought with them very high registration fees and a promise of future tax revenue. The city was careful, on the other hand, not to burden itself with more poor inhabitants than it already had. In the early years of the seventeenth century, sponsors often had to swear that immigrants who applied for citizenship would not become burdens on the poor relief agency (*Almosenkasten*).[23] There is only one record of such sponsorship after 1613, when the council established minimum wealth requirements for applicants. A craftsman had to have assets worth 200 fl., while all others were to have resources of 300 fl. to be accepted as citizens.[24] The Bürgerbücher leave little doubt that newly accepted people throughout the rest of the century had honorable occupations that should have made them independent of poor relief.

A final important criterion was the Lutheran religion of the immigrant. In 1628 the council decided not to accept any more Calvinists as either citizens or denizens in Frankfurt.[25] The Calvinist families which had already attained citizenship continued to flourish, however, and by the early eighteenth century there was also a large number of Calvinist denizens. Despite its apparent laxity toward denizens over the seventeenth century, the council probably admitted to citizenship only the Calvinists who married into the old Reformed families. On the other hand, it welcomed converts from Calvinism into both the Lutheran faith and the citizen body. In 1634, for example, a former Calvinist from Zweibrücken was accepted as a Frankfurt citizen free of charge—but with the clear understanding that, should he return to his former faith, he would lose his citizenship.[26] A bold law excluding Catholics from citizenship as the ordinance of 1628 had banned Calvinists would have been politically unwise for a city as closely tied to the emperor as was Frankfurt. But admission policy toward those of the Roman faith was in practice very much the same as with the Reformed. The first references to Catholics' being admitted as new citizens (without marriage into the old

---

brewers—to be dealt with in Chapter 6—shows the council much more merciful toward the dishonored: an example was its decision of 15 October 1711 in Bgmb 1711–12, 91v–92r, to force the brewers to accept as a master one Caspar Siegfriedt, despite the fact that he had been conceived before his parents' marriage. See also Ugb D24 L29.

23. See Bgb 1586–1607 and Bgb 1608–34, passim. The practice was even used for a few burgher sons.

24. The ordinance of 6 May 1613 may be found in Corpus Legum Francofurtensium oder Neue Sammlung derer Raths-Schöffen und Aembter Verordnungen . . . (a twelve-volume collection of original printed ordinances in the Frankfurt City Archive, cited hereafter as CLF), I, Nr. 82.

25. Bgmb 1627–28, 84r–84v (10 January 1628).

26. Bgb 1608–34, 327v (6 March 1634).

Frankfurt Catholic families) appear in the 1720's after the Italian denizens and the imperial commission had applied pressure to end the council's exclusion of Roman Catholics from citizenship.[27] At the same time, to admit a Jew to the citizenry would have been unthinkable. A Jewish convert to Lutheranism, on the other hand, seldom paid fees when he was ceremoniously accepted into citizenship. Frankfurt was an overwhelmingly Lutheran city, and the council's admission policy was designed to keep the community as Lutheran as possible.

We should look more carefully at the group of 20,393 burghers admitted in the period 1600 to 1735. First of all, the annual rate of admission (shown on Table 2)[28] seems to have followed, but only roughly, the general trends of the city's population curve. Admissions fluctuated

TABLE 2

Average Yearly Admissions to Citizenship, 1601–1730
(by decades)

Decade	Admissions	Decade	Admissions
1601–10	160.3	1671–80	148.5
1611–20	123.4	1681–90	143.4
1621–30	178.0	1691–1700	147.1
1631–40	153.8	1701–10	153.2
1641–50	118.8	1711–20	160.9
1651–60	139.5	1721–30	157.1
1661–70	133.3		

rather more sharply than the general curve in the first half of the seventeenth century. After mid-century the average number of persons accepted yearly climbed more slowly and less steadily. Table 3 shows the total number of admissions by specific historical periods.[29] It demon-

27. Bgb 1723-35, 73r (7 June 1726); 77v (?); 184r (23 February 1730); 190v–191r (10 May 1730); 318v (8 November 1734). See also Ugb D10 I, passim, but especially 552–587.

28. Table 2 is also based on my use of the Bürgerbucher; I should note immediately that my figures vary almost consistently from those of Dietz, *Bürgerbuch*, 187–193. I have attempted to learn the cause of our disagreement without much success; my feeling is that Dietz often counted the number of entries per year without checking to verify that they were actual citizenship registrations. This would account for some of his higher figures; where he is lower, the problem could be one of counting children. When sons or daughters coming in with immigrants are specifically named or enumerated as receiving Bürgerrecht, I have counted them into the total.

29. Native sons and immigrants do not quite add up to total admissions, because I have not put the very small number of independent native women on the table. A few words explaining the five subperiods are in order at this point: I used 1630 as my first cut-off date, because Frankfurt was first directly affected by the Thirty Years War

TABLE 3

Admissions to Citizenship, 1600–1735
(by historical periods)

Period	Total Admissions	Native Sons	Immigrants
1600–30	4776	1681	3088
1631–50	2726	862	1863
1651–75	3400	1526	1868
1676–1704	4320	2035	2278
1705–35	5171	2776	2379
1600–1735	20,393	8880	11,476

strates more clearly the increase after 1650 and gives an initial breakdown into native sons and immigrants, pointing to comparisons between
the two groups which Tables 4[30] and 5 elaborate.

Table 4 underscores my previous emphasis on the importance of immigration. The citizen body simply could not have sustained itself without a constant supply of newcomers. What is even more interesting,
however, is the clear tendency for the percentage of immigrants to decrease after mid-century, while the ratio of native sons increased. When
we consider only the male citizens in Table 5, this increase of native men
over newcomers seems even more impressive. Over the entire period of

TABLE 4

Admissions to Citizenship, 1600–1735
(percentages)

Period	Native Sons	All Immigrants	Immigrant Men	Immigrant Women
1600–30	35.2	64.7	55.5	—
1631–50	31.6	68.3	41.5	26.9
1651–75	44.9	54.9	31.1	23.7
1676–1704	47.1	52.7	32.6	20.2
1705–35	53.7	46.0	31.1	14.8
1600–1735	43.5	56.3	38.6	17.7

in the 1630's; 1631–50 may be taken as the years when the war was felt most strongly
in the city. I decided to use the period of the constitutional conflict as another sample,
then finally I divided the period between the war and the conflict into two parts to
make five relatively equal time spans.

30. The absence of native women means that totals will be not quite 100 percent.
The figure for immigrant women in the 1600–30 period would not be statistically
significant, since records on outside marriages by native sons seem to begin only in
1614–15 and fees for wives from outside began in 1623.

TABLE 5
Admission of Men to Citizenship, 1600–1735

Period	Admissions	Native Sons		Immigrant Men	
1600–30	4334	1681	38.8%	2653	61.2%
1631–50	1993	862	43.3	1131	56.7
1651–75	2589	1526	58.9	1063	41.1
1676–1704	3442	2035	59.1	1407	40.9
1705–35	4386	2776	63.3	1610	36.7
1600–1735	16,744	8880	53.0	7864	47.0

136 years the ratio between the two groups was completely reversed. The change undoubtedly reflected both the city's improved rate of natural population increase after the terrible losses of the Thirty Years War and the decline in the number of male immigrants who married into the community after 1705. But we must note immediately that the ratio between native and immigrant male citizens remained fairly stable after the real reversal of the mid-seventeenth century. In fact, the percentage of immigrant men within the entire citizenry (Table 4) remained almost stationary after 1650, and the decrease in immigrants resulted from a drop in the number of outside women brought into the community. Despite the small success of native Frankfurters in reducing the number of male immigrants who married into the community, the number of total immigrant men increased, and their relative position remained just above 30 percent of the citizens admitted after 1650. This fact shows that the council was increasing its outright grants of citizenship, while many burghers—particularly the artisans—were complaining of overpopulation and attacking the easy access to citizens' privileges provided by marriage into burgher families.[31] The corresponding decline in the percentage of women brought into Frankfurt as wives is especially striking when seen on Table 6.[32] The city showed a real dependence on outside marriages to survive the demographic crisis of the Thirty Years War and to recover its loss. But the percentage of men marrying outsiders declined dramatically after 1650, and even the ratio of immigrants bringing wives into Frankfurt decreased to one third of its mid-century point by the end of the constitutional conflict. Marriages outside the citizenry seem to have become less and less attractive. This change was probably the result of

31. This increase in outright grants is, of course, implied in Table 1, column three: if there was a drop in the percentage of immigrants marrying into Frankfurt from nearly 70 percent in the second, third, and fourth periods to 60 percent in the period 1705–1735, then outright grants had to increase correspondingly.

32. Again the figures for the 1600–1630 period are omitted because the limited data make them statistically insignificant.

a general sentiment among settled burghers that their city was being overrun by outside elements, but one of its more concrete causes was the system of fees which became increasingly discriminatory against immigrants.

The fees charged burghers when they were registered officially in the Bürgerbücher varied in an almost arbitrary fashion. The wealthy were charged very high rates, but the council often showed consideration for those of modest means by reducing their rates below normal. Pastors,

TABLE 6

Marriages With Outside Women

(percentages)

Period	Native Sons Marrying Outsiders	Immigrant Men Bringing Wives
1600–30	—	—
1631–50	21.6	12.7
1651–75	13.7	22.6
1676–1704	8.1	17.8
1705–35	3.0	7.7
1600–1735	8.7	10.4

physicians, and city employees were usually free from any payment; both Jacob Spener and Georg Philip Thelemann, to cite illustrious examples, became burghers free of charge during our period.[33] While remaining flexible in its application of the law, the council did establish certain standard rates which took into consideration the wealth, origin, and marriage of the newly registered citizen. The decrees of 1610 and 1621 on *Bürgergeld* called for a 50-percent reduction of the fees for a man who married a burgher widow or daughter; a new ordinance of 1636, however, made no such provision.[34] Reductions occurred after 1636 but less and less frequently. We have already seen that a council decree of 1699 made immigrant women subject to the same fees paid by outside men becoming burghers. Table 7 allows us to follow the minimum standard rates over the seventeenth century for both native sons and immigrants.[35] The rise of fees was steady until 1726, when those for

33. Bgb 1657–89, 180r (26 April 1669) and Bgb 1690–1723, 306v (24 July 1714) respectively.

34. Bgb 1608–34, front, for the decrees of 30 January 1610 and 24 April 1621; Bgb 1634–56, front, for the ordinance of 11 February 1636.

35. All fees are reduced to common coinage. There seems to be no specific decree for the increase that occurred in the 1660's. After the burgher leaders began administering the chancellery in 1717, the variations in fees stopped and very careful records

all burgher sons—rich and poor—were reduced to the 1 fl. level guaranteed in the Citizens Agreement of 1612/13. But there was no corresponding reduction for immigrants, who were forced instead to pay an extra 5 fl. for poor relief after 1717. Given the rise in fees and the literal en-

TABLE 7

Minimum Bürgergeld, *1610–1726*

Year	Native	Immigrant	Source
1610	1 fl.	6 fl.	Bgb 1608–34: decree of 30 Jan 1610
1613	1		Guaranteed by *Bürgervertrag*, Art. 31
1621	1½	9	Bgb 1608–34: decree of 24 Apr 1621
1636	3	9	Bgb 1634–56: decree of 11 Feb 1636
1660's	6	15	Bgb 1657–89: usual fee charged
1717	6	20	Bgb 1690–1723, 361r, ff.
1726	1	20	Bgb 1723–35, 75v. In accordance with the *Verbesserte Visitationsordnung*

forcement of all such regulations by the burgher leaders when they took over management of the chancellery in 1717, the decline in the percentage of immigrants becomes intelligible. The burghers who had complained in 1713 about the council's arbitrary increases over the seventeenth century in their sons' fees[36] found no reason to lighten the burden on immigrants who desired citizenship. Burgher administration of the fees left no loopholes for poorer immigrants or for reduction because of marriage with a burgher's son or daughter. The citizens were determined to make entrance into the community from outside as difficult as possible.

Before turning to the groups outside the Bürgerschaft, we should look

---

were kept of what happened to the revenues collected. Bgb 1690–1723, 361v, gives a specific breakdown of the total fee:

Specific Charges	Native Son		Immigrant	
Bürgergeld	fl. 6		fl. 15	
Leather pail (fire fighting)	1	12 kr.	1	12 kr.
Poor Relief	—		5	
Chancellery fee		30		30
Total	fl. 7	42 kr.	fl. 21	42 kr.

After August 1726 the leather pail had to be physically produced rather than paid for, so that the 1 fl. 12 kr. was removed from the fee. There is no mention of a chancellery fee before 1717.

36. Bavarian State Archive Würzburg: Mainzer Regierungsakten: Kaiserliche Kommissionen, Fascicle 138, 149v–150r: "Libellus Gravaminum" submitted to the imperial commission 14 March 1713.

briefly at the burghers' occupations. I have already pointed out that the burgher—unlike other, less privileged men in the city—could enter any type of economic activity. Undoubtedly the majority of citizens were artisans who produced items for the local market. Only the burgher could engage in both wholesale and retail commerce; theoretically, he might exploit both the Frankfurt market and the European market represented in the city's two yearly fairs. Table 8 divides all citizens admitted from 1600 to 1735 into seventeen occupational groups and allows us to compare the proportion of all burghers with the percentage of immigrants entering each category.[37] The table gives a good impression of the relative importance of different occupational groups (measured, of course, in terms of the numbers of men involved, not necessarily the

TABLE 8
Burgher Occupational Groups, 1600–1735
(percentages)

Occupational Group	All Burghers Entering Each Group	Immigrant Burghers Entering Each Group
Agriculture	9.7	3.8
Day labor	1.7	1.8
Luxuries	6.2	5.4
Textiles	2.3	2.4
Clothing	10.0	11.0
Leather	1.9	1.2
Woodworking	6.1	4.8
Construction	2.9	2.4
Earthenware	0.5	0.5
Metals	3.1	2.8
Publishing	1.4	1.6
Food	8.6	5.8
Commerce	10.0	9.4
Transport	2.3	2.7
Scholars	2.6	2.2
Artists	1.2	1.3
Officials	2.2	2.3
Women	17.9	31.5
Unknown	9.2	7.0

37. Tables 8–11 are also based on machine computations of material taken from the Bürgerbücher from 1600 to 1735. I have adopted the occupational categories used by Friedrich Bothe, *Entwicklung vor dem 30jK*, 142–157, in his analysis of the tax list of 1587.

economic profit or social benefits derived). We should notice immediately the high proportion of burghers providing the most basic services for the community: 18.3 percent in food growing and processing and another 10 percent in the clothing industries. If we add to them the men in construction trades—plus those in woodworking who also had a hand in building work—we arrive at about the same 35 to 40 percent of the population engaged in what W. G. Hoskins calls the "three fundamental groups" in the English provincial towns he has studied for the sixteenth century.[38] Here in Frankfurt we find the same "variety of urban economy" that impressed Hoskins in his study of what are commonly called "cloth towns" in England. Although Frankfurt's reputation rested on its role as a major commercial depot for Central Europe, only 10 percent of the burgher population devoted full time to commerce.

But Table 8 gives us too static a view of Frankfurt's occupational structure. It cannot show, for example, that the percentage of citizens

TABLE 9

Percentage of All Burghers
Entering Occupational Groups, 1600–1735

Occupation	1600–30	1631–50	1651–75	1676–1704	1705–35
Agriculture	8.5	8.1	9.7	9.5	11.8
Day labor	4.0	1.0	0.7	0.7	1.4
Luxuries	10.1	4.8	5.7	4.9	4.8
Textiles	2.6	2.2	1.8	2.2	2.6
Clothing	10.4	9.8	9.4	10.3	10.0
Leather	2.3	1.9	1.8	1.8	1.9
Woodworking	6.4	5.1	6.7	6.6	5.5
Construction	3.3	2.0	3.5	2.6	2.8
Earthenware	0.7	0.6	0.5	0.3	0.4
Metals	3.2	2.6	3.0	3.3	3.2
Publishing	2.6	1.1	1.5	0.9	1.0
Food	6.6	7.2	7.0	9.3	11.5
Commerce	10.3	7.6	6.9	10.3	12.6
Transport	3.0	2.3	1.8	1.7	2.5
Scholars	2.2	1.8	2.7	3.0	3.1
Artists	1.8	1.2	0.9	0.9	1.2
Officials	2.7	3.0	1.7	1.9	2.0
Women	9.3	26.9	23.9	20.3	15.2
Unknown	10.3	10.7	10.4	9.3	6.6

38. "English Provincial Towns in the Early Sixteenth Century," in his *Provincial England* (London, 1963), 80.

engaged in commerce dropped from 10.3 in the prewar period to only 6.9 after the Thirty Years War. Nor does it point out the steady increases to 10.3 and 12.6 in the periods before and during the constitutional conflict. Tables 9 and 10 present a more dynamic picture by showing the proportions of Table 8 over five historical subdivisions of the longer period of 136 years. The changes in the relative importance of the different occupational groups within the entire citizen body appear clearly on Table 9. Note the fairly steady increases for the food-producing groups; both had outdistanced the clothing industries in numerical importance by the early eighteenth century. Most occupations reflected the demographic slump after 1630, but though many stabilized themselves after 1675, some like the luxury industries or wage-earning labor never recovered their prewar positions. Yet stability is probably the best word to describe the overall impression gained from Table 9; the most noticeable changes occurred in the food-producing industries and that sector of the economy which made the city famous—commerce.

These three occupational tables, then especially Table 11, also permit comparisons between native-born and immigrant burghers. In general,

TABLE 10

*Percentage of Immigrant Burghers
Entering Occupational Groups, 1600–1735*

Occupation	1600–30	1631–50	1651–75	1676–1704	1705–35
Agriculture	6.2	4.0	3.6	2.5	2.3
Day labor	4.5	1.0	1.0	0.4	0.9
Luxuries	9.5	3.4	4.0	3.3	4.7
Textiles	3.0	2.1	1.4	2.4	2.4
Clothing	11.0	9.9	10.3	11.6	11.9
Leather	1.7	1.3	1.1	1.1	0.8
Woodworking	5.8	4.0	4.4	5.5	3.7
Construction	2.9	1.6	2.8	2.0	2.5
Earthenware	0.7	0.7	0.5	0.4	0.3
Metals	3.4	1.9	2.8	3.2	2.5
Publishing	2.9	1.0	1.8	0.7	0.8
Food	5.8	5.9	3.7	5.6	7.3
Commerce	10.4	7.4	6.1	8.9	12.9
Transport	3.5	2.6	2.2	2.0	2.6
Scholars	2.5	1.4	2.1	2.4	2.1
Artists	1.5	0.9	1.1	1.0	1.8
Officials	2.8	3.4	1.6	1.9	1.9
Women	14.1	39.3	43.1	38.3	32.2
Unknown	7.6	8.1	6.5	6.9	5.8

the proportion of immigrants entering the various occupations reflected the same tendencies we have noted for the entire citizenry. Immigrants showed more interest than native sons in clothing industries and commerce but considerably less participation in food producing. Much more revealing for our purposes is the comparison in Table 11 of the proportion of immigrant burghers to native-born citizens within each occupational group. The table demonstrates once again what I have previously emphasized: the importance of the immigrants to Frankfurt's economy as well as the tendency within the citizenry in the late seventeenth and early eighteenth centuries for native sons to weaken the economic position of their immigrant counterparts. There was only one occupational group (artists) in which the ratio of immigrants to natives was higher in the early eighteenth century than it had been a hundred years before. Only two others (luxuries and food processing) saw a higher ratio in the period 1705–1735 than in 1651–1675. Although the proportion was quite stable in the area of commerce between 1651 and 1735, in most categories there were sizable reductions in the period of the constitutional conflict

TABLE II

Proportion of Immigrants to Native Sons
Entering Each Occupational Group, 1600–1735

Occupation	1600–1735	1600–30	1631–50	1651–75	1676–1704	1705–35
Agriculture	22.3	46.7	33.5	20.2	13.7	8.9
Day labor	61.3	73.3	70.4	83.3	32.3	31.0
Luxuries	49.0	61.3	48.5	37.9	36.0	45.3
Textiles	58.2	75.8	66.7	44.3	58.5	43.9
Clothing	61.8	68.9	69.2	59.8	59.8	54.3
Leather	35.4	48.6	46.2	32.8	32.1	18.8
Woodworking	44.4	58.4	54.0	36.1	44.0	31.2
Construction	47.2	57.6	54.5	44.2	40.2	41.0
Earthenware	59.8	65.6	81.3	62.5	57.1	31.6
Metals	51.3	68.9	48.6	50.5	51.4	36.8
Publishing	61.1	74.6	62.1	63.5	45.9	37.7
Food	37.7	57.0	55.8	28.9	31.6	29.2
Commerce	53.1	65.0	67.0	48.3	45.2	47.0
Transport	65.5	77.3	75.0	70.0	60.0	48.8
Scholars	46.5	75.7	54.0	42.9	41.5	31.5
Artists	60.6	55.3	51.5	62.5	60.5	72.1
Officials	59.1	68.5	79.0	50.0	51.8	43.4
Women	98.9	98.4	99.9	99.3	99.4	97.3
Unknown	42.7	48.1	51.9	34.1	39.1	40.5

itself. Although immigrants revealed much the same general pattern as native sons in their choice of occupations over the entire period from 1600 to 1735, the significant change was the success of burghers in limiting the proportion of immigrants entering the labor market. Guarding the privileges of citizenship more carefully during the constitutional conflict made economic sense; it worked to the advantage of the settled burghers over newcomers, and, as we shall see later, it protected both against elements outside the citizenry.

III. The Outsiders: Denizens and Jews

The outsiders included the denizens, the transient foreigners called *Fremde*, the dependent villagers, and the Frankfurt Jews. Residents of the surrounding villages under the city's jurisdiction were villeins of the city until 1810.[39] Their communal administration was directed by Frankfurt's Office of Rural Affairs (*Landamt*), and the villagers had no political role or social position within the city.[40] The Jews and noncitizen foreigners were permitted to live inside the city walls according to specific regulations, codified for the Jewish community in its Stättigkeit. For the Christian foreigners—transient or settled—no clear code of regulations was enacted until 1708, when a Denizen Ordinance was passed after burgher merchants demanded firm action against the illegal economic practices of the outsiders.

Fremde could refer to any outsiders; when not using the term so comprehensively, Frankfurt legislation of the seventeenth century seems to have used it to denote transient foreigners. Such persons were to register their names with the Office of Inquisition and to pay a small fee (*Schutzgeld* or *Schreibgeld*); only on presentation of a receipt from that office were foreigners permitted to receive lodging in the city.[41] The numerous edicts (57, according to a quick and probably incomplete count for 1600–1735) forbidding burghers from renting rooms to unregistered foreigners suggests that the number of such transients was probably quite high and that the law was unenforceable. The city was flooded by refugees from the wartorn countryside in the 1630's and 1640's, but the council was unable to impress either burghers or foreigners with a need to register

---

39. Anton Horne, *Geschichte von Frankfurt am Main in gedrängter Darstellung* (Frankfurt, 1882), 152. Bücher, *Bevölkerung*, 673, counts 1417 souls in six of Frankfurt's eight villages in 1685.

40. Ruppersberg, "Aufbau der . . . Behörden," *Die Stadt Goethes*, 62.

41. See, for example, the ordinance of 29 September 1649 (renewing one of 7 March 1648) in CLF, III, Nr. 52. An ordinance of 20 January 1674 provided that inns do the reporting for their visitors each night; see Ugb B76 C, 44–45.

the guests and have them pay fees.[42] The sample of legislation I have seen indicates that the problem was not considered acute again until the mid-1670's. After 1674, frequent registration laws threatened burghers with penalties for lodging the outsiders; citizens certainly did not hesitate to take financial advantage of the fact that many foreigners were in the city. The size of the fees paid by foreigners to the city government remains unclear, and I am unable to learn whether there was any limitation on how long a transient might stay in Frankfurt without making more permanent arrangements.[43] But Fremde were forbidden from buying property or establishing a trade in the city, and if they had no intention of becoming burghers or denizens, they were urged to move on.[44]

Denizens were outsiders who made Frankfurt their residence. Regulation of their position in the community seems to have begun in the late sixteenth century, and in 1595 a special Office of Inquisition was created to oversee their admission and taxation.[45] In 1628 an oath of allegiance was first required for denizens, though the practice apparently fell into disuse and had to be revived in 1676.[46] The very existence of an oath— so important to the political life of medieval and early modern communities—demonstrates the formal and more binding attachment of the denizen to the city. He was permitted to reside anywhere in the city (in contrast to the Jews) and to earn a living in Frankfurt under the protection of its laws (in contrast to the Fremde). Yet his position was decidedly inferior to the burgher's privileged status. He could not own property in the city, and his economic activities were largely limited to dependent and wage-earning jobs, on the one hand, and to large-scale commercial enterprises on the other. The seventeenth century saw ever-increasing economic competition between denizens and burghers, and the citizens —led by the great wholesale dealers—fought hard to place more and more limitations on the outsiders' enterprises. The burghers' conflict with the denizens is the subject of Chapter 8; here I need only indicate

42. See Ugb B76 D1, a collection of ordinances on the foreigners from 1607 to 1684, passim, as well as Ugb B76 E1. 16 of the 57 ordinances I have quickly counted for the whole period 1600–1735 fell in the years 1635–48. An edict of 19 November 1640 found in this collection was passed after the Office of Inquisition complained that burghers didn't seem to know about the ordinances against lodging unregistered foreigners.

43. The city later created a legal category for transients: *Permissionisten* were allowed to reside in the city for one year. See *Hessisches Städtebuch*, 132.

44. See the ordinance of 29 January 1618 in CLF, II, Nr. 2; that of 15 July 1617 printed in Johann Conradin Beyerbach, *Sammlung der Verordnungen der Reichsstadt Frankfurt 1530–1806* (Frankfurt, 1798–1818), 1358; and Ugb B76 Rr for an order from the Office of Inquisition dated 9 June 1718.

45. Dietz, *FftHG*, IV, i, 159.

46. Ibid.; the ordinance of 25 May 1676 found in Ugb D76 D1 speaks of reintroduction of an old practice that had fallen into disuse.

that the resulting Denizen Ordinances of 1708 and 1735 capped a seventy-five-year process of diminishing the denizen's economic privileges. Whatever small competition he presented in handicraft corporations was eliminated, he was excluded from the city's retail market, and his commercial ventures were burdened with higher tolls and tariffs. Although they did not enjoy the economic privileges of burghers, denizens were subject to the same or sometimes higher taxes.

Why then would an immigrant coming to Frankfurt become a denizen rather than a burgher? The most obvious reason was the council's exclusion of non-Lutherans or of men who would not have had an independent position in a handicraft corporation. The arrangement may have offered some advantages to big commercial agents, even if they qualified for citizenship. Dietz argues that the most important immigrants became denizens, because they wanted a trial period in the city to see how their businesses would thrive in Frankfurt.[47] Hans Mauersberg also sees little willingness on the part of the largest wholesalers to assume citizenship, because their position as denizens allowed them the mobility necessary to their international commercial activities, while it also gave them greater political independence in times of war between France and the Empire.[48] Although the last argument is weak (the embargoes on trade with France were imperial not Frankfurt legislation), denizens were more mobile. They were not tied to the city by fixed assets and, as far as I know, were not subject until 1725 to the "Tenth Penny," a 10-percent tax on the holdings of any burgher who gave up his ties to the city.[49]

The basic fee for protection as a denizen of Frankfurt increased over the seventeenth century, but this increase did not stem the growth of the outside group attached to the community. In 1614 a single person paid 16 Sch. (or 2/3 fl.) *Schreib-* or *Schutzgeld*, while a married couple paid 1 fl. per quarter year.[50] An increase to 4 fl. for single men and 8 fl. for a married couple per year was applied after 1631 for the rest of the century to "common denizens."[51] Wealthier men were undoubtedly charged more, but I find no record of their rates until 1676, when they were ordered either to declare their total assets for purposes of paying a fixed percentage or to pay a flat rate of 50 Rtlr. (75 fl.).[52] The following year

47. Dietz, *FftHG*, IV, i, 157.

48. Mauersberg, 137–138.

49. Müller, *Frankfurt contra Frankfurt*, II, 130, for fees established for denizens by the *Verbesserte Visitations-Ordnung* of 1725. On the Tenth Penny in general, see Schnapper-Arndt, *Lebenshaltung*, I, 382.

50. Ordinance of 19 May 1614 in Ugb B76 D1.

51. Ordinance of 31 April 1631 in Ugb B76 D1.

52. Ordinance of 10 August 1676 and rejection of an appeal against that ordinance on 23 November 1677; both in Ugb B76 D1.

the council set a rate of .5 percent of their total assets for wealthy Beisassen, and to this was added the basic fee of 8 fl. for all denizen couples.[53] Finally, the Visitation Ordinance of 1725 set a flat rate of 100 fl. for the wealthiest denizens; a second category could pay 40 kr. for each 100 fl. assets, and the "commoners" were to continue paying 6 to 8 fl. yearly.[54] These fee increases do not in themselves explain the enormous rise in income enjoyed by the Office of Inquisition over the seventeenth century. Only a considerable increase in the number of denizens immigrating into Frankfurt could account for such striking change. Other evidence also points to an increase in the size of the denizen group: the ratio of denizen to burgher baptisms grew higher over the century, and burgher concern about the outsiders multiplied as the century passed.[55] Precise statistics on denizens are, however, sparse. Various counts were taken by the captains of the fourteen quarters, but no complete list is extant in the Frankfurt City Archive.[56] In the *Haus-, Hof- und Staatsarchiv* in Vienna there is a specification of the denizens in all fourteen quarters presented by the council to the Reichshofrat on 13 June 1714; since the scrupulous burgher officers supplied an appendix pointing out the denizens missed by the council, we may assume that the total of 1212 denizens for 1714 is fairly accurate.[57] Abraham Mangon has given another probably accurate figure for total denizens in his history of the Calvinist community, a manuscript now in the Frankfurt archive. As one of the few Reformed leaders of the burgher party in the constitutional conflict, Mangon had access to tax and Inquisition records to check for overdue payments. In January 1719 he apparently made a list of deni-

53. Ordinance of 30 January 1677 in Ugb B76 D1.
54. Müller, *Frankfurt contra Frankfurt*, II, 130.
55. Mauersberg, 136–138.
56. Ugb B76 is a list for 1657 consisting of reports from nine or ten quarters, some of which are very difficult to count: I get 276 persons, but Mauersberg, 137, gets 378. Ugb B76 U1 is a list of denizens who paid *Servizgeld* in 1669 and totals 392 persons; Mauersberg assures us that, despite the fact that all 14 quarters reported, the list is not complete, because all Beisassen did not have to pay the fee. Reports in Ugb B76 E2 from nine quarters for March, 1677, total 306 denizens taking their oaths. Dietz, *FftHG*, IV, i, 159, says there were 336 denizens paying taxes in December, 1676; the sizes of the partial lists suggest that the figure is too low for all denizens, and Dietz himself gives no indication what tax they were paying. He goes on to say that 225 of those denizens swore the *Beisasseneid* in May 1677; he gives no citation for his source and I cannot be certain whether he means the March list (Ugb B76 E2) or another now lost. Ugb B76 U1 is another partial list of denizens for only three quarters, but it is relatively more valuable because occupations were given. If we compare the lists for the fourth quarter for 1669 (Ugb B76 U1) and 1682 (Ugb B76 U2), we see an increase from 49 to 63 denizens—an increase of 28.6 percent.
57. HHSA Wien: RHR Decisa 2146, ad Nr. 47 and Nr. 48. Mauersberg is unaware of this specification, as he is of Mangon's estimate.

zens and the protection fees they paid. I am unable to locate the list itself, but his totals were:

99	Calvinists	paying fl.	3940 —	kr.
13	Important Catholics		863 —	
66	Important Lutherans		814 —	
1135	Common Lutherans and Catholics		5421	45
1313	Total Denizens	paying fl.	11,038	45 kr.

Mangon hastened to point out that his coreligionists were paying over one third of all the Schreibgeld collected.[58] We expect the Calvinists to appear on the list, and the high proportion of "commoners" is not surprising; the large number of "important" (read "wealthy," probably "merchant") Lutherans, on the other hand, demonstrates that some commercial people chose to remain denizens.

The specification of 1714 presents a unique opportunity to examine the occupations of Frankfurt's denizens. Other records show that many diverse kinds of economic activity were pursued by denizens,[59] but the enumeration of all Beisassen in 1714 with their occupations permits a statistical breakdown (Table 12). To the degree that the city's legislation on denizens was enforced, the 112 persons in commerce would have been wholesalers, not retailers. The majority of those engaged in the production of luxuries were involved in some way with the tobacco industry—a business tolerated only outside the city walls.[60] Although some persons in categories like scholars (three Calvinist ministers, for example) or artists might have been as respected or wealthy as merchants, most of the men whom I have listed in the individual categories had low-caliber positions. The denizens in clothing industries, to take another example, usually included shoe repairmen and not shoemakers. The high ratio of day laborers and menial transportation workers reinforces my earlier impression that denizens should be divided economically into a large number of dependent workers and a few men of high economic or social position. The polarization was undoubtedly clear to that good burgher Abraham Mangon when he divided his list into "important" and "common" denizens.

On the fringe of the community—physically and legally isolated from

58. Mangon's "Chronologische Darstellung, 1517–1728," v 171 of the Archiv der französisch-reformirten Gemeinde (deposited in the Frankfurt City Archive), 912–13. Mangon says his specification was written out in v 170, 213 ff., but it is unfortunately not there.

59. Ugb B76 U1, for example.

60. Friedrich Bothe, *Geschichte der Stadt Frankfurt am Main* (Frankfurt, 1913), 473; for its importance to Frankfurt's commerce, however, see Dietz, *FftHG*, IV, i, 56–61.

TABLE 12

Denizen Occupational Groups, 1714

Occupation	Total Denizens
Agriculture	36
Day labor	152
Luxuries	88
Textiles	58
Clothing	146
Leather	2
Woodworking	24
Construction	43
Earthenware	2
Metals	8
Publishing	29
Food	7
Commerce	112
Transport	137
Scholars	24
Artists	53
Officials	4
Women	170
Unknown	117
Total	1212

other groups in the city—lived Frankfurt's Jews. Their location within the city symbolized their legal and social position. The long, narrow ghetto stretched along the outside of a section of the twelfth-century *Staufermauer* which effectively cut it off from the Christian city. Semi-isolated in this southeastern corner, the Jews were still protected by the expansive fourteenth-century wall with its elaborate seventeenth-century fortifications. In 1372 the Emperor Charles IV had sold the Jewish community in Frankfurt, which was his fief, to the city itself. The city attained the right to tax the Jews and to establish the regulations (Stättigkeit) under which the Jewish community was permitted to remain in the city. These conditions could be changed but had to be submitted—along with the privileges of the citizens themselves—for the approval of each new emperor. Until 1685 the emperor reserved the right to repurchase the community for a fixed sum of money; he held *dominium eminens* over the Jews, while Frankfurt held *dominium utile*.[61] In addi-

61. These arrangements are fully treated in B. J. Römer-Büchner, *Die Entwicklung der Stadtverfassung und die Bürgervereine der Stadt Frankfurt am Main* (Frankfurt,

tion to this arrangement, the Jews of Frankfurt enjoyed special privileges in the entire Empire at the pleasure of the emperor. Tolls and customs previously fixed on Jews, for example, could not be raised; they did not have to wear special clothing identifying themselves as Jews when traveling; Frankfurt Jews could be tried only in Frankfurt or imperial courts.[62] Thus the Jews in Frankfurt still had two masters—both of whom were eager to acquire as much money from them as was feasible. The Jews were in a fairly good position, however, because they knew how to play off the two authorities against each other. When the emperor attempted to force extraordinary imposts from them, they appealed to the city council, which hastened to remind the emperor that he had sold it the right to tax the Jews. When the council acted against them, the Jews often went over its head to the emperor, who—in return for certain financial considerations—usually granted them special protection from the city. The history of the Frankfurt Jews will help to illustrate, in Chapter 4, the character of patrician government as well as the intricate relations between the council and the emperor.

Inside Frankfurt itself the Jews were forced to live in the crowded and unsanitary *Judengasse*. Between sunset and dawn (as well as on Sundays and holy days) they were not permitted outside the locked gates of the ghetto. They were allowed on the streets only in groups of two, and even then only when properly identified by the large yellow ring sewed on their clothing. Such were the regulations of the last Stättigkeit drawn up in 1616,[63] but these stipulations hardly give any picture of the actual situation of the Jews in Frankfurt—as analysis of the relations between the Jews and the burghers in Chapter 7 will show. Although the Stättigkeit tried to limit the Jewish population by allowing no more than 500 households in the ghetto, the number of Jews grew rapidly in the years before the constitutional conflict. They numbered just over 2000 in 1621, declined in the next twenty years to about 1540, and then increased to around 1800 by the end of the Thirty Years War.[64] Precise figures do not appear again until burgher concern led the council to conduct visitations of the ghetto in 1694, 1703, and 1709. The number of households had reached 436 by 1703, and it was to increase to 505 by 1709; the total population was 2364 and 3024 respectively.[65] Although the legal limit

1855), 78–81, and in Johann Heinrich Bender, *Der frühere und jetzige Zustand der Israeliten zu Frankfurt am Main* (Frankfurt, 1833), 13–14.

62. Isidor Kracauer, *Geschichte der Juden in Frankfurt am Main* (Frankfurt, 1927), II, 75–77, discusses the imperial privileges of the community renewed by Leopold I.

63. The Stättigkeit is most conveniently found in Bothe, *Entwicklung vor dem 30jK*, 247–317. For a discussion of the word and its different meanings, see Bücher, *Bevölkerung*, 528.

64. Kracauer, "Juden im 30jK," 131–132.

65. Bücher, *Bevölkerung*, 570; Kracauer, "Judengasse," 322–23. I rely throughout

on households was not passed until 1709, a population increase of 67 percent from the mid-seventeenth century to 1709 (and 25 percent from 1703 to 1709!) shows that burgher complaints about violation of the intention of the Stättigkeit were quite justified. By 1709 the ghetto faced a housing crisis which become a disaster with the great fire of 1711.[66] And Frankfurt burghers faced increased competition from Jewish retailers who illegally invaded their local market between the great spring and autumn fairs. The visitations of 1694 and 1703 provide occupational data which suggest that commercial activity was probably the only area where burghers and Jews conflicted (Table 13).[67] The growth of the professions is impressive at the beginning of the eighteenth century, but there is no evidence of clashes between professional Jews and Christians.

TABLE 13
Jewish Occupational Groups

Occupation	1694	1703
Commerce	267	288
Professions	33	59
Handicrafts	19	13
Day labor	9	12
Poor	7	9
Unknown	48	48
Totals	383	429

A few Jewish artisans provided the community with its special food requirements and made no attempt, to my knowledge, to sell to people outside the ghetto. The number of Jews engaged in commerce was high and their competition with burghers sharp, especially since the Jews switched after the Thirty Years War from their famous (or infamous) moneylending businesses into retail enterprises. The occupational data indicate strong concentration of Jewish efforts not in producing but in selling textiles, clothing, food products, and luxury items.[68] The Jews entered what the burghers considered their own sanctuary—the retail market—and earned their implacable hatred. The most important concern of the burghers in 1705 was, as I have previously pointed out, to

on Kracauer rather than Wilhelm Hanauer, "Zur Statistik der jüdischen Bevölkerung in Frankfurt am Main," *Zeitschrift für Demographie und Statistik der Juden* 6 (1910), 137, who seems to draw estimates for the seventeenth century largely from Dietz, *Bürgerbuch,* 191–93.

66. Kracauer, "Judengasse," 323–28.

67. Table 13 is based on Joseph Unna, *Statistik der Frankfurter Juden bis zum Jahre 1866* (Frankfurt, 1931), 29–30.

68. Ibid., 29.

eliminate this Jewish competition and thereby preserve the economic foundations of their own society.

IV. The Ordered Society and Its Instability

What kind of society were the burghers of Frankfurt trying to preserve? Their society was organized legally into a hierarchy of distinct social orders, but it faced changes which threw the relatively clear traditional stratification out of focus. A shuffling of the positions of different social groups in seventeenth-century Frankfurt called into question the old system of legal and honorific strata. During the constitutional conflict sumptuary legislation revising that system raised serious difficulties for the community. Yet no one questioned the existence of legalized social divisions among the Christian residents, and the burgher captains who asked the council to make the law clear and enforceable continued to think of Frankfurt's social hierarchy in terms of status groups and not economic classes. The orders of society were defined in the police and clothing ordinances which go back in the city's history to 1356.[69] Although such legislation aimed originally at combating luxury, it served primarily as a means of social differentiation after the imperial police ordinances were enacted in the sixteenth century.[70] Specific regulations concerning the clothing appropriate to each order (*Stand*) were probably unenforceable; they were flouted as styles changed or as men acquired new wealth or social aspirations. Yet the ordinances are valuable reflections of the social conceptions prevalent in the early modern period; "what they do tell us is how the authorities of a given community visualized its social hierarchy, and how groups were supposedly related to one another in terms of public status, even if their members refused to dress accordingly."[71]

The police ordinances of 1621, 1671, and 1731 defined Frankfurt's hierarchy over the seventeenth and early eighteenth centuries.[72] Table 14 indicates the city's system of five legal orders, as they were outlined

69. See Schnapper-Arndt, *Lebenshaltung*, I, 223–33, for an excellent brief discussion of the history of the ordinances; Karl Bräuer, "Frankfurter Polizeiordnungen im 17. Jahrhundert," *Alt-Frankfurt* 1 (1909), 58–61, is a popular sketch.

70. Schnapper-Arndt, *Lebenshaltung*, I, 224–25; cf. the general comments of Liselotte C. Eisenbart, *Kleiderordnungen der deutschen Städte zwischen 1350 und 1700* (Göttingen, 1962), 55–58.

71. Franklin L. Ford, *Strasbourg in Transition, 1648–1789* (Cambridge, Mass., 1958), 15. See also Schnapper-Arndt, *Lebenshaltung*, I, 227.

72. There were clothing ordinances passed in 1597, 1621, 1625, 1636, 1640, 1671, and 1731. The ones for 1621, 1671, and 1731 were parts of more comprehensive police ordinances, which may be found in CLF, II, Nr. 36; CLF, IV, Nr. 25; and Beyerbach, *Sammlung*, esp. 167–172.

TABLE 14
The Five Social Orders, 1621–1731

Order	1621	1671	1731
First	Members of first bench of the council The *Geschlechter* = old patrician families	First bench of council Other council members, the syndics, and noble families involved in government for a hundred years or longer Holders of the doctorate	First bench of the council The syndics and the second bench of the council Noble families involved in city government a hundred years who maintained their station Holders of the doctorate or the licenciate not undertaking work as notaries
Second	Other council members The most distinguished citizens and merchants	Members of the council's second bench not in the first order Most distinguished citizens and merchants involved in wholesale & banking enterprises	The council's third bench Most distinguished merchants and rentiers having at least 30,000 fl. assets Captains of the burgher militia

Third	Distinguished retailers Notaries, procurators, and others of approximately the same station	Council's third bench Notaries, procurators, artists, and retailers of approximately the same station and not in other orders	Procurators in the courts Merchants not in the second order Notaries, artists, and the most distinguished retailers Lieutenants and *Fähnrichs* of the burgher militia
Fourth	Common retailers All handicraft people	Common retailers Merchant assistants and all handicraft people	Common retailers Merchant assistants and all handicraft people
Fifth	All others not really handicraft or retail people; esp. coachmen, transport workers, day laborers, etc.	All others not really handicraft or retail people; esp. coachmen, transport workers, day laborers, etc.	All others not really handicraft or retail people; esp. coachmen, transport workers, day laborers, etc.

in the three laws. The social pattern shows no very startling changes from 1621 to 1731, nor was it static. Signs of group mobility appear only in the three upper strata—not in the fourth and fifth orders, which contained the large majority of the population. A look at the upper orders shows immediately that actual or potential participation in civic government was the organizing principle of the hierarchy; governing was probably regarded by all groups as the most important social function in the community. Although there was real consensus on that point, the aristocrats who controlled the first two benches of the city council had considerable difficulty by 1731 in arranging other groups in the hierarchy "according to their proximity to or distance from the style of life of the dominant group and according to the quality of services they rendered."[73]

Alterations in the three upper orders reflected some of the changes with which the city fathers had to cope. Perhaps the most striking development was the expansion of the first order to include not only the old patriciate but also other noble groups, in particular the university graduates and those Frauensteiner who could be counted as nobles. Although the two aristocratic societies remained distinct socially, their cooperation as the ruling clique in seventeenth-century Frankfurt found expression in the careful inclusion of as many Frauensteiner as possible in the highest legal order. The appearance of the educated elite (the syndics and the holders of the doctorate) in the first order by 1671 indicates its increasing prestige and political role in a century which, according to Hohenemser, saw rapid expansion of Frankfurt's bureaucracy.[74] The demands of the university graduates for more appointments in city government and for a higher social position than the Frauenstein Society afforded probably explains the upgrading in 1731 of the council's second bench, so that Frauensteiner who served there would continue to enjoy precedence over most doctors of law. The changing social rank of the artisan councilmen of the third bench is also revealing. The aristocrats who controlled the senate did not hesitate to lower the status of their artisan colleagues in 1671, but after the council's power in the community was challenged in the early eighteenth century, the third bench was elevated once more into the second order. The move paralleled the raising of second-bench senators into the first Stand at the end of the constitutional conflict and represented another attempt to buttress the social position of the entire council vis-à-vis the men who had successfully challenged its monopoly of political power in Frankfurt. And those

73. Roland Mousnier, *Problèmes de stratification sociale: Deux cahiers de la noblesse pour les états généraux de 1649–1651* (Paris, 1961), 16.

74. Paul Hohenemser, "Beamtenwesen in Frankfurt am Main um 1700," *Alt-Frankfurt* 3 (1911), 65–72.

men finally appeared in the official hierarchy in 1731; the city fathers simply could not ignore the officers of the burgher militia.

Several groups, listed only in general terms in 1621, were more carefully defined in 1671 and 1731. The nobles included in the first order were, at first, only the patricians; then those whose families had been involved in city government for a hundred years; and finally, in 1731, those who maintained as well an appropriate style of life. A similar clause which referred to maintaining the proper dignity of the order was added for holders of the doctorate in the last ordinance. The need to be more precise about the "most distinguished merchants" meant defining them first in 1671 as wholesalers and bankers and in 1731 as men with assets of at least 30,000 fl. This last change is doubly interesting: it introduced a purely economic factor into a classification based largely on political functions, and it tended to downgrade the big merchants by dividing them into two groups and lowering the status of some. Since this step was taken at the same time that the council raised the status of its own lower-bench members, the greater precision used by the magistracy to define the other groups in the upper orders had the net effect of making nonmembers of the council considerably less secure in their social positions. What happened to the noble who did not maintain his station? Did he fall into the second order as a distinguished rentier? What about a doctor of law who did notarial work occasionally to increase his income, or the merchant who suffered momentary losses which brought his assets below 30,000 fl.? The noble families of the Alt-Limpurg Society which did not have members in the council at the time could not bear the thought of having lesser rank than non-noble members of the council's second bench.[75] University graduates also resented the fact that a merchant sitting in the council might have precedence over them and that they were not permitted to engage in notarial activities.[76]

These and other groups petitioned the council to change their own positions in the last police ordinance, but the burgher officer corps chose instead to speak for the entire community in its trenchant criticism of the magistrates in August or September 1731.[77] Its statement contained

75. Ugb A51 Nr. 16, 326r–329v: Nr. 71, Alt-Limpurg petition to the council (13 September 1731).

76. Ugb A51 Nr. 16, 323r–325r: Nr. 70, "Notamina Doctorii" (7 October 1731); 350v–351v: Nr. 79, memorial of Lic. Clauer to a meeting of the Graduate Society (19 February 1732); 353r–355v: Nr. 80, Graduate petition to the council (19 February 1732); 360r–362v: Nr. 82a, Graduate petition to the imperial commission (4 March 1732).

77. I have used an undated copy of the captains' statement sent by the burgher deputies to the imperial commissioner Count von Schönborn 31 September 1731; it reached his estate at Wiesentheid on 4 October 1731 and was subsequently sent on

neither bitter demands for an equal voice in setting up the social hierarchy nor petty requests for self-advancement. The burgher leaders did not question the ultimate value of the legislation or the council's sole jurisdiction in the matter. They wanted not to delay implementation of the ordinance but to convince the council that eventual modifications of the law would be necessary to make men's social positions in the hierarchy entirely clear. They found two kinds of problems in the ordinance as it stood—innovations that would only cause disputes within the community and an unclear definition of the groups in the lower social orders. The captains showed particular concern over the elevation of status for members of the lower benches of the council; this change meant inevitable conflicts for public precedence among the councilmen, the holders of degrees, and merchants. The novel limitation on the notarial activities of the graduates of law did not recognize economic facts, and giving precedence to the handicraft masters of the council's third bench over the militia officers showed no grasp of political reality. Most harmful to the city's prosperity, however, was the "harsh" classification of merchants by wealth rather than their status as wholesalers and bankers. If his rank in society were determined by wealth alone, the merchant with temporary misfortune might well fall into the third order and thereby endanger his reputation and his chances of gaining the credit necessary to recover his losses. The division of the merchants (*Handelsstand*) into two orders also complicated the arrangement of marriage alliances between young men just starting in business (probably with less than 30,000 fl.) and older commercial families, whose tendency would be to marry their social equals. Perhaps the most significant of the captains' comments were their requests for clear explanations of just who were to be regarded as artists, distinguished retailers (*Crämer*), ordinary retailers and handicraft people, and subordinates ("welche diejenige seyen, so keine rechte Handwercker oder rechte Crämer sind").[78]

The burgher officers were entirely serious in asking the council to give more precise definitions of the groups in the lower orders; they were not simply attempting to burden the council with a new and impossible task which would end its whole project for revising the police ordinance. Initiative for the revision had come, in fact, from the burgher leadership and the imperial commission and not from the city fathers themselves.[79]

---

to the Reichshofrat. See HHSA Wien: RHR Decisa 2203, Nrus. 1617. The views of the captains and the deputies themselves were well outlined earlier in the 51er Protocolla 1731, 107–112 (meeting of 16 August 1731). I draw from both documents for the following discussion.

78. HHSA Wien: RHR Decisa 2203, Nrus. 1617.

79. See HHSA Wien: RHR Decisa 2201, Nrus. 1474, Petition of the burgher deputies

The captains clung to the concept of society legally divided into status groups, yet the demand for precise definitions of all groups made the task impossible. The careful spelling out of the upper orders had already caused many disputes, and an attempt to carry the process further would have raised innumerable problems. Count von Schönborn had already authorized publication of the police ordinance despite its difficulties: the commission's work was nearly over, several years had elapsed since the initial order for a revision of the law was issued, and he felt that problems could be worked out in amendments to the legislation once it had been published.[80] But amendments were never worked out, and the police ordinance of 1731 was the last in Frankfurt's history.[81] Fifty years later Johann Moritz wrote: "daily experience alone shows that even this police and clothing ordinance is no longer observed."[82] It was probably never carefully observed, and examination of the situation in which the ordinance was issued shows that Frankfurt's leading citizens, though they continued to think in terms of legal orders, could not see how the social groups of the community fit into a stratified hierarchy in any clear and satisfactory way.

The problem lay not in a simple lack of consensus between the council and its dissident burghers (they were, in fact, drawing closer together by 1731 in a common fight against denizens and against Calvinist moves to gain public worship in the city) but in a complex social situation that had blurred whatever clear vision of an ordered society men had previously had. Economic and social changes of the period after the Thirty Years War had complicated the relationships among different groups of the city's residents to such an extent that old social categories did not always conform with new reality. Were the most distinguished merchants to be assigned their social station as men with a certain level of wealth or as a group with fairly clearly defined commercial functions? "Every . . . economic transformation," wrote Max Weber, "threatens stratification by status and pushes the class situation into the foreground."[83] Yet we see Frankfurt at a point in its history when both class and status-group relationships must be used to explain the city's social life. Group actions were conditioned by traditional attitudes and the city's legal arrangements as well as by practical economic (Weber's "class") considerations. The artisans' struggle against the Jews, for ex-

to the Count von Schönborn (31 March/2 April 1731); title 11 of the Visitation Ordinance of 1725 in Müller, *Frankfurt contra Frankfurt*, II, 93; and title 7, number 17, of the Consistory Ordinance of 1728, ibid., III, 82.

80. HHSA Wien: RHR Decisa 2203, Nrus. 1618 (5 October 1731).

81. Schnapper-Arndt, *Lebenshaltung*, I, 226.

82. Moritz, II, 262.

83. Weber, "Class, Status, Party," 194.

ample, can be seen as a fight for the retail market in Frankfurt, but such an analysis scarcely begins the full story. Only when we have examined them as stratified occupational groups organized in handicraft corporations (*Handwerke*), understood their conception of the council's responsibility to protect their traditional status in the community, and seen their real goal as a minimum living standard (*Nahrung*) to maintain their burgher style of life—only then do we begin to grasp the complexity of the artisans' social and political status. And only against such a background of status-group analysis can we grasp the full implications of the economic challenges the artisans faced or their particular political responses to them. I propose to look at each of the major social groups in seventeenth-century Frankfurt in terms of both its class and its status-group relationships. I shall begin at the top of the hierarchy—with the aristocracy.

PART TWO

THE URBAN ARISTOCRACY

Wir haben gethan, was Regenten thun dürfen.
a patrician (1616)

Was Kaiser? Wir sind Kaiser hier und der
Kaiser ist Kaiser zu Wien.
a syndic to a burgher captain (1706)

Chapter 3

The Aristocratic Societies

The dominant element of Frankfurt's "mixed" constitution was the aristocracy. The city's most important families were organized in the seventeenth century into three different groups—the Limpurg, Frauenstein, and Graduate societies. Besides their joint political power in the city council, the aristocrats enjoyed first rank in the social hierarchy and were free from service in the burgher militia.[1] Although I shall use the term aristocracy to embrace all three groups, the city's "best men" made fairly clear distinctions among themselves which reveal much about the nature of social status and social mobility in one of the Empire's more conservative cities.

The Limpurger were the most important aristocrats, for they were recognized by all Frankfurters as the city's ancient and noble patriciate. Although many Frankfurt historians have accepted the claim (made first in the mid-eighteenth century) that the Frauensteiner too were patricians, such high rank was not acknowledged by their fellow citizens in the early modern period. Many Frauensteiner, as holders of university degrees or special patents, were nobles, but they differed from the patriciate in their willingness to engage in commerce. They were less exclusive than the Limpurger, and they had a certain parvenu quality that did not enhance social prestige in the seventeenth century.

1. Moritz, *Frankfurt*, I, 215, 219, 220.

A group of university graduates in law and medicine formed the Free Society in 1613 to comply with the Citizens Agreement, article three of which had ordered all burghers into social corporations.[2] In 1616 the society changed its name to the *Collegium Graduatorum*, but it did not generate the strong corporate sense that characterized the other two groups of aristocrats. In contrast to the Limpurger and the Frauensteiner, the Graduates owned no lodge hall in which to hold regular social meetings. The lawyers and physicians met only in special sessions to consider issues important to them as a status group in Frankfurt.[3] Yet the prestige of the Graduates increased considerably over the seventeenth century, and by 1705 they claimed higher qualification for public office and precedence in public ceremonies over the Frauensteiner. The legal battle which ensued shows that the social position of the Frauensteiner was vulnerable to attack from the educated elite. But neither group of the aristocracy presumed to challenge the high position of the Limpurger as Frankfurt's noble patriciate.

I. The Patricians or Urban Nobility

The Alt-Limpurg Society was formed probably in the mid-fourteenth century, when Frankfurt's guilds were attempting to wrest a share of political power from the patricians.[4] The patrician families themselves (*Geschlechter*) were neither so ancient nor so high in original status as their seventeenth- and eighteenth-century chroniclers presumed. Lersner, the most famous of these writers and a patrician himself, admitted that the exact origins of the Geschlechter were unknown, but he assumed that Frankfurt was among the towns in which Henry I had established "important men" in 924. The proud Lersner was certain that these men stemmed from the rural nobility and that they rendered knights' services to the emperor.[5] Such a view of their history undoubtedly bolstered the self-esteem of the patricians as well as their position

2. Article 3 of the Citizens Agreement is found in Bothe, *Entwicklung vor dem 30jK*, 496. It was nullified by the Transfix of 1616, and only the three aristocratic corporations remained when the guilds and other societies were abolished.

3. Römer-Bücher, *Stadtverfassung*, 247–248; Ugb A51 Nr. 16: Nr. 82b, "Aufsatz . . . von dem Nützen und Vortheil des Collegii Graduatorum," passim, indicates that no strong corporate sense held the Graduates in a lodge in the same way it did the Limpurger and Frauensteiner.

4. Franz Lerner, *Die Frankfurter Patriziergesellschaft Alten-Limpurg und ihre Stiftungen* (Frankfurt, 1952), 24–27.

5. Lersner, *Chronica*, I, i, 295–296; compare Lerner, *Alten-Limpurg*, 11, who cites a "Geschlechter Chronica" written in the mid-seventeenth century by Johann Faust von Aschaffenburg in his discussion of the patrician myth of its ancient and noble ancestry.

in the community; in the seventeenth century, their *Alt*-Limpurg Society was generally regarded by Frankfurters as both *uralt* and noble. Though a present-day historian like Franz Lerner would modify this version of the patricians' medieval past, he would not deny their noble status. Lerner's research on the Limpurger fits nicely into recent interpretations of the origin of the urban patriciate not from the rural nobility or even from ministerial administrators but from a diverse group of men usually common in origin but gaining great wealth and prestige through commercial activities.[6] Lerner traces Frankfurt's great families back to peasant origins in the twelfth and thirteenth centuries.[7] Their rise as wholesale merchants secured them complete domination of the city in the thirteenth century; commercial profits were channeled into land purchases and moneylending businesses. Eventually these families risked no more than one fourth of their holdings in commercial ventures, keeping the rest in property and coin. In time, a high proportion of city property and housing was in the hands of the patricians, and other residents were often their tenants or their debtors.[8]

This powerful group—soon, like its counterpart in most imperial cities, an amalgam of different social elements including merchants, ministerials, patricians from other cities, and some rural nobles—took

6. Research on the problem is admirably summarized in Rudolf Hiesel, *Die staatsrechtliche und soziologische Stellung des Stadtadels im deutschen Mittelalter, hauptsächlich in den oberdeutschen Städten* (Dissertation; University of Mainz, 1952), 16–34; see particularly 20–21 for the view, best represented by Hans Planitz, that commerce was the real economic base for the medieval patriciate. The ministerial theory, which has now received such impressive support from recent work on the Nürnberg patriciate, does not belie the importance of commerce for medieval patriciates but only posits a different legal status for the original group of families which later formed themselves as patricians. Ministerials were, in fact, not only military men but also stewards with many economic activities under their supervision. That they were concerned very early with trade and commerce now seems clear to most students of the problem, though Lerner insists on their sharp separation from merchants in Frankfurt. For essays that emphasize the diverse social origins of patricians, see the collection edited by Hellmuth Rössler, *Deutscher Patriziat 1430 1740* (Limburg/Lahn, 1968); Gerhard Hirschmann, "Das Nürnberger Patriziat," 258, treats the issue in an exemplary manner, for he draws from the masterful analysis of Hanns Hubert Hofmann, "Nobiles Norimbergenses: Betrachtungen zur Struktur der reichsstädtischen Oberschicht," in *Untersuchungen zur gesellschaftlichen Struktur der mittelalterlichen Städte in Europa*, ed. Theodor Mayer (Konstanz, 1966), esp. 63–68.

7. Lerner, *Alten-Limpurg*, 21; Lerner specifically rules out any possibility that ministerial types mixed with the rural freemen as the latter gained tremendous wealth and prestige as merchants. He admits only that social integration occurred at some later point. Heinz F. Friedrichs, "Sippe und Amt in der Reichsstadt Frankfurt," *Genealogie* 13 (1964), 51, emphasizes the diverse social status of patricians at the time they entered the Limpurg Society and does not comment on their more distant pasts.

8. Lerner, *Alten-Limpurg*, 17–18.

the lead in developing the civic institutions it was to control for many centuries. Its combination of economic and political power gave Frankfurt's patriciate noble status as early as the fourteenth century. The disdain for commerce which characterized patricians of the seventeenth century was absent from their medieval forerunners, and commercial enterprise did not derogate their status as noblemen of the empire.[9] Social mixing with the rural nobility occurred regularly by the fourteenth century, when Frankfurt's patricians were seen as its equal in birth and its superior in economic strength.[10] About the same time, the patricians organized themselves in social lodges or corporations.

Franz Lerner sees the formation of merchant and patrician societies in the mid and late fourteenth century as a response to the political challenge presented by handicraft tradesmen, many of whom were already organized in guilds.[11] The newly formed lodges provided other groups in the city the same kind of institutional framework for their religious, economic, social, and political activities. Several lodges for nonguild people grew up in the fourteenth and fifteenth centuries, and the families which can be identified as patrician in the thirteenth century probably joined different societies rather than favoring only one. Membership in the five lodges of the fifteenth century—Limpurg, Laderam, Löwenstein, Frauenstein, and the *Krämerstube*—was fairly open, and patrician families participated in the four societies which were not specifically for retailers.[12]

The most significant development of the late fifteenth century, however, was the gathering of all patrician families into the Limpurg Society. The Laderam and Löwenstein societies died out, the patrician families flocked to the lodge that had probably always held a majority of their numbers, and a small group of newer families kept up the Frauenstein Society.[13] Retailers' lodges persisted up to 1616, but the two important groups after the fifteenth century were the Frauensteiner and the Limpurger. The social and political position of the Limpurger remained much greater than that of the Frauensteiner throughout the old regime in Frankfurt, even though, as we shall see, the younger group

9. Hiesel, *Stellung des Stadtadels*, 1–15; compare the classic article by Siegmund Keller, "Der Adelsstand des süddeutschen Patriziates," *Festschrift Otto Gierke* (Weimar, 1911), 741–758, passim.

10. Lerner, *Alten-Limpurg*, 37–38; the views of Römer-Büchner, *Stadtverfassung*, 236–238, contrast sharply with those of Lerner and must be attributed, I think, to his nineteenth-century liberal prejudices.

11. Lerner, *Alten-Limpurg*, 24–27.

12. Ibid., 33–34; cf. Bücher, *Bevölkerung*, 67–68, on the absence of hard and fast lines in the fourteenth and early fifteenth centuries between guilds and lodges as well as among the lodges themselves.

13. Lerner, *Alten-Limpurg*, 34, 28; Römer-Büchner, *Stadtverfassung*, 225.

showed greater vitality and dynamism in the seventeenth and eighteenth centuries. As far as I can learn, however, the Frauensteiner made no claim to equal social status with the Limpurger before the mid-eighteenth century. While the Frauensteiner and the university graduates became part of Frankfurt's governing aristocracy after the Fettmilch Uprising, the term "patriciate" referred only to the Limpurger.

The history of the patricians after they all came together in one society contrasts strikingly with their medieval past. Several tendencies must be traced over the sixteenth and seventeenth centuries: their turn away from commerce, their imitation of the landed nobility, and their greater exclusiveness made the patricians something different from the vigorous class which had forged the city's economy and constitution in the Middle Ages. Economic predominance slipped from their hands, as the Limpurger chose a new style of life and relied on their noble status as the buttress of their power.

The gathering of all patrician families into the Limpurg Society was the first step toward a policy of greater exclusiveness. From the end of the fifteenth century, patrician status depended on admission by the older families to that "ancient and noble" society. Lerner emphasizes, however, that upward mobility into the patriciate had been fairly high in the late Middle Ages and that this openness continued into the first half of the sixteenth century. The institutional framework for exclusion was not its cause; the prerequisite was a change in values which occurred sometime during the sixteenth century. Lerner traces the change to a large influx of lawyers into the society:

> In the sixteenth century the fully-developed patriciate at the height of its power experienced a fundamental transformation which led in a few generations to its decline. Along with the jurists and the humanistic education, there penetrated other previously alien elements which led on the one hand to a heightening of intelligence and on the other to a criticism of the traditional way of life. Commerce was no longer fine enough for these minds; only politics seemed [an] adequate [challenge]. In simpler souls the result was arrogance and emphatic exclusiveness.[14]

Patricians with humanistic educations probably shared many interests with the jurists. Since imperial law placed both groups in the same general social order (the lower nobility), admission of legists brought no dishonor to the patrician society. Sixteen of the thirty-five new names on the Alt-Limpurg roster from 1510 to 1575 belonged to lawyers.[15] Lerner

14. Lerner, *Alten-Limpurg*, 118.
15. Ibid., 53; Lerner points out that only two of those sixteen families (Ficard and Lersner) survived into the seventeenth century.

believes that these jurists—men of less distinguished origins and without the self-confidence of the old, established patrician families—went on to emphasize Alt-Limpurg's complete equality with the rural nobility and to dissociate the patriciate from its commercial past.

If the lawyers were responsible for initiating this change of attitude and life style within Frankfurt's patriciate, they were only leading their colleagues along the path that most German patricians would take in the early modern period. The vigorous assertion of their social equality with rural nobles was a natural reaction to the denial of that status by knightly orders and societies. Especially during the late fifteenth century, the imperial knights had asserted that the commercial activities of the Geschlechter disqualified them from such noble privileges as participation in knightly tournaments or membership in religious foundations.[16] The pretensions of the knights to a higher station than their urban cousins probably reflected their own insecure economic and political position, but the effect was to put the Geschlechter on the defensive. Patricians became eager to produce tangible evidence of nobility: certified coats of arms, long and honorable pedigrees, and patents from the emperor confirming their status.[17]

The transformation from the merchant-knight of the late Middle Ages to the early modern patrician with few or no commercial connections was gradual and varied from city to city. Nürnberg's classic patriciate of forty-two families became a closed corporation in 1521, for example, but many of its members remained active businessmen until the late seventeenth century. Ulm's patricians, in contrast, no longer engaged actively in commerce after the end of the fifteenth century.[18] In Frankfurt this transformation occurred during the second half of the sixteenth century. In 1558 the Limpurg Society instituted its official record of patrician coats of arms, perhaps the best expression of a new, more self-conscious posture as members of the imperial nobility.[19] Exclusion of retailers had probably always been the rule, but after 1584 an applicant for membership had to prove that none of his ancestors for two generations had practiced a trade or engaged in retail commerce.[20] At no time did Alt-Limpurg rules explicitly bar large wholesalers from membership, but practice gradually eliminated even commercial giants from patrician

16. See Hofmann, "Nobiles Norimbergenses," 74–75.

17. Cf. Keller, "Adelsstand des Patriziates," 754–756, on the imperial patents sought by old patrician families to confirm their noble status.

18. On Nürnberg's patricians, see Hofmann, "Nobiles Norimbergenses," 75–78, and Hirschmann's essay in *Deutsches Patriziat*, 265–268; on Ulm, see Albrecht Rieber's essay, ibid., 305–306.

19. Lerner, *Alten-Limpurg*, 58.

20. Ibid., 63–64. In 1636 this rule was changed to include the third generation of ancestors; see ibid., 76.

ranks. Table 15[21] shows the pattern of admissions over several centuries and points clearly to the exclusion of merchants. The turning point was

TABLE 15

Admissions to the Alt-Limpurg Society

Period	Total Number of Families Admitted	Jurists	Others Noncommercial	Merchants
Before 1406	37	—	—	37
1406 – 1495	56	2	1	53
1496 – 1550	28	7	1	20
1551 – 1612	18	11	2	5
1613 – 1692	8	2	3	3
1733 – 1806	11	—	9	2
1807 – 1866	16	—	16	—
After 1866	7	—	7	—

the period 1551–1612—precisely the time of Frankfurt's second great commercial boom. The great prosperity of the fourteenth century, which had helped solidify the position of the original patrician families, was succeeded by a long slump over the fifteenth and early sixteenth centuries. The wave of religious refugees after 1554 revitalized the city's economy, but, in sharp contrast to their earlier history, the patricians had no part in this economic revival. As Alexander Dietz wrote:

> While Frankfurt's medieval commerce . . . was in the hands of an industrious and enterprising patriciate, the picture changes completely in the middle of the sixteenth century. The patriciate stepped off the stage and, in proud retirement, left commerce to the immigrants from the Spanish Netherlands, who dominated almost all areas of trade . . . in the period from 1554 to 1630.[22]

Nor did the Alt-Limpurg Society admit the wealthy and well-born immigrant merchants who had enjoyed patrician status in their native cities.[23] Only three of these new families were eventually accepted in the next century—exceptions, as Lerner says, to an "unwritten rule."[24] Religious prejudice cannot explain the change in admission policy, for many of the most important immigrants were Lutherans. The reluctance of the Limpurger to have anything to do with commerce and merchants was the decisive factor in this whole development.

21. This table is based on Lerner's Table 1, ibid., 120; I have added the fifth column for merchants.
22. Dietz, *FftHG*, II, vii.
23. Lerner, ibid., 61.
24. Ibid., 134; the families were Scholier (1625), Kayb (1636), and Ruland (1675).

Occasionally a patrician family did engage in commerce in the seventeenth century, but a silk wholesaler like Fleckhammer von Aystetten was an exception in Limpurg ranks. His colleagues were very critical of his business activities and urged him to stop retailing Venetian glassware.[25] Fleckhammer himself had entered the Frankfurt patriciate in 1636, after he had received a patent of nobility elsewhere in 1613.[26] Such a patent was clearly the chief recommendation for admission to Alt-Limpurg after the early seventeenth century. Sometimes it was even accompanied by the emperor's personal letter urging the applicant's admission to Alt-Limpurg. But neither the patent nor the Kaiser's intervention guaranteed acceptance by the society. Although Leopold I's recommendation was influential in gaining membership for Nicolaus Ruland in 1675, the Limpurger successfully resisted the efforts of the distinguished Frauenstein family Fleischbein von Kleeberg to use an imperial order as an entree.[27] With seemingly impeccable credentials as members of the Frauenstein Society before the turn of the seventeenth century, city councilmen with very distinguished public careers since 1615, recipients of patents of nobility duly confirmed by the emperor in 1639, and bearers of Leopold's own order that Alt-Limpurg should admit them to the patriciate in 1676—even with such credentials the Fleischbeins were not acceptable. Their continuance in commercial enterprises was an important hindrance, but so too was an old political grudge against the family because of its moderation during the Fettmilch Uprising. The Limpurger disliked the emperor's intenvention in what they regarded as a local matter, and they probably also wished to maintain the social gap between themselves and the Frauensteiner. They took their case to the Reichshofrat and argued that, since the Fleischbeins enjoyed access to city offices and were already nobles, there was no reason to force the patriciate to take them in. Since Alt-Limpurg no longer monopolized civic power after 1612, its membership should not be a public issue (as it might be in Nürnberg, Ulm, or Augsburg, where patricians exercised tighter control). Nor could the patrician society be

25. Ibid., 77; Lerner and Römer-Büchner, *Stadtverfassung*, 240, agree that there were other patricians engaged in commerce, but they name no particular men and assert that such business activity was frowned on by the large majority of Limpurger.

26. Lerner, *Alten-Limpurg*, 151.

27. Ibid., 78; detailed information on the Fleischbein family is found in Friedrichs, "Sippe und Amt," *Familie und Volk* 5 (1956), 100–103, 146–150, 180–183. Erwin Riedenauer, "Kaiser und Patriziat: Struktur und Funktion des reichsstädtischen Patriziats im Blickpunkt kaiserlicher Adelspolitik von Karl V bis Karl VI," *Zeitschrift für bayerische Landesgeschichte* 30 (1967), 526–655, uses the Fleischbeins as one of several case studies; though I disagree with his analysis of the situation in Frankfurt on some points, here I rely heavily on his account of the dispute between Alt-Limpurg and the Fleischbeins before the Reichshofrat.

expected to admit every nobleman living in Frankfurt or even every man who might marry into one of its families. Except for having imperial favor behind them, the Fleischbeins represented no extraordinary case, and the Limpurger asked the emperor not to use his authority to force new members on their private corporation. They were careful not to question Leopold's right to elevate men into the patriciate, so the decision was not swayed by a need to assert the imperial prerogative. In 1680 the emperor accepted Alt-Limpurg's argument that, as a private association, it should determine whom it would admit to its own ranks. The society did not choose to accept the Fleischbeins until 1755! A special combination of factors hindered their admission in the seventeenth century, but their case symbolized the difficulty of entering the city's most respected social group.

The patriciate of the seventeenth and early eighteenth centuries had excluded most active merchants and lawyers; it had become an increasingly closed circle of old Frankfurt families living as *rentiers*. No period in their history saw the patricians so exclusive as the years from the Fettmilch Uprising to the end of the constitutional conflict. Even jurists, so freely admitted in the sixteenth century, began to disappear from their ranks, as increasing emphasis was placed on a member's noble pedigree. In fact, only eight new families were admitted between 1613 and 1692, then no new people came into the society until after the long conflict waged by the burghers against patrician rule.[28] At the very time when their government faced its most determined opposition, the patricians cut off the possibility that new elements might strengthen their own ranks. Table 16[29] shows the decline in the number of patricians, until it reached only thirteen families and twenty-six members by 1733. Of the twenty Geschlechter in Frankfurt in 1706 (Table 17),[30] eight had been

28. Lerner, *Alten-Limpurg*, 80.

29. Table 16 is taken from Lerner, 122, with two additions for 1622 and 1797 from Hans Körner, *Frankfurter Patrizier: Historisch-Genealogisches Handbuch der Adeligen Ganerbschaft des Alten-Limpurg zu Frankfurt am Main* (Munich, 1971), 426–470. The table is designed to give a notion of the relative number of members, and Lerner himself warns against accepting the figures as absolutely accurate. The information is drawn from various lists found among the material left after World War Two, some of which—if my own experience working with lists of Frauensteiner is typical—may be incomplete. Lerner has found a list of 19 families for 1692, for example, but Lersner, *Chronica*, I, i, 255–256, lists 20 for the year 1706. We know that there were no admissions between 1692 and 1733, so Lerner's 1692 list may well be incomplete.

30. The list itself appears in Lersner, *Chronica*, I, i, 255–256, and I have taken the dates of reception into the society either from Lerner's first appendix, *Alten-Limpurg*, 143–176, or from the genealogical compilations of Körner, *Frankfurter Patrizier*, passim. Körner's more detailed work provides a few corrections to Lerner's information on specific families (like the Humbracht, Zum Jungen, von Hynsperg, and Schaden

Limpurger from the fifteenth century or earlier, while six families dated from each the sixteenth and the seventeenth centuries.

A fair picture of the style of life led by these noble families emerges

TABLE 16

Number of Members in the Alt-Limpurg Society

Year	Families	Members
1407	29	60
1466	35	78
1514	76	106
1610	22	42
1622	29	51
1636	20	31
1692	19	54
1733	13	26
1797	8	13
1838	19	37
1881	21	56
1899	19	73
1925	19	53
1951	14	33

TABLE 17

The Patrician Families in 1706

(with the date of reception into Alt-Limpurg)

von Holtzhausen	before 1406	Faust von Aschaffenburg	1560
von Glauburg	before 1406	Lersner	1566
Humbracht	1427	von Günterod	1588
Zum Jungen	1430	von Stettin	1596
Völker	1447	Schaden	1603
von Hynsperg	1459	Bauer von Eyseneck	1622
Stallburger	1468	Fleckhammer von Aystetten	1636
Steffan von Cronstett	1462	Kaib	1636
Kellner	1518	von Damm	1661
Fichard	1539	Ruland	1675

families in Table 17), but his book adds little or nothing to the general interpretation of the history of the patricians as a social group. The author has written a genealogical handbook that can provide specific examples of the tendencies noted by Lerner and other historians, but his failure to delineate all Limpurg families and to clarify his principle of selection means that the book cannot serve historians as a basis for a careful statistical analysis of marriage, educational, or career patterns.

from Lersner's chronicle, Körner's genealogical handbook, and Franz Lerner's two books on the most venerable of all the Limpurger—the Holzhausens.[31] Lersner emphasized the interests of his fellow Limpurger in scholarly pursuits, travel, warfare, and government. He was also quick to point out that Frankfurt's patriciate shunned all commerce and carefully inspected the genealogical acceptability even of its members' wives.[32] A young patrician usually attended the local *Gymnasium*, after which he might either study law at a university or embark directly on a military or diplomatic career outside the city. Although he might enroll in such universities as Altdorf, Giessen, Marburg, Tübingen, or Strassburg, he seldom bothered with the formality of taking a law degree.[33] His future was secure with only some elementary instruction in jurisprudence, and he saw greater advantage in broadening his experience and his contacts through travel to various courts or famous cities. He then faced at least three career opportunities. Many Limpurg sons chose to become officers in either imperial or territorial armies, while others entered some kind of diplomatic service. This latter career might mean leaving Frankfurt permanently, but it could also involve staying in the city and representing princes or other cities at the frequent political conferences held there. The third possibility for the young Limpurger—the one his family regarded as most important—was a career in Frankfurt government. Lersner's own family demonstrates the usual tendency for patricians to send sons into all three fields of endeavor. His father, Heinrich Ludwig (1629–1696), studied in Strassburg and Tübingen before returning home to enter the Frankfurt city council. Two of Heinrich's sons, the oldest Johann Heinrich (1658–1713) and the chronicler August Achilles (1662–1732), followed him on the council, but their youngest brother Philipp Ludwig died as a captain in an imperial army before Belgrade in 1690. The chronicler's son, Georg August (1701–1749), never held office in Frankfurt, though he lived there as the representative of the Counts of Kirberg and of Wied-Neuwied. His son, in turn, chose a military career in the army of the Westphalian Circle and died in 1767 in a hunting accident. The chronicler's nephew, Friedrich Maxmilian (1697–1753), served in both the Danish and imperial diplomatic services before becoming the family's most influential politician in Frankfurt

31. See his *Gestalten aus der Geschichte des Frankfurter Patrizier-Geschlechtes von Holzhausen* (Frankfurt, 1953) and *Beiträge zur Geschichte des Frankfurter Patrizier-Geschlechtes von Holzhausen* (Frankfurt, 1953).

32. Lersner, *Chronica*, I, i, 299–300.

33. Lersner, 298–299, affirms that many noble families had taken degrees—but only two hundred or so years earlier, when popes and emperors had asked them to save the arts from *Barberey*. Körner has recorded the university matriculations of the Limpurger included in his book.

during the 1740's.[34] Although such military or diplomatic careers were important to most Limpurg families, their real life's work as patricians was to govern their own city. The dominant figures in each generation were those who settled in their native city and devoted their time to managing their own households and to ruling Frankfurt. They tended to marry women from the local aristocracy or from noble families outside (curiously enough, seldom from the patriciates of other imperial cities), and they led a cultivated and very civilized existence.[35] I shall examine their control of the city government in the next chapter; here I need only point out that these men needed a certain degree of wealth before they could even hope to pursue a career in the city council.

Most patricians lived off inherited wealth—property and houses in the city, sometimes a small estate in the country, and various kinds of investments such as storage of wine and loans to fellow citizens.[36] These assets were probably enough to give all patrician families the independence necessary to public life. Yet the investigations of the imperial finance commission during the constitutional conflict leave no doubt that officeholding itself was an important source of income for the men who controlled the council and its several administrative agencies. Not only were salaries paid for government service but extraordinary fees and gifts multiplied its financial rewards several times.[37] Careful investments, advantageous marriages, favorable leases of farms on their rural estates (which otherwise were summer places in the country), and general administrative skills enabled some families to increase their assets over the seventeenth century.[38] When Johann Hector von Holzhausen died in 1668, for example, he left an estate valued roughly at 58,378 fl.; the estate was worth 96,575 fl. when his nephew Johann Georg entailed it fifty years later.[39] Thus the patricians did not have to remain merchants to increase their wealth during the century, and we should not think of them as an economically depressed group. Despite possible absolute increases in their holdings, however, the nobles' relative position had de-

34. On career patterns in general, see Lerner, *Gestalten*, 149–150; for the individual members of the Lersner family, Körner, *Frankfurter Patrizier*, 169–207.

35. Fine libraries serve as one measure of patrician interests: Lerner, *Gestalten*, 147–148, admires Johann Hector von Holzhausen's 328 volumes of classics and travel literature (especially on the Orient and the Turks); the library of Johann Maximilian zum Jungen—a man of deep scholarly bent—was presented to the city in 1690, according to Schnapper-Arndt, *Lebenshaltung*, I, 19–20. On marriage patterns, see Lerner, *Gestalten*, 149–150, and Körner, *Frankfurter Patrizier*, passim, but esp. XII.

36. See, for example, the inventory of the Holzhausen estate in 1721 when it was entailed: Lerner, *Beiträge*, 115–118.

37. The best discussion is Schnapper-Arndt, *Lebenshaltung*, I, 28–33.

38. Lerner, *Alten-Limpurg*, 71–72.

39. Lerner, *Gestalten*, 146–147, and *Beiträge*, 115–118. Both of Lerner's estimates are conservative.

clined from its previous high level. The Limpurger were no longer the wealthiest or the economically most important group in Frankfurt. At the beginning of the sixteenth century, thirty of the forty-two taxpayers with assessments over 10,000 fl. were Alt-Limpurger. Their ratio of men in the top income group declined from this 72 percent to only 44 percent by the early seventeenth century.[40] The patricians had been outflanked by the immigrant merchants of the late sixteenth century, and they were never to regain economic ascendancy.[41] The large Holzhausen assets of 96,575 fl. do not begin to compare with the estate of between 700,000 and 800,000 Rtlr. left by Frankfurt's wealthiest merchant, Johannes Ochs, in 1677.[42]

With its relative economic position diminished, the patriciate relied heavily on its special noble status to maintain its social and political power. The basic fact that Frankfurt's prosperity and importance lay in its far-flung commercial enterprises could not work to the advantage of the Limpurger. They remained a wealthy class; but had economic strength alone been decisive in the constitutional conflict, the patricians could never have retained their place in city government or in the local social order. Their power was buttressed by their political alliance with the other aristocrats (all the Frauensteiner and many of the Graduates), by the skillful tactics of council leaders during the last years of the conflict, and by the essentially conservative character of their opposition. The goal of burgher leaders was not to remove the patricians but to share power with them. The burgher movement put a halt to aristocratic, and especially patrician, fiscal and social irresponsibility; it created political institutions that would safeguard its interests. Yet it did not seek to deny the Limpurger their rightful place in the constitution— and an old and honorable place it was. Economic strength enabled a new elite to demand a voice in governing Frankfurt, but its conception of the community as a society protected against outside incursions relied heavily on traditional constitutional arrangements. How could burghers constantly emphasize the special privileges citizenship bestowed on its holders and, at the same time, deny the unique status of the men who had epitomized from time out of mind the community's existence as an almost independent polity and society? They could modify the old order, but they could not destroy it.

The economic position of the patricians was certainly damaged by the reforms (though they succeeded in extracting handsome salaries at the end of the conflict), but they emerged from the battle still strong politically and still at the very top of the social hierarchy. No other single

40. Lerner, *Alten-Limpurg*, 57, 69.
41. Ibid., 58, 72.
42. Dietz, *FftHG*, IV, i, 98.

group within the *Bürgerschaft* enjoyed more power than the Limpurger even after the constitutional conflict, and their prestige remained such that Frauenstein families continued to attempt the climb up into their august company. As a status group enjoying the less tangible but no less important advantages of honor and prestige in a tradition-bound community, the Limpurger were still unmatched. And, of course, honor and prestige were not so intangible in early modern times. In the city police ordinances as well as in the ostentatious public ceremonies that mirrored Frankfurt society, the Alt-Limpurger always enjoyed absolute precedence.

II. The Frauenstein and Graduate Societies

The best approach to the Frauensteiner and the university graduates—about whom little has been written and documentary evidence is sparse—is an examination of their fight over second place in the community behind the Limpurger. The Frauenstein Society, like Alt-Limpurg, originated in the last half of the fourteenth century. When the patrician families gathered into the Limpurg Society in the late fifteenth century, the Frauensteiner seem to have fallen quite naturally into a position just beneath that of the urban nobility.[43] The social gap between the two groups was probably still rather wide during the sixteenth century, but it narrowed gradually over the next two hundred years. One result of the Fettmilch Uprising was more active participation of the Frauensteiner in city government, and their prestige and power in Frankfurt increased steadily after 1612.[44] The Frauensteiner of the seventeenth and eighteenth centuries were either wealthy merchants or university graduates. Table 15 has already shown the virtual exclusion of lawyers from the Limpurg Society after 1612; a small group of jurists and physicians were admitted to Frauenstein ranks, but the majority seem to have remained without a regular social lodge. From the early seventeenth century to the end of the constitutional conflict, there were only three instances when the university graduates acted collectively. Fifteen lawyers and physicians formed the Free Society in 1613, and in 1640 seventeen Graduates petitioned the city council for preservation of their exemption from militia duty and from the quartering of troops.[45] No further

43. Römer-Büchner, *Stadtverfassung*, 209–210, finds the earliest records of a lodge "zur güldenen Schmiede" in 1382; in 1423 the group moved into Haus Frauenstein from which it eventually took its name. On the position of the families left in the lodge at the end of the fifteenth century, see Lerner, *Alten-Limpurg*, 34.

44. Heinz F. Friedrichs, "Sippe und Amt," *Familie und Volk* 5 (1956), 100; Dietz, *FftHG*, IV, i, 33.

45. Ugb A51 Nr. 16: Nr. 63 and Nr. 64 are copies of the petition of 10 June 1613; for that of 20 May 1640, see ibid.: Nr. 29b.

2. Dr. Johann Christoph Ochs von Ochsenstein, leader of the city council during the constitutional conflict.

(Courtesy of the Frankfurt City Archive)

3. A street scene centered on the Hauptwache, headquarters of the burgher militia.

(Courtesy of the Frankfurt City Archive)

record of their activities is known until 1705, when the Graduates challenged the position held by the Frauensteiner as Frankfurt's second most important citizens.

The occasion was the same ceremony chosen by the burgher militia captains to launch their attack on the city council—the swearing of the oath of fealty to the new emperor, Joseph I. For this most important of all public ceremonies, the council published a set procedure that established the proper arrangement of all citizens in the square before the city hall. As Count Solms took his place directly in front of the *Römer* to receive the oath on behalf of the emperor, the Limpurger were to stand at his right (directly in front of their lodge hall), while the Frauensteiner were on his left. The Graduates were relegated to a position just behind the Frauensteiner, and other citizens were to stand in the square facing the emperor's representative and Frankfurt's aristocracy. This order of precedence reflected traditional practice, as the council later argued, but the Graduates appealed over the council's head. Arguing that both imperial and local police ordinances gave Doctors precedence over commercial people, the Graduates convinced Count Solms to reverse the places assigned the two groups during the actual ceremony.[46] This dramatic move by the lawyers and physicians seems to have taken the city by surprise, but it did not lead the council to give them precedence over the Frauensteiner in local matters.

Had quarrels over precedence been empty gestures of vanity, the Graduates might have been satisfied to have their way in the imperial ceremonies in 1705 and again in 1712. But the council's failure to follow through in Frankfurt's own governmental agencies (particularly in the offices which administered public charities) caused the Doctors such pain that they decided to appeal once again to higher authorities. In 1706 they asked the Reichshofrat to confirm their privileges, specifically to assure them precedence over the Frauensteiner and greater consideration for posts in the city government. The vague language used in the confirmation drawn up in 1712 evaded both questions, however, and neither seems ever to have been resolved to the satisfaction of the Graduate Society. Issuance of the vague document would have been so costly, in fact, that the Graduates did not bother to have the chancellery in Vienna publish it until the city became concerned in 1726 with drawing up a new police ordinance. In that year the council assured the Graduates that it would maintain the privileges granted them by the imperial constitution and Frankfurt's own laws, as long as they themselves refrained from attempts to extend their rights too far beyond the em-

46. A good description of these events is the general memorial prepared by the Graduates in Ugb A51 Nr. 16: Nr. 3; cf. Römer-Büchner, *Stadtverfassung*, 251–254.

peror's intentions.[47] The statement meant nothing less than another denial of Graduate claims to precedence over Frauensteiner, and the angered lawyers and physicians took their grievances to Count Schönborn's imperial commission. The issue then seems to have become part of the whole insoluble problem of producing a police ordinance with a system of social orders satisfactory to all groups in Frankfurt. As the imperial commission was concluding its work in 1732, the Graduates presented Schönborn with a strong complaint about the ordinance of 1731 which gave members of the council's second bench (and hence many Frauensteiner) precedence over Doctors. Even after the constitutional conflict itself was over, the Graduates were still demanding a more prominent role than Frauensteiner and other merchants in the city council.[48]

The events of the years 1705 to 1732 show clearly that the Graduates assumed an aggressive position vis-à-vis the Frauensteiner; they did not question the superior station of the Limpurger, but they sought to sandwich themselves between the patricians and the Frauensteiner in the social and political hierarchy. The two older lodges controlled the council, however, and were able to maintain the Frauensteiner's traditional prestige against the challenge from the Doctors. As late as 1785, Johann Moritz wrote that the Frauensteiner gave place only to the Limpurger.[49] It seems quite reasonable to believe, moreover, that the Graduates' strong attack on their position in the early eighteenth century led the Frauensteiner to claim the same patrician status enjoyed by the Limpurger. Loen's *Kaufmannsadel* (1751), for example, argued that wholesale commerce did not derogate nobility, and Johann Philipp Orth, another Frauensteiner and the city's most important jurist of the enlightened century, asserted that both Limpurger and Frauensteiner together had *always* made up Frankfurt's patriciate.[50] Orth's position has

47. I draw here from several documents in the collection Ugb A51 Nr. 16; the most important are Nr. 13b, a council report to the RHR (13 November 1706); Nr. 22, the official confirmation of Graduate privileges (3 May 1712) along with the costs involved; and Nr. 42, the council decree (8 August 1726) pledging to maintain those privileges for the Graduates, "so fern sie solche privilegia zu weit und über die Kaysserl. allergerechteste Intention zu extendiren Sich enthalten würden."

48. See ibid.: Nr. 52, the "power of attorney" given by the Graduates to their leaders (16 September 1726); Nr. 54 (11 December 1726) and Nr. 55 (4 September 1728), petitions to Count Schönborn; Nr. 80, a petition to the council (19 February 1732); Nr. 82a, a petition to the imperial commission (4 March 1732); and Nr. 88, the petition to the emperor (27 September 1742) on the question of council seats.

49. Moritz, *Frankfurt*, I, 219, says this was the situation even in the important ceremony of swearing fealty to the emperor.

50. On Loen's book, see Römer-Büchner, *Stadtverfassung*, 214. Orth's "Umständliche Nachricht . . ." on the equality of the Frauensteiner with the Limpurger appears in his *Nöthig- und nützlich-erachtete Anmerckungen über die . . . so genannten*

been echoed by numerous writers of the nineteenth and twentieth centuries, even though it was not accepted either by Limpurger or Graduates in the early modern period. What concerns us here, however, is not Frauenstein claims of the mid-eighteenth century but their controversy with the Graduates during the constitutional conflict.

The Frauenstein Society responded to the initial challenge from the Graduates in 1705 with a short tract explaining why its members enjoyed greater prestige and power in the city.[51] First the Frauensteiner raised the issue of the unclear, probably heathen roots of the scholars' practice of taking degrees. This speculation about general origins was quickly followed, however, by a more concrete comparison of social backgrounds. The Graduates were children of handicraft people and thus from the lowest families of the community, while the Frauensteiner were among Frankfurt's most distinguished families—those eligible for election to the city council (ratsfähig). The contrast was carried still further: the Frauensteiner considered themselves broader in composition and outlook. Their inherited wealth (emphasis on housing and property here) placed them far above the petty considerations of the Graduates, who could scarcely scrape together enough to keep up their social pretensions. We should note that, in contrast to the Limpurger and even to Johann Philipp Orth later in the eighteenth century, the Frauensteiner of 1706 stressed their great wealth rather than an ancient or noble heritage. Table 18[52] suggests the wisdom of this approach, for only two of

TABLE 18

The Frauenstein Families in 1706
(with the date of reception into the society)

	von Barckhausen	1683	Glock	1677
§	Bender von Bienenthal	1669	Grams	1626
	Clemm	1692	Horst	1669
	Dieffenbach	1662	Mohr v Mohrenhelm	1667
§	Eberhard gen. Schwind	1655	§ Orth	before 1601
	Fischer	1609	§ Seyffart v Klettenburg	1635
§	Fleischbein von		§ Uffenbach	1614
	Kleeberg	before 1601	Werlin	1692

---

erneuerten Reformation der Stadt Franckfurth am Mayn, Dritte Fortsetzung (Frankfurt, 1751), 902–952.

51. For the following discussion, I rely most heavily on Ugb A51 Nr. 16: Nr. 8 (the Frauenstein tract) and Nr. 9 (the Graduates' response), both written in October 1705.

52. Table 18 is taken from Lersner, *Chronica*, I, i, 256; I have added the dates of admission to the society from Philipp Malapert, "Frankfurter Genealogien" (unpublished manuscript in the Frankfurt City Archive), II, 224 and 239; compare also his

the fifteen Frauenstein families listed by Lersner in that year antedated the seventeenth century. In fact, only six of them had become members of the society before 1655. Little wonder they could still be regarded by the venerable Limpurger as upstarts!

The fact that there were only fifteen families in the Frauenstein Society—compared with twenty in Alt-Limpurg—does not suggest very broad composition. Table 19[53] shows that the Frauensteiner, like the Limpurger, were a small group of families, becoming more and more exclusive in the late seventeenth and early eighteenth centuries. Their total membership of seventeen in 1722 does not compare with the seventy-four Graduates listed in the "Catalog of Doctors" in 1726—or even with the forty-two men most actively supporting the moves to gain precedence over the Frauenstein "merchants and shopkeepers."[54] The

TABLE 19

Number of Members in the Frauenstein Society

Year	Families	Members	Members Holding Degrees
1609	18	23	1
1629	21	27	2
1637	16	20	1
1651	14	19	2
1660	15	22	4
1670	16	28	7
1694	15	25	9
1700	15	21	9
1706	15	—	—
1712	11	18	5
1722	10	17	4
1734	10	18	5
1741	13	19	—
1750	11	15	—

list of all members of the society from 1405 to 1685, Ugb C25 Bbb. The sign § indicates that the family had obtained an imperial patent of nobility; see Erwin Riedenauer, "Kaiserliche Standeserhebungen für reichsstädtische Bürger," in *Deutsches Patriziat,* 65.

53. The figures in Table 19 are counts of individual lists: 1706 comes, of course, from Lersner, *Chronica,* I, i, 256; 1609 and 1629 are from the same source, II, i, 104 and 105; the other lists from 1637 to 1722 appear in the Frauenstein Protokolle 1598–1717, from which I have extracted those which seem to be complete rather than simply lists of members present at particular meetings; finally, membership lists were published each year after 1734 in *Raths- und Stadt-Calender* (Frankfurt, 1734 ff.).

54. See the "Catalogus Doctorum et Licentiatorum" in Ugb A51 Nr. 16: Nr. 26;

claim to broader composition and outlook was based not on numbers of members, however, but on the fact that the Frauenstein Society embraced both university graduates and big merchants. At their high point in 1694, Frauensteiner holding degrees made up more than one third of the society's members, but usually graduates fell below that figure. They were always outnumbered by wholesale merchants—not retailers, as the Graduate Society liked to claim.

Most Frauensteiner have their histories told in Dietz's *Handelsgeschichte*, which contrasts their society with Alt-Limpurg as vigorous, open, and progressive.[55] This picture has to be modified somewhat. Frauensteiner were among the most important merchants of the seventeenth and early eighteenth centuries, their membership saw much more rapid turnover than Alt-Limpurg's, and they had absorbed many of the rising, ambitious families which had immigrated in the late sixteenth century but had been rejected by the more exclusive patricians. Yet we must not think of the Frauenstein Society as open to all new merchants; Calvinists were not accepted, and, while the city's population was increasing rapidly, the society declined in membership before and during the constitutional conflict. When the chamber of commerce took shape in the early eighteenth century, none of its leaders were Frauensteiner.[56] Their social aspirations were indicated, at least in part, by the patents of nobility sought and obtained in Vienna by six Frauenstein families during the seventeenth century (compare Table 18), and their position in the constitutional struggle from 1705 to 1732 was with the Limpurger as defenders of the established political order against other elements of the citizenry. Despite these basic reservations about the "progressive" Frauensteiner—despite their tendency to become by the early eighteenth century an exclusive status group identifying itself more and more as an established, ruling aristocracy—it remains significant that the Frauensteiner did not dissociate themselves from commerce. Though Dietz often notes a tendency for second-generation Frauensteiner to live a more genteel existence than their entrepreneurial fathers, they always remained proud of being merchants. Their combination of commercial activity with government made them, so they argued, Frankfurt's most important families.

The Graduate Society naturally regarded the learned professions

---

ibid.: Nr. 24 and Nr. 52 indicate that between 42 and 44 Graduates were actively involved in the conflict.

55. See esp. *FftHG*, IV, i, 33–34; cf. Friederichs, "Sippe und Amt," *Genealogie* 13 (1964), 51, who sees the Frauensteiner as the "democratic and dynamic" element in city government.

56. See the list of its first leaders printed in *Geschichte der Handelskammer zu Frankfurt a. M. (1707–1908)* (Frankfurt, 1908), 104 ff.

more important than commerce, even in a center of international trade. Scholarly men knew more about public affairs than merchants; their degrees were signs of proven merit, a distinction not at all clear about membership in a social lodge or about inherited wealth. The Graduates argued that they represented a larger portion of the community than did the Frauensteiner. In terms of total membership figures for the early eighteenth century, we have already seen that this assertion was true. The Graduates were, of course, either lawyers or physicians, and the former seem to have predominated two to one. In 1640 there were twelve advocates and five medical men; approximately the same ratio is seen in the 1726 "Catalog of Doctors" with its fifty-one lawyers and twenty-three physicians. Whether or not the Graduates were broader in outlook or wiser in judging the public interest than Frauensteiner, they took great care to defend their social position vis-à-vis the merchant society. Men of low extraction who were able to rise to the top through hard work and intelligence deserved to be proud; those who earned their money were no less dignified than those who inherited it. Such arguments sound like admissions of the validity of Frauenstein charges about the origins and wealth of the Doctors, though detailed genealogical work would be necessary to evaluate them. Whatever their origins or their wealth, however, Graduates argued that the holding of a doctor's degree (or a licentiate) made all the difference between them and the Frauenstein merchants. Perhaps the Frankfurt city council and the Frauensteiner did not recognize this simple fact, but the emperor and all the imperial princes did. Doctors were nobles and, as such, members of the highest imperial councils, the imperial courts, territorial chancelleries, and religious foundations. Their privileges—including precedence over merchants—were written into both imperial and local law. Frankfurt's great legal code (called the Reformation), the Citizens Agreement of 1612/13, and local police ordinances from 1640 to 1671 had all placed the Graduates with the noble patriciate in the first social order. Frauensteiner holding degrees or patents of nobility belonged in the highest order as well, but the society's members who engaged in commerce had been assigned quite properly to the second rung of the hierarchy. The essential question was why the city council did not enforce Frankfurt's laws and place the Graduates as a group before the Frauenstein Society, which had mixed social character.

Frauenstein responses to these hard facts were couched in terms of traditional local practice. There were in Frankfurt only two "public societies and fulcrums of the city"—Alt-Limpurg and Frauenstein—both of which served as seminaries for the public magistracy. The Frauenstein Society was a corporate unit preserving old and distinguished families devoted to and trained for public service. The dignity of its members went beyond the personal prestige bestowed by a university degree and was second only to that of patrician families. No one in the city had previously challenged their special place: it was recognized in the city council, in all public offices, and in Frankfurt churches. Frauensteiner had always preceded Graduates in the past; why should there be a sudden change in 1705? The Graduates were, after all, not even a real society. No corporate bonds united them: they did not have frequent meetings where public issues might be discussed, nor were they able even to create harmony in their own ranks. Here the Frauensteiner may have touched a sore spot, for it became clear later that not all Graduates supported their society's moves against the Frauensteiner. Only forty-odd Doctors attended the important meetings concerned with the precedence issue; when invited to cooperate, twenty-eight others refused.[57] As late as 1738, Graduate leaders were still attempting to bring the society together for regular meetings rather than just extraordinary sessions to discuss specific, important topics.[58]

Admitting that they had no regular social lodge like the Frauensteiner, the Doctors asserted that all university graduates everywhere formed a large society with its own rules and standards. True, the local advocates and physicians did not have organized leadership to give continuity to their group, but such careful organization was beside the point. The printers in Frankfurt formed a corporation with leaders and regular meetings, yet no one was foolish enough to argue that they might have precedence over Doctors. Membership in the Frauenstein Society alone was not enough to give a merchant precedence over a Graduate or even enough to make him suitable for election to the city council. Not the aristocratic societies but the entire citizenry schooled men of high merit for service on the council; not traditional custom but written law was the proper criterion for public practice. With the enunciation of these notions about Frankfurt's government, the Graduate Society touched basic issues of the coming constitutional struggle.

The Graduates' arguments in this fight for precedence in 1705 were not meant to be formal statements of constitutional principle, but they do indicate what direction most (but not all) Doctors would take as the burgher deputies challenged the aristocrats' virtual monopoly of the city council. Precedence was a social issue behind which political problems loomed: many Graduates believed that their group—even though it was part of the city's aristocracy—did not enjoy an adequate share of power. Their demand for greater consideration for vacant council positions overshadowed the issue of precedence as the constitutional conflict progressed. Many Graduates supported the efforts of the burgher party

57. Ugb A51 Nr. 16: Nr. 25.
58. Ibid.: Nr. 82b.

to open the doors of government service to a broader circle of citizens; in fact, the burgher deputies to the imperial commission employed as their own legal advisers men who also served on the Graduate Society's executive council.[59] But just as a large number refused to cooperate in the fight over precedence, many Doctors undoubtedly refused to join the burgher leaders against the entire council. We must not neglect one of the most striking facts about the twenty-six-year conflict: the most intelligent and powerful leader of the council itself—Johann Christoph Ochs (later Ochs von Ochsenstein)—was neither Limpurger nor Frauensteiner but a Graduate.

While the Graduates remained divided throughout the years 1705 to 1732, the Frauensteiner shared power with Alt-Limpurg in the council and defended the established order of which they were an important part. They undoubtedly intended to make their own social position more secure, when, in the police ordinance of 1731, the members of the council's second bench were given precedence over Graduates.[60] The old controversy with the Doctors was certainly not forgotten during the long constitutional conflict, even though it had been pushed into the background by larger political issues. And, interestingly enough, the council fought those basic constitutional issues with arguments similar to ones used by Frauensteiner in 1705 against the Graduates. While burgher leaders demanded a stubbornly literal adherence to the law as confirmed by the emperor, the aristocratic council fought to preserve traditional arrangements worked out by the city's privileged groups during the seventeenth century. The clash of principles seen as early as 1705 took on larger dimensions, because Frankfurt's written constitution clashed sharply with governmental practice. How then did the council govern the city?

59. Compare Ugb A51 Nr. 16: Nr. 26 with the 51er Protocolla 1726–28, passim, and 51er Protocolla 1732, 159–162.
60. See Table 14, 62–63.

Chapter 4

The Character of Aristocratic Government

Before the constitutional settlement of the early eighteenth century, the city council or senate exercised all legislative, judicial, and administrative authority in Frankfurt. The council sent representatives to the imperial diet and to meetings of the Upper Rhenish Circle (the imperial military district to which the city belonged); it negotiated treaties, levied taxes, collected tolls and tariffs, coined money, and enacted laws—all insofar as the emperor permitted. The senate established administrative departments to implement its policies and courts to enforce its laws. All these bodies were in the hands of council members or were very closely supervised by them. The council itself co-opted replacements for its deceased or retired members, and whoever could control the city council could control Frankfurt very effectively.

After the Fettmilch Uprising of 1612 to 1616, the Limpurger and Frauensteiner shared political power in the council. Their government of the city in the seventeenth century showed parallel tendencies toward an increased particularism and an absolutism unresponsive to the demands of the burghers. Frankfurt's aristocrats took a very independent attitude toward the emperor and a very haughty attitude toward their fellow citizens. The council managed in the course of the century both to alienate all other groups in the city and to prejudice its own position of favor with the emperor. The burgher party presented its grievances after 1713 to imperial agencies already prepared to believe that the council had overstepped its proper authority. Strong burgher opposition combined with imperial sympathy for their cause to alter the power structure which had controlled Frankfurt for over a century.

I. Aristocratic Control of City Government

Each Tuesday and Thursday morning the forty-three members of the city council met in plenary session. Although they always met and voted together, the councilmen were formally seated in three groups or "benches," each of which included fourteen men. The first bench was the city's principal court as well; its fourteen jurors (*Schöffen*) were joined by Frankfurt's highest official, the *Schultheiss* or chief justice, who was the odd forty-third man on the council. The Schöffen, from whose ranks the elder burghermaster was elected each year, enjoyed the highest prestige and the strongest political position in the city. They were the council's senior members, and almost all of the Schöffen had previously served on the second bench before their election to the higher post. The first and second benches were occupied almost exclusively by aristocrats, while representatives of nine of the city's thirty-odd handicraft associations sat on the third bench. Why those nine guilds had received positions when the third bench was formed in 1315 is not clear, but the council maintained their traditional representation throughout the early modern period. Of course, the third benchers were not chosen by their fellow tradesmen. The entire council elected suitable men from the Handwerke to fill the two seats to which the weavers, butchers, smiths, bakers, and shoemakers were each entitled as well as the single seats allotted to the gardeners, furriers, tanners, and fishermen. To find the honorable and prosperous men required for the council seems to have been difficult in some handicrafts: positions were often left vacant until the proper man was found, and merchants were generally substituted for the weavers, whose trade had declined sharply after the late Middle Ages.[1] We may be certain, moreover, that suitability for the lowest bench depended not only on the wealth and good reputation of the candidate but on his docility as well. The third-benchers counted very little in the city's power structure, and their presence on the council was a formality. They never received important administrative posts, and, in fact, upward mobility within the council itself was denied the handicraftsmen. During the period 1570 to 1762, only five members of the third bench advanced to the higher benches, and those five men were merchants, not artisans representing their own handicrafts.[2] When they

1. See Lersner, *Chronica*, II, i, 157–161, for examples.
2. My calculations from lists of council members printed in Lersner, *Chronica*, I, i,

presented their grievances to the imperial commission in 1713, the artisans of Frankfurt looked for leadership not to the third-bench men but to the burgher captains outside the council. Count Schönborn considered the third-benchers so unimportant in the city government that he referred to them as an unnecessary financial burden to the citizens.[3]

Although an almost unbridgeable gap separated the third from the upper benches of the council, the two higher levels showed no sharp functional or social differentiation. While the Schöffen enjoyed greater prestige than second-bench men, most of the senators from that bench eventually became jurors. Usually a man was elected to the second bench and served there several years before he was promoted to a vacancy in the first bench. More significant than their division into separate benches was the councilmen's social status. Table 20 indicates the general social composition of the entire council from 1570 to 1762, while Table 21 provides a detailed breakdown for the upper benches.[4] Both tables offer graphic evidence of the predominance the two aristocratic lodges enjoyed before the constitutional changes of the early eighteenth century. We should look more closely, however, at their division of power and at their relation to other burghers—particularly the Graduates—in the upper benches of the council.

TABLE 20

Men Entering the Council, 1570–1762

	1570–1611		1612–1724		1727–1762	
Total entering	102		283		88	
Third-benchers	37	36.3%	93	32.9%	35	39.8%
Limpurger	54	52.9	92	32.5	11	12.5
Frauensteiner	7	6.9	52	18.4	12	13.6
Other Burghers	4	3.9	46	16.2	30	34.1

278–294; II, i, 156–164; and Friedrich Krug, *Diarium der Frankfurter Raths-Wahlen . . . oder Chronologisches Verzeichniss aller Raths-Glieder vom 11. März 1727 an . . .* (Frankfurt, 1846), 7–25. Cf. the remarks of Lersner, *Chronica*, I, i, 257.

3. Schönborn's report to the emperor (18 July 1731) published in Hohenemser, *Verfassungsstreit*, 439–440.

4. Tables 20 and 21 are based on my calculations from the published lists of council members mentioned in note two, above. These readily available lists begin with 1570, so I have taken the men entering in the years 1570 to 1611 as a sample representative of the period before the admission of the eighteen new members from the *Bürgerschaft* in 1612. The years from 1612 to 1724 represent the heyday of joint rule by the Limpurger and the Frauensteiner; there were no council elections between 1724 and the introduction of new electoral procedures in 1727. Finally I have used a thirty-five-year period for a sample of men entering the council after the reform.

TABLE 21
Men Entering Upper Benches of Council, 1570–1762

	1570–1611		1612–1724		1727–1762	
Total entering	65		194		52	
Second bench only	20		60		18	
Limpurger	17	85.0%	27	45.0%	1	5.5%
Frauensteiner	2	10.0	14	23.3	5	27.8
Other Burghers	1	5.0	19	31.7	12	66.7
First bench	45		134		34	
Limpurger	37	82.2	65	48.5	10	29.4
Frauensteiner	5	11.1	38	28.4	6	17.6
Other Burghers	3	6.7	31	23.1	18	52.9
Chief Justices	3		15		3	
Limpurger	3	100.0	7	46.7	0	0.0
Frauensteiner	0	0.0	5	33.3	0	0.0
Other Burghers	0	0.0	3	20.0	3	100.0

The most significant result of the otherwise unsuccessful Fettmilch Uprising of 1612–1616 was the breaking of the virtual monopoly previously enjoyed by the Limpurger over the upper benches. Article 2 of the Citizens Agreement of 1612/13 provided for a temporary expansion of the council to include eighteen new members selected by the councilmen from a slate of thirty-six nominees put forward by the burghers. The eighteen were to enjoy equal access to administrative posts, and, after enough members had died to restore the original size of the council, future elections were to ensure that no group receive special electoral privileges.

> . . . as soon as the usual number is restored and then one or more councilmen, whether from the common citizenry or the patricians, should die, another native-born, wealthy person qualified under the imperial constitution—and graduated persons shall not be excluded —shall replace [the deceased member] without discrimination, and the election shall proceed according to the usual old custom; likewise, since suitable persons are to be found in the two old Limpurg and Frauenstein societies, such persons, as is customary in well-ordered communes and city governments, shall also be considered, in such a manner, however, that the Limpurger have no more than fourteen persons in the council at any one time and—above everything else—that the impropriety of close family relationship and the disquieting partiality which results therefrom be avoided, thus that

in the future no brothers, fathers and sons, fathers and sons-in-law be either presented for or elected to vacant council positions; if, however, a man already in the council should then come into such a relationship through marriage, he shall not be forced for that reason to give up his council seat.[5]

During the constitutional conflict of the early eighteenth century, the meaning of this article was hotly disputed. The issue was whether the Agreement had guaranteed the Limpurger fourteen council seats or had simply forbidden them from having more than that number. Although the emperor sided with the burghers in 1725 and accepted the latter, more literal explanation of the passage, the council had followed its own interpretation throughout the seventeenth century.[6]

The eighteen new members joined the council a few weeks after the Citizens Agreement was reached; their election gave the Frauensteiner and Graduates a secure foothold in the council. Of the twelve new men to enter the upper benches, five were Frauensteiner and seven were founders of the Graduate Society a few months later. The change began a new phase of the council's history in which the Limpurger shared power, especially with the Frauensteiner.[7] The council's usual practice between 1612 and 1724 was to have fourteen Limpurger and seven Frauensteiner sit in the upper benches. With the vote of the chief justice—usually one of their members—the two societies enjoyed majority control of the entire council.[8] The Citizens Agreement had made no reference to a specific number of Frauensteiner, and its only provision for Graduates was that they not be excluded from consideration for council seats. Table 22 shows that the number of Doctors increased considerably in the seventeenth century. Graduates did not receive the special consideration given Frauensteiner, however, and only twelve lawyers or physicians were among the forty-six members chosen from the citizenry-at-large before the change in electoral procedure in 1727. These two facts help explain the vehemence with which some Graduates attacked their fellow aristocrats during the constitutional conflict. The new procedures introduced in 1727 ended the joint control exercised by the two aristocratic

5. Printed in Bothe, *Entwicklung vor dem 30jK*, 495–496.

6. See Article 3 of the First Imperial Resolution (22 November 1725) in Müller, *Frankfurt contra Frankfurt*, I, 9; on the council's practice during the seventeenth century, see Hohenemser, *Verfassungsstreit*, 187–188, where the report of the imperial commissioner is summarized.

7. Dietz, *FftHG*, II, 77–78; the author was incorrect, however, when he assigned the Frauensteiner six regular seats in the council after 1612. No specific number was mentioned for the Frauenstein Society during the Fettmilch Uprising, and the limitation of its representatives to no more than six men occurred in 1725.

8. Lersner, *Chronica*, I, i, 255; Hohenemser, *Verfassungsstreit*, 188.

TABLE 22
Graduates in the Council, 1570–1762

	1570–1611	1612–1724	1727–1762
Total in council	3	26	21
As Frauensteiner	0	14	2
As Other Burghers	3	12	19
First bench total	3	22	15
As Frauensteiner	0	11	2
As Other Burghers	3	11	13

lodges in the seventeenth century, and the Graduates won a large share in the redistribution of power which followed.

Such changes during the early eighteenth century resulted from burgher grievances concerning both the structure and the character of government exercised by the Limpurger and the Frauensteiner for almost a hundred years. Let me outline the machinery of government before I turn to the larger issue of its quality. The council was the center from which all governmental functions proceeded. Although its legislation was subject ultimately to possible imperial interference and immediately to the practical problems of effective enforcement, the council's laws could affect every aspect of the citizen's life. The councilmen regulated local prices, wages, and working conditions; set up guidelines for suitable clothing as well as baptism, marriage, and funeral ceremonies for each social order in the population; tried to protect the city from foreign invasion and from disease; looked after orphans, widows, and the unemployed; and guided the burgher's communal social and religious life. Much of the council's power was delegated to specific administrative agencies, but plenary sessions still passed laws and read petitions from citizens on minor as well as major issues. All decisions from individual city offices could be appealed to the council itself. The growth in the number of offices staffed or overseen by councilmen as well as the general increase in the work load of most members meant a transformation of the council itself over the seventeenth century. A large population increase usually entails the expansion of governmental activities, and the growing interest taken by the Frankfurt aristocrat in public service undoubtedly helped the process along. In any case, the councilman in the upper benches, who had accepted a council seat at the time of the Fettmilch Uprising as an honorary post beside his principal occupation, had become a career man in city government by the early eighteenth century.[9] The attempt in 1614 to limit a councilman's

9. Paul Hohenemser, "Beamtenwesen in Frankfurt a. M. um 1700," *Alt-Frankfurt* 3 (1911), 66.

income to a small fixed salary was unsuccessful, and his salary was richly supplemented during the seventeenth century by honoraria, by the fees he charged for his administrative services, and by the gifts he received from petitioners.[10] Although the imperial resolutions of 1725 and 1732 met burgher demands and eliminated all payments except the regular salary, they also recognized that council membership had become a full-time occupation. Because of the sizable increase in the council's work load over the previous century, the Reichshofrat raised salaries in 1732 even above the recommendations of Count Schönborn to a level which, according to Hohenemser, should have enabled the councilman to live comfortably without the aid of an independent income.[11]

The council delegated authority to various committees (deputations) of its own members and to lower officials who served in offices closely supervised by the councilmen. A regular Council Deputation (consisting of all the jurors, the syndics, the junior burghermaster, and two representatives from each of the two lower benches) met on Monday, Wednesday, and Friday mornings to prepare the agenda and make general recommendations for the plenary sessions held on Tuesday and Thursday mornings.[12] Such a group was undoubtedly very influential, but it probably did not enjoy the power exercised behind the scenes by the Secret Deputation appointed in 1705 to combat burgher opposition.[13] Two burghermasters elected yearly from the upper benches headed the city's regular administrative machinery. The Schöff who served as senior burghermaster presided over council or deputation meetings and oversaw the paper work handled by the city chancellery; both he and his junior colleague from the second bench took care of matters such as law enforcement which did not fall under the authority of particular offices.[14] During the seventeenth century Limpurger and Frauensteiner controlled both posts; only one physician and six lawyers served as burghermasters in the hundred years before the constitutional conflict.[15]

Most administrative tasks fell to a series of special offices created by the council. By the early eighteenth century there were at least forty-five offices, more than half of which collected the various indirect taxes and

10. Ibid., 67; Schnapper-Arndt, *Lebenshaltung*, I, 33.

11. Hohenemser, "Beamtenwesen," 69; *Verfassungsstreit*, 364.

12. Otto Ruppersberg, "Der Aufbau der reichsstädtischen Behörden," *Die Stadt Goethes*, ed. Heinrich Voelcker (Frankfurt, 1932), 56. The essay is the best general discussion of the city administration, but it concerns city government after the constitutional changes of the early eighteenth century and must be used with caution for the seventeenth century itself.

13. Hohenemser, *Verfassungsstreit*, 19–20.

14. Ruppersberg, "Behörden," 56, 57. Moritz, *Frankfurt*, II, 166, says the burghermasters were responsible for law enforcement.

15. Hohenemser, "Beamtenwesen," 69.

tariffs levied by the city (Table 23).[16] The *Renthen-Amt* oversaw the money collected by those offices, while a special *Schatzungs-Amt* collected direct taxes, and the *Rechney-Amt* acted as a general city treasury. Other administrative agencies included the Office of Inquisition, which oversaw the affairs of denizens and other outsiders; the *Zeug-Amt* and

TABLE 23

The City Offices, 1717

Regular Offices	Special Offices for Indirect Taxes
Das Rechney-Amt	Das Renthen-Amt
Das Schatzungs-Amt	Das Tuch-Schau-Amt
Inquisitions-Amt	Das Standt-Amt
Zeug-Amt	Das Holz-Amt
Stadtbau-Amt	Das Fleisch-Amt
Land-Amt	Weinsteuer-Amt
Korn-Amt	Würz-Stoss-Amt
Sehnten-Amt	Safran Schau-Amt
Fortifications-Amt	Freyzeichen-Amt
Fisch-Amt	Der Rosszoll
Sanität-Amt	Zoll am Fahrthor
Feuer-Amt	Zoll am Leonhards-Thor
Acker-Gericht	Zoll am Mezger-Thor
Forst-Amt	Zoll am Bockenheimer-Thor
Marstall	Zoll am Friedberger-Thor
Casten-Amt	Zoll am Allerheiligen-Thor
Catharinen Closter	Zoll an der Brück
Hospital	Das Leinwandshauss
Weisfrau Closter	Die Bestätter-Dienste
Scholarchat	Die Staat-Waag
	Die Eisen-Waag
	Die Mehl Waag
	Die Butter-Waag
	Die Heu- und Güter-Waag
	Das gestempelte Papier

16. I take this enumeration from the Guarantee signed by eight burgher leaders (12 December 1714) that citizens could administer the city better than the council had done previously; see Müller, *Frankfurt contra Frankfurt*, I, 72. The offices were divided into two categories according to whether they were to be farmed out to burghers (those involved with indirect taxes) or left under the control of the regular bureaucracy with close burgher inspection. Note that the chancellery (*Stadt-Cantzley*) was not included in this listing. Augsburg, a city with a population about as large as Frankfurt's in the early eighteenth century, had a comparable number of offices in its bureaucracy; Bátori, *Augsburg*, 58–59.

the Fortifications Office, which organized defenses; the *Stadtbau-Amt,* which supervised all construction within the city; the Grain Office; the Forestry Office; and various offices to administer charitable foundations.[17] To each of these agencies the council appointed between two and six of its own members as decision-makers and supervisors of lower officials. A system of rotation by which a councilman served in an office three years and then moved into another agency became customary in the course of the seventeenth century. Although this practice was probably designed to acquaint the councilman with all facets of the administration, it left the lower officials named by the council to provide continuity within each office.[18] Some of the lower bureaucrats did receive free housing and payments in kind from the city, but they joined all other officials in relying for a livelihood on the incidental fees charged by each office for the services it rendered Frankfurt residents and visitors. The men who received small salaries (the councilmen, for example) gained supplements from the office funds, while those without salaries were forced to live off the incidentals they managed to collect. Arbitrary fees and improper accounting were characteristic practices of this growing bureaucracy until the reforms of the early eighteenth century.[19] The size of the administration itself before the reform period would be difficult to estimate, but Heinrich Voelcker believed that there were about five hundred men in the bureaucracy in the mid-eighteenth century.[20]

In the seventeenth century the highest positions went increasingly to those with legal training. Many councilmen of the upper benches knew a smattering of law, and they surrounded themselves with chancellery officials and court clerks who had taken doctorates or licentiates.[21] The

17. Ibid. Ruppersberg, "Behörden," 68–81, discusses the work of the more important offices *after* the reforms of 1716 and 1725.

18. Hohenemser, "Beamtenwesen," 66.

19. Ibid., 66–69. Hohenemser explains in *Verfassungsstreit,* 265–266, that the salaries of council members and administrative officials set in the Visitation Ordinance of 1614 had not been confirmed by the emperor, and the council felt in no way bound by its agreement with the burghers. Even though general opinion held council positions to be honorary posts, salaries were raised throughout the seventeenth century. Likewise the salaries of lesser officials increased from the early seventeenth to the early eighteenth centuries: the total amount of these salaries for lower officeholders increased from 5107 fl. to 18,669 fl., and some specific increases were even more impressive: Rechney, from 79 fl. to 5462 fl.; Schatzungs-Amt, from 402 fl. to 1792 fl.; and the Bau-Amt, from 62 fl. to 1374 fl. paid to their salaried employees. In no case, however, were the regular salaries the only, or even the chief, sources of income for officeholders.

20. Heinrich Voelcker, "Berufliche and soziale Gliederung der Einwohner," *Die Stadt Goethes,* 95. Bátori, *Augsburg,* 58, estimates that there were only 120 or 130 officeholders in that city.

21. Hohenemser, "Beamtenwesen," 72.

most important lawyers were the syndics, the special legal advisers of the council and the jurors' court. While they were appointed by the senate and served at its pleasure, they became the most powerful men in Frankfurt outside the council itself. Before the introduction of Roman law, the syndic had usually been a cleric with little higher status than other chancellery officials; lawyers began to assume the position in the sixteenth century, and they gained exclusive control during the seventeenth. By the time of the constitutional conflict, their special place in the city's power structure was symbolized by the fact that the syndics enjoyed uncontested precedence in public ceremonies over second-bench councilmen.[22] Their duties ranged from representing Frankfurt in diplomatic missions to Vienna, Regensburg, and Wetzlar to drafting legislation and court decisions. Although the syndics enjoyed no official decision-making position and no vote in the council, their opinions were sought on all important issues, and they played an important role in shaping government policy. These duties increased so much that four regular syndics were necessary by the end of the seventeenth century, and a fifth was taken on half time in 1691. The syndics were comparatively well paid and usually came from outside Frankfurt.[23] A few syndics were accepted into the Frauenstein Society during the century, and some were even elected to regular council seats.

Administrative and judicial functions were not sharply distinguished in Frankfurt: the Schöffen were the most influential legislators; they supervised the most important Ämter; and they sat as the city's highest civil court. Each office resolved disputes within its administrative sphere as well as issuing directives to implement council legislation. The Sehnten-Amt investigated, pronounced judgment on, and punished sexual offenses, violations of the clothing and luxury ordinances, and any other offenses against public morality.[24] A rather confusing system of regular courts exercised civil jurisdiction: that of the Oberstrichter handled cases involving property of less than five Gulden value and was court of first instance in cases involving larger sums. The latter cases might be appealed to the Burghermasters' Audience or finally to the entire Jurors' Court.[25] The same fourteen Jurors led by the Chief Justice sat as three different courts—one to decide ordinary civil (especially inheritance) disputes, another to deal with special cases like adoption or appointment of guardians for orphans which fell under its jurisdiction,

22. Ibid.; unfortunately there is no study for Frankfurt comparable to Martin Ewald, *Der hamburgische Senatssyndicus* (Hamburg, 1954).
23. Hohenemser, "Beamtenwesen," 71. The syndics are listed in Lersner, *Chronica*, I, i, 227 and II, i, 133.
24. Ruppersberg, "Behörden," 67.
25. Ibid., 57.

and a third to hear appeals from the lower courts. Criminal cases, on the other hand, went before the entire council for judgment.[26] The highest judicial official—the *Schultheiss* or Chief Justice—held the most prestigious position in Frankfurt. The medieval Schultheiss had been appointed by the emperor as his representative in the city, and, although the council purchased the right to select the Justice in 1372, he still enjoyed the prestige of an imperial official. Two important changes in his position took place in the seventeenth century: in 1606 the Chief Justice received his office as a lifelong appointment rather than one of only a few years' duration, and, after the last decades of the sixteenth century, he was always a Frankfurter rather than a nobleman of the surrounding area.[27] Table 24[28] shows that the Limpurger controlled the post more often than other aristocrats, while only four justices before the constitutional conflict held university degrees. This feature of aristocratic government in Frankfurt, like many others, was to change after the reforms of the early eighteenth century, and we must now examine the character of that government to see why it aroused burgher discontent and imperial disfavor.

II. Alienation of the Citizenry and the Imperial Government

The most serious charge made by the citizens during the constitutional conflict was that the council's rule was arbitrary. We have already seen in Chapter 1 the complete disagreement between the council and its citizens over their own political relationship. Burgher leaders argued that all Frankfurt's misfortunes stemmed from the council's mistaken notion that it exercised lordship over the citizens rather than a simple mandate to administer the city in their behalf.[29] That view enabled the senate to disregard the Citizens Agreement of 1612/13 and to rule Frankfurt according to its own standards. Burghers used the term arbitrary in both its connotations: the council's rule disregarded the wishes both of the emperor and of the citizens, and it was unpredictable. The charge applied to all areas of government from court decisions to the fees assessed by administrative offices and the tolls levied at the city gates.

26. Ibid., 65–66.

27. Hohenemser, "Beamtenwesen," 69–70.

28. I have checked the affiliations for the list published by Georg L. Kriegk, "Urkundliches Verzeichnis der Frankfurter Schultheissen," *Deutsches Bürgerthum im Mittelalter nach urkundlichen Forschungen und mit besonderer Beziehung auf Frankfurt a. M.* (Frankfurt, 1868–71), I, 517–519.

29. See section 5 of *Historische Nachrichten* (n.p., 1715); Hohenemser, *Verfassungsstreit*, 112–113.

TABLE 24
Chief Justices, 1571–1771

1571–1574	Hans Eitel von Carben	
1575–1576	None	
1576–1589	Johann Kellner	Limpurger
1589–1591	None	
1592–1606	Christoph Stallburger	Limpurger
1606–1614	Johann von Martorff	Limpurger
1614–1615	Dr. jur. Niklaus Weitz	Graduate
1616–1634	Johann Martin Bauer	Frauensteiner, later Limpurger
1634–1639	Hieronymus Steffan von Cronstetten	Limpurger
1639–1647	Hektor Wilhelm von Günterrode	Limpurger
1647–1648	Johann Schwindt	Frauensteiner
1648–1662	Hieronymuss Stallburger	Limpurger
1662–1666	Christof Bender von Bienenthal, Lic.	As Burgher
1666–1686	Hieronymus Peter von Stettin	Limpurger
1686–1689	Philips Wilhelm von Günterrod	Limpurger
1689–1693	Adolff Ernst Humbracht	Limpurger
1693–1695	Dr. jur. Johannes Thomas Eberhard genandt Schwindt	Frauensteiner
1695–1696	Henrich Ludwig Lerssner	Limpurger
1696–1716	Dr. jur. Johann Erasmus Seiffart von Klettenberg	Frauensteiner
1716–1721	Johann Georg von Holtzhausen	Limpurger
1721–1747	Johannes Christophorous Ochs von Ochsenstein Doctor	As Burgher
1747–1771	Johann Wolfgang Textor Doctor	As Burgher

The most sensitive issue, however, was arbitrary taxation. The burghers listed three general grievances in 1715: regular imposts were four to six times their early seventeenth-century levels, so that the cost of food had doubled over the century; the council had imposed extraordinary taxes—some seventeen special assessments between 1661 and 1715—without the consent of the burghers; and finally, all this increased taxation had done nothing to lower the city's debts.[30] The Citizens Agreement had established fixed tax rates on items like wine, flour, and malt, but the council ignored the agreement and failed to consult the burghers about increases.[31] The extraordinary assessments of the late seventeenth and early eighteenth centuries were presumably levied to pay Frank-

30. Section 5 of *Historische Nachrichten*.
31. Hohenemser, *Verfassungsstreit*, 118–119, gives specific examples.

furt's share of imperial defense costs,[32] and burgher leaders did not deny that some tax increases were necessary over the hundred-year period. What offended the citizens was not the high level of the taxes but the fact that the increases were arbitrarily levied and not properly administered.[33] The lack of clear financial records and the truth of burgher suspicions about the mismanagement of public funds were later demonstrated by the investigations of the imperial finance commission. Count Schönborn found the account books so confusing that estimates of the city's income or of its debt had to be guesswork, but he did conclude that the mismanagement of funds in the Rechney alone had meant a loss of 90,000 to 100,000 fl. over the seventeenth century.[34] Such a state of affairs, as both the burgher leaders and the imperial commissioner agreed, resulted from another arbitrary decision by the council. In 1616 it had decided to interpret the Transfix that abolished Frankfurt's guilds as also ending the mandate of the Committee of Nine set up in 1613 to oversee the city's finances on behalf of the citizens.[35]

Burgher leaders also complained that arbitrary interpretation of Article 2 of the Citizens Agreement had permitted the Limpurger and the Frauensteiner to control three fourths of the upper-bench seats in the council.[36] The two societies often controlled more than the twenty-one seats to which they felt Article 2 entitled them, and they did not implement the provisions of the article against the "impropriety of close family relationship and the disquieting partiality which results therefrom." In April 1713 the burgher deputies submitted to the imperial commission a report on the council members to show that a small circle of closely related families completely controlled the important upper benches (Table 25).[37] Only one of the councilmen (Grambs) seems to have been unrelated to any of the others, and even the men who entered as common burghers were closely tied to councilmen from the two lodges. This latter fact indicates that an increase in the ratio of burghers in the council from about 4 percent before 1612 to 16 percent in the period 1612–1724 cannot be interpreted as bringing much new blood

32. Moritz, *Frankfurt*, II, 375–376, presents a list of the extraordinary assessments between 1631 and 1713.

33. Hohenemser, *Verfassungsstreit*, 260.

34. Ibid., 222–231.

35. Ibid., 228–229.

36. See the *Tractatio Gravaminum* (30 December 1707) summarized in Hohenemser, *Verfassungsstreit*, 126; *Historische Nachrichten* (1715), section 5; cf. above, 99–100.

37. Bayerisches Staatsarchiv Würzburg: Mainzer Regierungsakten: Kaiserliche Kommissionen, Fasz. 138, Bll. 340 and 341: lists of council members as of 11 April 1713 submitted by the burgher deputies to the imperial commission. I have supplied the material in brackets from other sources.

into the council.[38] Since the councilmen co-opted their own new members and they all shared the lucrative rewards of officeholding, burgher charges of nepotism could scarcely be denied. Burgher leaders decried the tendency to regard council positions as an opportunity to make money, and they deplored the mismanagement and corruption that were the legacy of aristocratic nepotism in the seventeenth century.

Did councilmen and their employees in the Ämter view their posts as opportunities to better their financial conditions? We have no direct admissions of that attitude from officeholders, but evidence uncovered by burgher leaders shows that men were at least willing to bribe the councilmen both for election to the council itself and for positions in the city bureaucracy. A baker named Reichardt had paid 2500 fl. for a seat in the third bench, a judgeship had cost 4000 fl., and a clerk in the Grain Office had paid 3000 Taler for his position.[39] The burghers charged that two Jews, Löw Ochs and Löw Speyer, acted as financial agents for aspiring sons of aristocratic families who wished especially rapid election into the council and promotions into important supervisory posts.[40] Although the attraction to government positions lay, at least in part, in the prestige attached to them, the added financial enticement was not the official salaries but, as I pointed out earlier, the "incidentals." Burgher discontent becomes comprehensible when the income which a city official, say the senior burghermaster, derived from sources outside his salary is spelled out:

Installation present as senior burghermaster
Installation present as juror
Honoraria for attendance at meetings of council and offices
Presents from people who received special concessions at the fairs
Presents at major public festivals (May Day, the fairs)
Payments in kind: wood from city forest, six *Schweinspiesse*, five hens, twelve wax candles, lanterns, office supplies, etc.
Private gifts from Jews, from men becoming masters in *Handwerke*, and from officials in the bureaucracy
Official gifts from various Ämter in the bureaucracy[41]

The incidental income for Schöff von Glauburg (who administered the Rechney, the Schatzungs-Amt, the Fortifications Office, and the charities of St. Catharine's Cloister in the early eighteenth century) totaled 1778 fl. 20 xr. yearly; only 560 fl. were honoraria, and well over two thirds of

38. Cf. Table 20.
39. See Hohenemser, *Verfassungsstreit*, 121–122.
40. Ibid., 126.
41. Schnapper-Arndt, *Lebenshaltung*, I, 28–31.

TABLE 25

Family Relationships Among Upper-Bench Councilmen, 1713

First Bench

Name	Society	Relationship
Schultheiss Seiffart v Klettenburg	Frauensteiner	[Brother-in-law of v Barckhausen]
Joh. Adolph v Glauburg	Limpurger	Brother-in-law of v Stalburg
Heinrich v Barckhaussen	Frauensteiner	Brother-in-law of the Schultheiss and of Fleischbein; cousin of Dr. Ochs
Ph. Hein. Fleckhammer v Eychstätten	Limpurger	Father-in-law of Bauer v Eyseneck
Joh. Georg v Holzhausen	Limpurger	Brother-in-law of v d Bürgden and Hironymus v Glauburg
Matt. Carl Steffan v Cronstetten	Limpurger	Related *allerseits*
Joh. Philip Orth	Frauensteiner	Brother of Syndic Orth; cousin of the Fleischbeins
Joh. Martin v. d. Bürgden	Burgher	Son-in-law of former Schultheiss v Günterod; related to all Limpurger, esp. to Holzhaussen and v Glauburg
Joh. Jacob Grambs	Frauensteiner	Not related to the others
Joh. Heinrich Werlin, U. J. D.	Frauensteiner	Nephew of Müller; cousin of Dr. Ochs
Fr. Max. Bauer v Eysseneck	Limpurger	Related to all Limpurger
Joh. Ph. Kellner	Limpurger	Related to all Limpurger; brother-in-law of recently deceased Syndic Glock
Con. Hier. Eberhardt gen. Schwindt, M.D.	Frauensteiner	Related to various Frauensteiner
Hieronymus Humbracht	Limpurger	Brother-in-law of Glauburg; related to other Limpurger
Ludwig Adolph Siverts	Burgher	Uncle of Fleischbein; [later brother-in-law of Stallburger]

Second Bench

Joh. Christoph v Stetten	Limpurger [Frauensteiner]	Related to several Limpurger
Bartholomäus v Barckhaussen	[Burgher]	Related to Lud. v Lersner but also to other Limpurger
Joh. Christian v d Bürgden	Limpurger	Married d. of Fleckhammer after he entered the council
Georg Chr. Faust v Aschaffenburg	Limpurger	Brother-in-law of Schöffen Holtzhausen, Bürgden, and Humpracht
Hironymus v Glauburg		
Joh. Christoph Ochs, J.U.D.	[Burgher]	Brother-in-law of Syndic Klemm; uncle of Werlin; cousin of Schöffen v Barckhausen and Fleischbein
Joh. Hector v Limpurg	Limpurger	Related to most Limpurger; came into council while brothers-in-law Cronstätten and Fleischbein were there
Joh. Dan. Fleischbein v Kleeberg	Frauensteiner	Brother-in-law of Schöff Barckhausen; nephew of Joh. Ph. Fleischbein; cousin of Dr. Ochs and Syndic Klemm
Friedrich Ludwig Müller	[Burgher]	Came into council as Burgher, then married d. of Schöff Lersner, so Joh. Lud. Lersner is his uncle; uncle of Werlin and of Fleischbein's wife
Joh. Chr. v Stalburger	Limpurger	Brother-in-law of Schöff Glauburg and Siverts; uncle of Fleischbein and father-in-law of Schöff Bawer
Joh. Henrich v Lersner	Limpurger	Related to all Limpurger
Joh. Ph. Fleischbein v Kleeberg	[Frauensteiner]	Married d. of Lersner, thus related to Stalburg and Siverts; nephew of Müller and Joh. Dan. Fleischbein; [related to] other Limpurger
Joh. Ludwig v Lersner	Limpurger	Related to v d Bürgden, Müller, and Fleischbein
Vacant		

the total income derived from fees charged for special services rendered or from fringe benefits.[42] Although the sums for lower officials were smaller, the principle was the same from top to bottom in the city administration. Investigations by the imperial finance commission proved difficult because of the poor bookkeeping in all Ämter, but they revealed incidentals totaling 50,000 fl. yearly. Burgher leaders estimated that from 1600 to 1717 well over two million Gulden went into the pockets of councilmen and bureaucrats as incidentals, and that estimate could not take the income from court fines into account, because fines were not recorded in the account books at all.[43]

Burgher leaders argued that mismanagement of city offices made the aristocrats on the council incompetent to govern Frankfurt unassisted. Nothing in the administration seemed well-regulated: tolls, which serve as a good example even though burghers did not pay them, varied from gate to gate in the city. The burghers resented the arbitrary fees and the lack of any consistent schedule of charges, both of which left the door open to corruption. They attacked the Office of Construction (*Bau-Amt*), because it had sold many public buildings and had allowed others to fall into disrepair. The office did not maintain adequate supplies of wood for building purposes, its work on street and harbor maintenance was minimal, and the councilmen who ran the office usually had the city's employees repair their own property.[44] Alienation of city property without consultation with the Committee of Nine was, according to the burghers, another violation of the Citizens Agreement, but equally serious was the fact that councilmen themselves had purchased much of the property at very favorable prices.[45] Charges of incompetent administration and intentional misuse of the resources of the city's charitable foundations were so numerous that the emperor appointed a third commission to investigate them.[46]

The parallel accusations of incompetence and corruption became even stronger as the finance commission began its examination of the accounts of the city treasury and of the individual offices. According to the records of the Ämter, the average annual income of the city in the years 1700–1710 was 257,243 fl., but the books kept by the treasury showed an average of only 223,058 fl. The accounts were full of mathematical errors and showed the persistent tendency to carry over to the next year's records a sum considerably less than the surplus of the cur-

42. Hohenemser, *Verfassungsstreit*, 270–271.
43. Ibid., 254.
44. These are charges in the *Tractatio Gravaminum* summarized by Hohenemser, *Verfassungsstreit*, 122.
45. Ibid., 201–204.
46. Ibid., 122–124, 332–339.

rent year. For 1706–1707 a surplus of 894 fl. became 38 fl., and the 2610 fl. surplus of 1710–1711 was reduced to 926 fl. Most of these yearly reports were unsigned, and specific blame was difficult to assign. Records on the extraordinary taxes levied after 1678 were also unclear; no one could tell who had paid his entire assessment and who still owed arrears. The seventeen levies from 1678 to 1718 should have netted 1,228,366 fl., but only 1,164,199 fl. were accounted for in the Rechney ledgers; this meant a loss of 64,167 Gulden. The records did show, however, that the six councilmen responsible for collection of the extraordinary levies received special allowances for their efforts: low tax assessments on their own property and rewards of 200 fl. each.[47] Count Schönborn's investigations proved the situation even worse than the citizens had charged before he began his work in 1713.

While some of the burgher accusations seem to have been farfetched, their basic grievances were entirely justified. Perhaps Seiffart von Klettenberg and Steffan von Cronstetten did not steal a casket of gold and silver in 1692 (the year they served as burghermasters), and I doubt that several councilmen accepted two caskets of gold in 1698 in return for their help in a plot to turn the city over to the French.[48] The existence of such rumors, however, shows how cynical burghers had become about the integrity of their aristocratic council. Burgher leaders appealed to the emperor for redress of their many grievances against the aristocrats, and the solution they proposed was even more thorough reforms than had been written into the Citizens Agreement of 1612/13. Their success in achieving the most important constitutional changes in Frankfurt's history depended partly on the validity of their own charges about the council's misconduct and partly on the receptivity to their views shown by imperial officials.

While the council alienated its own citizens over the last half of the seventeenth century, it also annoyed the emperor enough to make his government responsive to burgher appeals for change. The council's haughty attitude toward its citizens and its independent attitude toward its superior, the emperor, were epitomized in a statement made by one of the syndics. When Captain Fritsch—later a leader of the burgher party—threatened to appeal to the Kaiser for justice in a court case brought before the Schöffen, Syndic Clemm replied: "What emperor? We are emperor here, and the emperor is emperor in Vienna."[49] Of course, such sentiments were never expressed to the emperor or to im-

47. For this entire discussion of financial records, I draw heavily from Hohenemser, *Verfassungsstreit*, 260–261.

48. Georg L. Kriegk, *Deutsche Kulturbilder aus dem achtzehnten Jahrhundert* (Leipzig, 1874), 23.

49. Quoted in Kriegk, *Kulturbilder*, 23.

perial officials, yet many of the actions of the council showed that it did not really accept the wishes of its liege lord. The council defended its sole right to tax the Jewish community; it opposed every effort of the financially weak emperor to exact special taxes from Frankfurt Jews. The council even argued that, if the emperor taxed one of Frankfurt's most important sources of income, the city itself could not pay him very high taxes.[50] The aristocrats bitterly opposed the intentions of many imperial officials to move the Reichskammergericht from its war-threatened seat at Speyer to the much safer Frankfurt. They feared that the imperial court would mix in matters under the jurisdiction of the city government. The council was so stubborn in its refusal to provide facilities for the body that, when it fled Speyer in 1688–1689, the chief court of the Empire was situated in Wetzlar instead of Frankfurt.[51] The aristocratic council also opposed the emperor's policy of enforcing his own embargoes on the importation of French goods during the first war with Louis XIV. The embargo of 1676–1679 was rigidly enforced in Frankfurt by the Archbishop of Mainz acting as an imperial commissioner for that purpose. The council felt, however, that it could enforce embargoes in its own territory, and it did so during the embargo periods 1689–1697 and 1703–1714.[52] In 1694 the council opposed the emperor's establishment of a commission on coinage for the Circle of the Upper Rhine. It forbade its citizens from taking money matters to the commission for settlement and protested to Leopold I that he was violating the Peace of Westphalia.[53]

The emperor himself showed much displeasure and some willingness to move against the particularistic attitude of the Frankfurt council. In 1695, furious with the council's attitude toward his coinage commission, Leopold implemented earlier plans and established an imperial resident in the city to observe the situation there and report any usurpation of the imperial prerogative.[54] He further punished the council's presumptuousness by fining it 1000 marks and warned that it should never again treat him as if he were merely "one of the neighboring *Stände*."[55] The emperor often made decisions embarrassing to the council's sense of its own importance. An excellent example is seen in the relations of the council with the Jewish community. After long negotiations between the council and the emperor over the latter's threat to repurchase *do-*

50. Kracauer, *Geschichte der Juden*, II, 7 and passim.
51. Otto Ruppersberg, "Frankfurt am Main und das Reichskammergericht," *AFGK* 4th series, 4 (1933), 81–106.
52. Dietz, *FftHG*, IV, i, 136–147.
53. Hohenemser, *Verfassungsstreit*, 136.
54. Ibid., 137–138; see also the documents in the city archive labelled Räthe und Residenten, III, 1–23.
55. Hohenemser, *Verfassungsstreit*, 137.

minium utile over the Jews, the emperor was persuaded by very liberal bribery in 1685 not to make the change. In the course of the correspondence, the council referred to the Jews as the "bondsmen and serfs of the city."[56] When Jewish leaders learned of this nomenclature, they feared possible moves by the city against their customary privileges. They appealed to the emperor, who decided that, although legally the Jews were serfs of the city, the council was not to tamper in any way with the traditional privileges, such as freedom of movement or marriages without special permission, which the community enjoyed.[57] Although it had no intention of limiting the privileges of the Jews, the council found the emperor's statement somewhat distasteful and was furious with the Jewish leaders for carrying the matter over its head to Leopold I. The leaders were ordered to surrender all documents granting them privileges and to swear that they would never appeal to the emperor's latest declaration. The Jews refused. Immediately the council imposed on them an extraordinary and unexplained tax of three thousand Taler. Jewish leaders once again appealed to Vienna, but the city government sent a wagon through the ghetto collecting enough valuables to pay the tax. Leopold then decided that the unexplained tax was illegal and that the Jews' property had to be restored to them or credited against future tax payments. The council was utterly humiliated by this decision; it took revenge on the Jews by passing bothersome regulations on their life in Frankfurt. Privately many aristocrats expressed the opinion that the emperor was an ingrate in spite of all their loyalty and services to him.[58] Such attitudes and actions probably predisposed the imperial government to give a favorable hearing to burgher appeals against the aristocrats in the early eighteenth century.

III. The Effects of the Constitutional Reforms

The constitutional reforms sought by the citizens and granted by the emperor meant a loss of power for the Limpurger and Frauensteiner and a fundamental reorganization of Frankfurt's government. Although some of the eighteenth-century changes went beyond a simple restoration of the Citizens Agreement, the establishment of a balance of power between the aristocrats and other citizens envisaged in 1612/13 remained

56. Kracauer, *Geschichte der Juden*, II, 88. This incident is related in great detail ibid., 78–93.

57. This declaration as well as Leopold's original decision in 1685 not to repurchase tax rights over the Jews are published in *Privilegia et Pacta des H. Römischen Reichsstadt Franckfurt am Mayn sammt der Goldenen Bulla Caroli IV* (Frankfurt, 1728), 496–504.

58. Kracauer, *Geschichte der Juden*, II, 99.

the essential goal. There was no question of excluding the two aristocratic societies from the council, even though their government of the city during the seventeenth century had aroused so much opposition from all sides.[59] New procedures for council elections ensured that a broader representation of the Bürgerschaft came into the council as old members died. Rules against close family relationships were extended to include cousins and brothers-in-law, and the eligibility of men in the aristocratic lodges was thus sharply reduced. So that the Limpurger and Frauensteiner would not misinterpret his intentions, the emperor explicitly set fourteen and six as their maximum and not their minimum numbers of representatives sitting in the council at one time. A complicated system of nominating Graduates and merchants as well as men from the two lodges for vacant council positions and then of electing them by lot was designed to open council seats to more burghers and to eliminate any possibility of manipulating the election results. The reforms were capped by the establishment of a burgher Committee of Three to oversee the nominations and elections which the council itself continued to conduct.[60]

The composition of the council changed only gradually; Table 26 shows that the first bench was still largely controlled by the Limpurger

TABLE 26

The Schöffen, *1742*

Schultheiss Joh. Chr. Ochs v Ochsenstein	Graduate
Conrad Hier. Eberhard genand Schwind	Frauensteiner
Johann Carl von Kaib	Limpurger
Johann Philipp von Syvertes	Limpurger
§ Antonius Schaaf	Graduate
Johann Philipp von Kellner	Limpurger
Johann Adolph von Glauburg	Limpurger
§ Johann Wolfgang Textor	Graduate
Nicolaus von Uffenbach	Frauensteiner
Joh. Georg Schweitzer Edler von Widerhold	Merchant
Friederich Maximilian von Günderode	Limpurger
§ Johann Carl von Fichard	Limpurger
§ Friedrich Maximilian von Lerssner	Limpurger
§ Friedrich Wilhelm von Völcker	Limpurger
§ Carl Ludwig von Lersner	Limpurger

59. See once again section 5 of *Historische Nachrichten* (1715).

60. These reforms are summarized in Hohenemser, *Verfassungsstreit*, 303–304. Most of them were promulgated in the First Imperial Resolution (22 November 1725), reprinted in Müller, *Frankfurt contra Frankfurt*, I, 8–15.

fifteen years after the new electoral procedures were introduced in 1727.[61] Only six of the Schöffen had entered the council under the new rules by 1742, so a later vantage point is needed to evaluate the effects of the reforms. Tables 20 and 21 include figures for the men entering the council for thirty-five years after 1727, and they show clearly the impressive increase in the percentage of burghers from outside the two exclusive lodges. Because these burghers could not have been as closely related to Limpurger and Frauensteiner as their counterparts before 1727, the increase of their ratio to 52.9 percent of the Schöffen indicates a much more significant gain for the common burghers. Who were these "commomers" in the first bench? About two thirds were Graduates, who did not think of themselves as ordinary burghers and should be considered part of the aristocracy, and the others were important merchants. The change meant a certain liberalization of Frankfurt politics: an expanded yet small elite exercised power in the eighteenth century.

Fundamental changes by the emperor in Frankfurt's governmental structure meant that the city's affairs were much better administered after the constitutional conflict. Burgher leaders argued and then proved that they could manage city finances better than the old council, and after 1717 the restored Committee of Nine exercised a possible veto and constant inspection over all financial matters handled by the council and its offices. Fixed salaries for everyone in the city government, the fees charged for official services, and all incidentals were worked out in the most detailed fashion, with great precautions against arbitrary decisions and possible corruption. The administrative offices were consolidated; many of those collecting indirect taxes were farmed out to citizens, and the other Ämter remained under the council's control. In either case, the citizens enjoyed joint supervision of the Ämter, because a newly created Committee of Fifty-One was empowered in 1732 to receive reports from the men who farmed the indirect taxes and tolls and to appoint special inspectors (*Gegenschreiber*) to each office under the council's direct control. The Fifty-One also advised the Committee of Nine on financial policy and the council itself on any important matters. While the council maintained the initiative in legislation and in administration, its power was effectively checked by the burgher committees set up during the constitutional conflict. Such was the victory of the burgher party to which we now turn.

61. I have added Schultheiss Ochs to a list found in Ugb A51 Nr. 16, 425v. Those Schöffen marked with an § came into the council under the new electoral procedures.

PART THREE

THE BURGHER OPPOSITION

Party actions are always directed toward
a goal which is striven for in a planned manner.
This goal may be a "cause" (the party may aim at
realizing a program for ideal or material
purposes), or the goal may be "personal" (sinecures,
power, and from these, honor for the leader and
the followers of the party). Usually the party
action aims at all these simultaneously.
Max Weber

Chapter 5

The Burgher Militia and Its Leadership

The existence of a burgher party which sought to share power with Frankfurt's aristocracy after 1705 depended, as I have already argued, on two parallel developments—the rise of a vigorous group of capable leaders and the articulation of a concrete program to remedy the grievances that had united various groups of citizens in opposition to the council. The burgher militia provided the institutional framework within which this opposition developed its cohesive strength, found its original spokesmen, and organized its struggle for a share of civic power. Although important leadership did come from other burghers, the militia officer corps was the nucleus of the citizens' movement. Previous writers have emphasized the fact that most officers were artisans, but a close look at burgher leaders during the constitutional conflict shows how diverse their social backgrounds were. Not only were merchants represented in the officer corps from the beginning of the conflict, but active direction of the burgher party came at first from the most enterprising craftsmen and retailers and later from big merchants. Burgher officers were usually wealthy men and enjoyed high prestige in the community; their shrewd sense of political tactics enabled them to gain from the emperor most of the goals for which they fought. Not least among their aims were the "personal" goals to which Max Weber referred, for the burgher officers—together with the members of the newly formed committees to oversee the city's finances and administration—constituted a second elite vying with the aristocratic societies for power and honor in Frankfurt.

I. The Militia and the Officer Corps

When the council reorganized the city militia in 1614, it unwittingly created the institution which was, in the course of the century, to replace the guilds as the vehicle for burgher political activity. Precisely because the guilds had served as the principal agents of insurrection from 1612 to 1616, the imperial government destroyed them as self-governing corporate units. The only formal organizations left the artisans were handicraft corporations over which the aristocratic council exercised complete control. The new Handwerke had none of the powers of guilds: they could not make or enforce any economic regulations, correspond freely with local or foreign corporations, or even hold unapproved meetings.[1] The leaders of the Handwerke were chosen by the council from men who would swear allegiance to it and who would see that the aristocrats knew about everything happening in the corporations. As a result, these official spokesmen for the artisans lost the respect of most citizens.[2] At the same time the new militia system in Frankfurt brought burghers together in well-organized units and, most importantly, produced during the century a corps of officers who represented the burghers' views rather than those of the council.

Frankfurt maintained a small garrison of professional troops from early times, but beyond this force the city depended for its defense on an armed citizenry. As early as 1373 the burghers were organized into fire-fighting and military squads (Rotten), and the burgher militia participated in the ill-fated aggressive campaign against Cronberg in 1389 as well as in the defense of the city against its besiegers in 1552. Before 1614 the militia squads were voluntary units not organized by districts inside the city; the fact that a burgher might join a squad distant from his own house made mobilization for emergencies slow and inefficient. When the traditional units proved unable to prevent guild apprentices from plundering the Jewish ghetto in 1614, the council determined to reorganize the citizen guard.[3] The city was divided into districts called quarters (at first sixteen, later fourteen), and those eligible for the mili-

1. See the Transfix of 1616 in Bothe, *Entwicklung vor dem 30jK*, 676–679; cf. Hohenemser, *Verfassungsstreit*, 10–11.

2. Ibid., 11; Römer-Büchner, *Stadtverfassung*, 187.

3. Rudolf Jung, "Das Frankfurter Bürgermilitär im XVIII. Jahrhundert," *Alt-Frankfurt* 4 (1912), 40.

tia had to serve in squads within their local quarters. The change made possible more rapid preparation for duty. Men living in ten consecutive houses made up a squad, and all the units of a quarter could be mustered quickly into a single company under unified local command.[4]

What groups were subject to this compulsory muster, however, is not entirely clear. The Watch Ordinance of 1640 exempted councilmen, the syndics, physicians, holders of doctorates or licentiates, ministers, and the top personnel in the *Cantzley*, the *Rechney*, and the *Schatzungs-Amt*. Noble persons resident in Frankfurt were free from personal service but had to pay substitutes for watch duty.[5] Although I find no ordinance to support Rudolf Jung's view that the most important commercial people (as part of the second order of the community) were also legally exempt, a statement of the burgher captains to the Reichshofrat in 1733 does indicate that the "most respectable citizens and merchants" were given the option of providing substitute watchmen.[6] Neither the Watch Ordinance of 1669 nor the renewed Quarter Ordinance of 1708 mentions this option, and it probably grew as an informal custom in the seventeenth century.[7] Although the practice may have eliminated a large number of merchants from the citizen guard, there were also many wealthy commercial men in its officer corps. Both Isador Kracauer and Jung believe that denizens served along with the burghers in the militia during the eighteenth century, but I am unable to find any evidence of denizen participation before the constitutional conflict.[8] If the citizens did have denizens among their ranks, they at least maintained strong control of the militia, for all the officers were burghers.

The chain of command in each quarter ran from three high officers—the captain, a lieutenant, and an ensign—through a group of lower officers varying from eight to eighteen in number down to the individual squad leaders (*Rottmeister*). The council's military ordnance department (*Zeug-Amt*) appointed the officers and presumably should have chosen men, like the leaders of the handicraft associations, loyal to the

4. Ibid.; Hohenemser, *Verfassungsstreit*, 7.

5. I have used a copy of the Watch Ordinance of 1640 appended to documents presented by the burgher captains in December 1733 to the RHR as a dossier against the claims of Frankfurt notaries to exemption from watch duty; HHSA Wien: RHR Decisa 2075, Lit. B of "Gegen Vorstellung und Bitt" (2 December 1733).

6. Ibid., the "Gegen Vorstellung und Bitt" itself. See Jung, "Bürgermilitär," 41; Isador Kracauer, "Das Militärwesen der Reichsstadt Frankfurt a. M. im XVIII. Jahrhundert," *AFGK* 3rd series, 12 (1920), 99, does not include wholesale merchants in the group of privileged citizens exempted from service in the militia.

7. The two ordinances are published in Beyerbach, *Sammlung der Verordnungen*, 1683–1692.

8. See Kracauer, "Militärwesen," 99, and Jung, "Bürgermilitär," 41; cf. Kriegk, *Kulturbilder*, 21.

aristocrats. In the course of the war-torn century, however, appointments to the officerships became customary advancements up the ranks as higher officers resigned or died. While the Zeug-Amt maintained the power of formal appointment, the right to nominate leaders accrued to the higher and lower officers themselves. By 1669 one aristocrat, Jacob Bender von Bienenthal, warned against the council's lax attitude toward the important matter of commissioning captains, but the customary practice continued, and the officers of the fourteen quarters came to be, in effect, the chosen leaders of those burghers who served in the militia.[9] While seniority was probably also an important criterion for appointments, the most significant aspect of advancement was the confidence enjoyed by the officer among his colleagues.

There is every reason to believe that the officer corps gained increased respect from citizens during the seventeenth century, for by its end the higher officers constituted a self-conscious burgher leadership. Their independence from the council undoubtedly enhanced their prestige: the officers had a relatively free hand in organizing both watch and fire patrols. There was no professional fire-fighting unit in the city, so that important function fell under the officers' supervision. They also oversaw minor administrative tasks such as maintaining up-to-date quarter lists used by the Schatzungs-Amt when it assessed direct taxes, and the captains organized honorific ceremonies for visiting dignitaries.[10] The expanded military duties of the citizen guard—first during the Thirty Years War but especially during the last third of the century—brought the burghers together in concerted and disciplined action for a long period of time. The discipline involved in their militia service probably gave the burghers greater group consciousness and greater respect for the leaders who planned and personally directed their efforts. Most officers were masters of handicraft trades and thus shared the economic problems and social views of the majority of citizens. Close association in planning city defenses provided ample opportunities for discussion of the grievances that became increasingly intolerable for burghers toward the end of the century. Self-assurance and a very conscious role of party leadership gradually developed; the officers, charged with responsibilities which took much time and money, also fostered esprit de corps by holding huge feasts on occasions of special importance to their quarters.[11] As early as 1704 several officers gave assistance to a group of bur-

9. See "Merckwürdige Aufsäze und Bemerckungen die Stadt Franckfurt betreffend von Jacob Bender von Bienenthal 1669" (Manuscript in the Frankfurt City Archive: Leonhardi Nachlass, Kistchen 27), 216. On the appointment of officers in general, see Hohenemser, *Verfassungsstreit*, 8, and Jung, "Bürgermilitär," 42.

10. Jung, "Bürgermilitär," 47–48.

11. Ibid., 44.

gher shopkeepers who were determined to go over the head of the council and seek imperial action against Jews who violated the city's ordinances on their commercial ventures.[12] When they approached Count Solms in 1705 to request renewal of the burghers' privileges as stated in the Agreement of 1612/13, the officers clearly regarded themselves instead of the council as the real representatives of the citizens of Frankfurt.

Quite as important as this evolution of burgher leadership in the last half of the seventeenth century was the development of a remarkable astute sense of political tactics. I have already referred to the most important tactical decision made by the burgher leaders—to fight the council in legal terms rather than by insurrection. Their appeal to the emperor was intelligent: as his loyal vassals they sought his protection against the aristocrats who had been asserting a large degree of independence from imperial control. The officers moved carefully through the channels of administration, bribing the correct people but also pointing to the fact that the Frankfurt council threatened the emperor's control over his vassals.[13] They showed real persistence in arguing the burgher case before imperial officials. When their initial appeal to Joseph I met with failure, the officers refined their legal arguments and kept reminding Vienna that its interest lay in putting down the political pretensions of the council. They fought for six years before the citizens had won even their first request: the appointment of a commission to investigate their charges against the council. Such stubborn insistence that their cause was correct enabled the burgher officers to wage a twenty-six-year conflict.

The perseverance of the burgher party is less difficult to understand than its keen legal intelligence, its astute political patience, and its strong financial resources. These traits would not usually be associated with artisan movements, yet most of the burgher officers were handicraftsmen. Frankfurt historians have previously emphasized this fact, however, without closely examining the social composition of the officer corps.[14] Information on individual militia leaders of the seventeenth century itself seems to be nonexistent, but, beginning with various lists of the higher officers during the constitutional conflict, I have been able to gather data on ninety-seven of the officers who served in the early

12. See the minutes of the council's investigations into the captains' role, Ugb D49 Nr. 7.

13. Hohenemser, *Verfassungsstreit*, 131 and passim.

14. See for examples Kriegk, *Kulturbilder*, 20; Jung, "Bürgermilitär," 41; and even Hohenemser, *Verfassungsstreit*, 9, 16, 28. Hohenemser was aware, of course, that there were merchants in the officer corps and that lawyers cooperated with it, but his interest in political and administrative history seems to have overridden any serious consideration of the social composition of the movement.

eighteenth century.[15] Table 27 shows that the picture of the officers as "simple artisans" (Hohenemser) must be modified considerably. Not quite half of these men practiced a single handicraft, although several officers combined artisan enterprises with other occupations. Only four crafts contributed more than two men to the officer corps: the bakers led the field with ten (plus one more who combined baking with selling flour), and the brewers followed with nine officers who only brewed beer. If we add the four men who combined brewing with other occupations, the brewers were the largest group of artisans in the corps. With their contribution of five officers, the dyers fell into third place, but we should note that these five were not ordinary *Färber* but men who worked with silks and fine fabrics (*Seiden- und Schönfärber*)—a cut above their fellow dyers in wealth and prestige. The fourth large group of artisans is instructive for our purposes: there were only two simple coopers among the officers—no more than there were blacksmiths, butchers, or cutlers—but six men combined their cooper's trade with other pursuits. Most artisans in the officer corps were men in food-producing industries (having probably more daily contact with other burghers than most craftsmen), men of higher standing than the average master in their craft, or men whose positions were enhanced by their combining two occupations. Table 28 indicates these combinations and also shows that innkeeping was involved in nine of the seventeen cases. Add to these nine the five innkeepers counted as retailers and we have another fourteen men, like the bakers and brewers, whose contact with their fellow burghers would probably have been fairly frequent, especially since the

15. I have drawn the names of the high officers from five lists: a list for 1705 is published in Lersner, *Chronica*, II, i, 538, and in Hohenemser, *Verfassungsstreit*, 5; in 1713 all the officers signed a *Vollmacht* for their deputies, found now in the Bavarian State Archive in Würzburg: Mainzer Regierungsakten: Kaiserliche Kommissionen, fascicle 138, Nr. 6; another list for 1716 is in the Frankfurt City Archive: Leonhardi Nachlass, Kistchen 2, ii; the officers present at the official publication of the imperial resolutions of 1732 are listed in the Extractus aus Kommissions Akten zur Geschichte des 51er Kollegs (a manuscript which extracts information from volumes 22 to 42 of the imperial commission's papers, which were burned in World War Two; cited hereafter as Extractus), 4r–4v; and the final list I have used was one for 1734 published in the *Raths- und Stadt-Calender* for that year. The lists provide the names of 99 men, but I can find no information on a Heinrich Jung (the lieutenant of the fourth quarter in 1705 and its captain by 1711), and I cannot properly identify a Jacob Riesen (presumably the ensign for the twelfth quarter in 1713, though he appears not on the list for that year but in the same fascicle of papers in the Würzburg archive, Nr. 27, Bl. 270). Information on the political activities of the officers is found in the records of the various burgher committees (cited later in this chapter) and in the lists of councilmen (cited in Chapter 4, note 2, above). Occupational and genealogical information was generously supplied to me by an expert Frankfurt genealogist, Mr. Georg Itzerott. My debt to Mr. Itzerott is very great indeed, not only for this kindness but also for many others extended to me in the course of my research.

TABLE 27
The Burgher Officer Corps, 1705–1734

Total Number of Officers	97
Occupations	
Artisans (including two gardeners)	46
Retailers (including innkeepers)	8
Merchants	25
Stocking manufacturer	1
Combinations	17
Origins	
Native sons	67
Immigrant citizens	30
Religious Affiliations	
Lutherans	92
Calvinists	5
Catholics	0
Family Relationships	
With other officers	47
With burgher leaders not officers	8
With council members	15
With other city officials	8
None found	19
Political Careers	
Burgher deputies	20
Burgher committees	27
Council	6
Bureaucracy	4
None traced	40

TABLE 28
Occupational Combinations Among Burgher Officers, 1705–1734

Brewer–Innkeeper	4
Cooper–Winedealer	4
Cooper–Innkeeper	2
Tobacco dealer–Innkeeper	1
Confectioner–Spice Dealer	1
Barber–Innkeeper	1
Baker–Flour Dealer	1
Bookbinder–Publisher	1
Gingerbread Baker–Innkeeper	1
Spice Dealer–Tobacco Manufacturer	1

handicraft corporations sold their guild halls in 1616 and held meetings thereafter in taverns and inns.[16] With the innkeepers we have moved into non-artisan occupations: 34 percent of the officers were retailers and merchants having no direct involvement in handicraft production.

A closer look at the role of nonartisans in the burgher party will follow shortly, but first a few comments on other social characteristics of the officer corps are in order. The high ratio of native sons to immigrant citizens in the corps is to be expected in a burgher party which showed increasing alarm at the number of outsiders entering Frankfurt. Of special interest in the next section, however, will be the strong role played by the immigrant officers during the constitutional conflict. The presence of five Calvinists among the Lutheran officers is a surprise, and even more impressive is the fact that two of the five were immigrant burghers. Four of these men were merchants, while the fifth was a wealthy silk dyer.[17] The usual prejudice of the Lutheran majority made itself felt, however, in the fact that only one Calvinist (Jacob Passavant) enjoyed a political career as a result of the burghers' victory: when the Committee of Fifty-One was set up in 1732, he was elected—almost as an afterthought—as its fifty-first member.[18]

Another revealing characteristic of the officer corps is the fact that 48.5 percent of its members enjoyed the close family relationships they condemned among councilmen. The large number of marriages among officers' families is a clear sign that the corps constituted not simply a political unit but a cohesive social group as well.[19] Johann Heinrich Krauss, a brewer and the captain of the thirteenth quarter after 1728, provides an interesting, though perhaps exaggerated, example. Son of a captain of the thirteenth quarter, Krauss married in 1695 Anna Bilger, the daughter of his father's successor, Captain Matthias Bilger. After her death Johann Heinrich took as his second wife the sister of Johann Moritz Adami, an officer in the fourteenth quarter (both quarters were in Sachsenhausen). Krauss's daughter Ottila later married Johann Jacob Fritsch, nephew of Captain Fritsch of the fourteenth quarter and son of

16. See Schnapper-Arndt, *Lebenshaltung*, I, 333, on the special importance of the taverns in the social life of Frankfurt's artisans after 1616. On the sale of guild halls, see below, 141.

17. The five Calvinists were Matthias Beytals (the silk dyer), Jacob Passavant, Bartholomäus Schobinger (from St. Gallen), Johann Henrich Stern (from Bad Kreuznach), and Christian Ziegler.

18. 51er Protocolla 1732, 210–216.

19. Cf. Roland Mousnier, "Problèmes de méthode dans l'étude des structures sociales des seizième, dix-septième dix-huitième siècles," *Spiegel der Geschichte: Festgabe für Max Braubach zum 10. April 1964*, ed. K. Repgen and S. Skalweit (Münster, 1964), 552: "La marque extérieure du groupe, ce serait le mariage de ses membres entre eux."

one of the burgher movement's nonofficer leaders, and, finally, Krauss's son Carl married the daughter of Johann Simon Grodt, the ensign of the first quarter.[20] Most of the officers' families were not so carefully matched within the corps itself as were the Krausses, but it is difficult to escape the impression that in many quarters a small circle of closely related families controlled the officerships. A glance at the first quarter illustrates the point: Captain Wüstenhöffer's successor was Johann Daniel Büchel, who married the sister of his own Lieutenant Johannes Bischoff (half-brother of Lieutenant Peter Bischoff of the eighth quarter and a stepson of Captain Wüstenhöffer himself). Bischoff's daughter Anna married the ensign of the quarter, Johann Simon Groth (whose brother Peter was, incidentally, the ensign of the neighboring second quarter).[21] Table 27 shows that family relationships extended to other groups such as the council itself, but by far the most important ties were those which linked nearly 57 percent of the burgher leaders (officers and non-officers) as a social elite within the citizenry.

But all members of this elite did not share political power equally. Only 20 percent of the officers served as burgher deputies—the men who spearheaded the attack against the council during the constitutional conflict. When burgher committees were set up to participate in governing Frankfurt, only 27 percent of the officers enjoyed membership in the new bodies. Since there was considerable overlapping between these two groups, the number of active political leaders to come out of the officer corps probably did not exceed 40 percent.

II. Social Background of the Burgher Leaders

To understand which elements of the officer corps participated most actively and to learn what other groups of burghers enjoyed the fruits of victory, we must now examine the development of burgher leadership during the conflict. Just as the council set up a Secret Deputation to handle the day-to-day maneuvering of the constitutional conflict, so too the burgher officers established an executive committee in 1706 (Table

20. Johann Heinrich Krauss's marriage with Anna Bilger on 17 June 1695 is recorded in Traubuch (hereafter, Trb) 7 (1693–1701), 176; his second marriage with Maria Adami took place 28 September 1697 and is found ibid., 364. Trb 9 (1707–1718), 854, records the union of his daughter Ottila with Johann Jacob Fritsch on 19 April 1718, while his son Carl's wedding with Anna Maria Grodt on 4 September 1736 is found in Trb 12 (1736–1750), 63. References to the marriage records here as well as in the next note were generously supplied by Mr. Itzerott.

21. For Büchel's marriage with Antonnette Elisabeth Bischoff on 28 July 1690, see Trb 6 (1687–1692), 320v; their daughter Anna married Johann Simon Groth on 22 June 1723, according to Trb 10 (1719–1727), 312a–313.

29) to present their case to imperial officials.[22] This first *Ausschuss* was not very active, since the main task during the opening years of the conflict was to persuade the emperor to appoint a special commission to investigate burgher charges that the council had been violating the Citizens Agreement for almost a century. The leading figures of this precommission period of the struggle were Captain Dietrich Stein, Johann Jacob Böhler, and especially Captain Johann Wilhelm Fritsch. While the first two men were not on the Ausschuss, Fritsch was its most important member and the man to whom Hohenemser credits burgher success in finally having an imperial investigation undertaken in 1713.[23] All three men were native sons: Böhler was a dyer, and Stein and Fritsch

TABLE 29
The Burgher Deputies, 1706

Name	Age	Occupation	Origin
Capt. Joh. Jost Leinweber	—	Baker	Immigrant
Capt. Georg Körber	63	Brewer	Immigrant
§ Capt. Joh. Wm. Fritsch	47	Brewer–Innkeeper	Native son
Capt. Moritz Petri	—	Druggist	Immigrant
Capt. Josua Lemmé	54	Silk Dyer	Immigrant
§ Lt. Peter Bischoff	44	Cutler	Native son
Lt. Jacob Freidhoff	52	Confectioner-Spice Dealer	Native son
Lt. Joh. Peter Müller	—	Blacksmith	Native son
Ensign Johannes Klotz	46	Dyer	Immigrant
§ Ensign Joh. Mart. Wüstenhöffer	42	Merchant	Native son
Ensign Joh. Con. Siegling	57	Innkeeper	Native son
§ Ensign Joh. Reinhard Kistner	46	Brewer–Innkeeper	Immigrant
Ensign Joh. Ulrich Rücker	38	Gingerbread Baker	Native son
Heinrich Abraham Vahrentrapp	44	Silk Merchant	Immigrant

22. Hohenemser, *Verfassungsstreit*, 65–66. The table itself is based on information gathered from Mr. Itzerott's genealogical records for the men named in Hohenemser. The men with a sign § before their names were related. Fritsch and Kistner were brothers-in-law, since both had married daughters of Andreas Eisenacher; see Trb 6 (1678–1692), 86v and 267r. Wüstenhöffer's marriage with Anna Catharina Bischoff recorded in Trb 7 (1693–1701), 14, made him Peter Bischoff's step-father. We should note in passing the other structural resemblances between the officer corps and the city council: both consisted of three groups of fourteen men, the upper group in each—the captains and the Schöffen—enjoyed the greatest power and highest prestige, both relied for legal advice on men outside their own ranks, and both were so large that they often delegated authority to smaller committees of their own members.

23. Paul Hohenemser, "Bürgerkapitän Fritsch und der Beginn des Frankfurter Verfassungskampfes 1705–1712," *Alt-Frankfurt* 2 (1910), 13.

both combined brewing with innkeeping. Böhler's financial situation remains unclear, but Stein and Fritsch were enterprising businessmen who had become quite wealthy. Stein's total holdings were worth about 62,000 fl. in 1707, and Fritsch estimated shortly before his death in 1712 that he had spent 40,000 fl. for the burghers' cause.[24] All three men had been involved since 1700 with the efforts of the "Christian Shopkeepers Committee," which sought imperial help against the Frankfurt Jews, and they emphasized the burghers' complaints against the Jews as much as their grievances against the council.[25] Jewish competition was a crucial issue for local retailers, as we shall see in Chapter 7, and the earliest leaders of the burgher party represented wealthy handicraft and retail interests above everything else.

The burgher deputation of 1706 seems to have disintegrated, however, and only a few officers supported Fritsch's stubborn campaign in its darkest days in 1707 and 1708. Most council opponents were fairly well cowed into submission by the magistrates, until support came from imperial officials (especially the imperial resident, Völkern, and the Schönborns) and won Captain Fritsch his investigating commission.[26] But Fritsch himself died shortly after the decision to appoint a commission, and the burgher party had to regroup itself. The actual process of reorganization is not completely clear, though the officer corps certainly provided continuous leadership throughout the entire conflict from 1705 to 1732. The captains of each quarter assembled their burghers in February 1711 to obtain signed approval of their leadership and program, and, as the imperial commission began its sessions in March 1713, another collection of signatures gave the officers the support of more than four fifths of the citizenry.[27] On March 28, 1713, the officers presented to Count Schönborn a statement giving their deputies full power to represent the burgher cause, but whether the deputies themselves had been elected in 1713 or at some earlier time I do not know.[28]

24. Ibid. Fritsch seems to have paid Böhler's expenses while both represented the burghers in Vienna from 1706 through 1710. On Stein's wealth, see Hohenemser, *Verfassungsstreit*, 104.

25. See the documents in Ugb D49 Nr. 7; Hohenemser, "Fritsch," 6, and *Verfassungsstreit*, 16, 30. For Böhler, Jew-baiting seems to have become an obsession: his tracts against the Jews and against the council made it too dangerous for him to return from Vienna with Fritsch at the end of 1710, and in 1722 the emperor and the imperial vice-chancellor agreed with the council that his fanatical pen had to be stopped; Hohenemser, *Verfassungsstreit*, 292–293.

26. Ibid., 113, 80.

27. Ibid., 397–398, for quarter totals. The lists themselves are now in the Würzburg archive: Mainzer Regierungsakten: Kaiserliche Kommissionen, fascicle 138, Nrs. 7 to 20 (Bll. 48–145) with notarized copies, Nr. 26 and Nr. 27 (Bll. 201–272).

28. The Vollmacht for the burgher deputies is also in the commission papers at Würzburg, ibid., Nr. 28.

The Ausschuss of 1713 (Table 30) was more important than its predecessor in 1706, because it was a standing and active committee.[29] The deputies hired legal consultants and appeared with them at all commission sessions, sent a regular representative (Dietrich Notebohm) to Vienna, held meetings at least twice a week and kept minutes of these proceedings (extant from 1726 on), and consulted the entire officer corps for instructions on issues on which they had not already received policy guidelines. As the burgher party won its demands from the emperor, the work of the deputies increased. After they gained the reestablishment of the Committee of Nine to oversee city finances, the deputies concentrated their administrative efforts on supervising the city offices. They selected the "admodiators," who farmed out indirect taxes, and the inspectors in other offices; they also took reports on city administration to the commission and to the council itself. Besides these assigned duties,

TABLE 30

The Burgher Deputies, 1713

Name	Age	Occupation	Origin
Capt. Dietrich Stein	49	Brewer–Innkeeper	Native son
Capt. David Düring	71	Brewer	Native son
Capt. Joh. Peter Körber	—	Brewer	Immigrant
§ Capt. Joh. Peter Müller	—	Blacksmith	Native son
§ Lt. Johannes Klotz	53	Dyer	Immigrant
§ Lt. Paul Henrici	40	Dyer	Native son
Lt. Joh. Conrad Siegling	64	Innkeeper	Native son
Lt. Joh. Mart. Wüstenhöffer	49	Merchant	Native son
Ensign Joh. Ulrich Rücker	45	Gingerbread Baker	Native son
Ensign Jacob Riess	61	Cooper	Native son
Ensign Joh. Dietrich Notebohm	42	Merchant	Immigrant
§ Ensign David Klotz	49	Dyer	Immigrant
Joachim Hoppe	48	War Provisioner	Immigrant
Their legal consultants:			
Dr. Benjamin Lehnemann	41	Lawyer	Native son
Dr. Johannes de Neufville	47	Lawyer	Native son
§ Dr. Ehrenfried Klotz	58	Lawyer	Immigrant

29. The names of the deputies appear in the Würzburg papers, ibid., 41r, and in Hohenemser, *Verfassungsstreit*, 165, 220. The other information on the deputies comes from Mr. Itzerott's genealogical records, and the names of the legal consultants are taken from Extractus, 1ar. Again the sign § indicates family relationships: the three Klotzes were brothers, and J. P. Müller was Paul Henrici's son-in-law. For Müller's marriage with Anna Judith Henrici on 24 February 1718, see Trb 9 (1707–1718), 844.

the Ausschuss often heard the grievances of citizens on private matters and intervened on their behalf with the magistracy.[30] In the course of the constitutional conflict, then, the deputies undertook not only the presentation of the burgher case before the commission and in Vienna but also those functions which were to fall to the permanent Burgher Committee of Fifty-One (the *Bürgerausschuss*) when it was created in 1732.

Although the political activity of the burgher executive committee increased considerably after 1713, its social composition did not change much between 1706 and 1713. Only five men of the original group remained in the second Ausschuss, but there was little difference in the occupations represented: the number of artisans increased from seven to eight, and merchants increased from two to three, while the number of retailers (two) and men combining different occupations (three) declined to one each. Immigrant citizens and native sons were fairly evenly balanced in both groups, though immigrants declined from 50 percent in 1706 to 40 percent in 1713. These percentages gave immigrant burghers a larger role than we might have suspected, however, when we saw on Table 27 that they constituted only 31 percent of the entire officer corps. Even the average age of the deputies changed by only three years (48.5 to 51.5).

The significant difference between the two groups of deputies lies not in their general social composition but in the smaller circle of most important leaders within each committee. While the first committee had been controlled by wealthy artisan and retail interests, the Ausschuss of 1713 came under the direction of very wealthy merchants. There was considerable personal rivalry within the second group between 1713 and 1716: the three Klotz brothers together with Wüstenhöffer and (from outside the Ausschuss) Lieutenant Büchel attempted to assert leadership, but they were soon challenged by the two men who became the top leaders of the burgher party—Dietrich Notebohm and Joachim Hoppe. The Klotz brothers apparently opened themselves to charges of forming a clique of closely related and self-interested men; they pushed through the appointment of their brother Ehrenfried as legal consultant and burgher representative in Vienna in 1713.[31] Resentment within the officer corps against this grasping for power undoubtedly benefited Notebohm and Hoppe, though their own ability to aid the burgher cause finan-

30. A review of these activities appears in the "Kurtze Nachricht Was es mit denen bürgerl. Deputirten zu Franckfurth am Mayn und derer noch immer continuirenden Zusammenkünfften vor eine beschaffenheit habe," an anonymous manuscript dated 1730 and presumably written by or for the deputies, found in the city archive: Geheime Deputation and Correspondenz VI.

31. Hohenemser, *Verfassungsstreit*, 287.

cially was certainly the most significant factor in their growing popularity. When the burgher leaders were required in 1714 to place 100,000 fl. collateral on their promise to net that amount if they were allowed to administer all city offices, Hoppe and Notebohm were the most important contributors (Table 31).[32] In October 1716 thirty-six officers supported the two merchants in their demand to have Ehrenfried Klotz withdrawn from Vienna. Their success over the Klotz brothers in 1716 represented the victory of the wealthiest merchants in a struggle for control of the Ausschuss, and Hoppe and Notebohm enjoyed unchallenged command of the burgher movement throughout the remaining years of the constitutional conflict.[33]

The men who vied for leadership of the second Ausschuss were probably all wealthier than Captains Stein and Fritsch, and, in contrast, they were immigrant burghers. True, these immigrants had resided in Frankfurt for an average of thirty years, but the Klotz brothers came to the city as boys, while Notebohm and Hoppe spent their formative years in the north (Lippstadt and Harburg). Whether the broader outlook on Frankfurt politics and the better perspective on imperial affairs shown

TABLE 31

Burghers Who Guaranteed the Admodiation in 1714

Name	Occupation	Origin	Amount
Capt. David Düring	Brewer	Native son	fl. 5000
Lt. Peter Bischoff	Cutler	Native son	4000
Lt. Johannes Klotz	Dyer	Immigrant	10,000
Lt. Joh. Con. Siegling	Innkeeper	Native son	5000
Lt. Paul Henrici	Dyer	Immigrant	5000
Ensign Diet. Notebohm	Merchant	Immigrant	15,000
Ensign David Klotz	Dyer	Immigrant	6000
Deputy Joachim Hoppe	War Provisioner	Immigrant	50,000
		Total	fl. 100,000

32. Müller, *Frankfurt contra Frankfurt*, I, 73, supplies the names of the contributors and the amounts they raised. Occupations and places of origin were, once again, obtained from Mr. Itzerott's genealogical records.

33. Hohenemser, *Verfassungsstreit*, 288. As we shall see in Chapter 8, Notebohm did come into serious disagreement with the officer corps on the two issues of denizens' privileges and the right of Calvinists to hold public worship services in Frankfurt. The disagreements occurred in the last years of the constitutional conflict (1726–1732), but even when the officers became very angry with Notebohm, they stopped short of revoking his mandate to represent them in Vienna until after the imperial commissions had concluded their work. See esp. 51er Protocolla 1729 (which are really the protocols for the deputies' meetings until 1732), 261–265 (10 November 1729), and 51er Protocolla 1732, 176–177 (7 July 1732).

by the latter two was a result of their early experiences outside the city, of natural intelligence, or of the wide connections they enjoyed as wholesale merchants is difficult to judge. The two wholesalers clearly had greater wealth and higher social station than any other members of the 1713 deputation. Notebohm's commercial activities are not specifically recorded even in Dietz's *Handelsgeschichte*; he is always referred to simply as a "merchant" and may have engaged in different types of commercial enterprise. Since he married the daughter of a Frankfurt broker and later gave his own daughter to a prominent banker, we can be sure that his professional and social contacts with financial circles were very important. While Notebohm probably inherited money from his father (a merchant and bailiff in Lippstadt), Joachim Hoppe seems to have been a self-made rich man. He started as a tailor when he came to Frankfurt in 1687, but he made a large fortune as a military provisioner during the wars at the turn of the century. Hoppe wielded influence among imperial officials and was appointed Provisions Commissioner for the Upper Rhenish Circle.[34]

The two merchants who controlled the Ausschuss after 1716 inspired greater confidence among professional and commercial interests in Frankfurt than Stein and Fritsch had done and led the movement in a somewhat different direction. The earlier leaders had not been able to gain the assistance of Frankfurt lawyers and had had to hire legal advisers from outside the city.[35] Now the deputies employed local lawyers and gained the support of some of the most influential members of the Graduate Society.[36] The issues emphasized after 1713 reflected the change in leadership: the problem of Jewish retail activities—so crucial to Fritsch, Stein, and Böhler—was scarcely given even passing mention by the second Ausschuss. The interests of the handicraft associations were well presented, but chief attention went to questions like corruption, financial mismanagement, and administrative incompetence in the aristocratic government. In contrast to the matter of Jewish infringements of the burghers' retail market, these issues involving the possibility of increasing city and imperial revenues were of great concern to the government in Vienna. But they were also of overriding interest to the big merchants and financiers, who bore a large share of the tax burden and who expected city government to be efficient and to operate in the black.

34. Information on Notebohm and Hoppe is sparse and has been gleaned from various sources brought to my attention by Mr. Itzerott. For Notebohm, see Bgb 1690–1723, 109r, and Trb 7 (1693–1701), 261; on Commissioner Hoppe, see Bgb 1657–1689, 393v, Taufbuch 22 (1706–1708), 730–731, and, most importantly, Totenbuch 17 (1736–1743), 1139.

35. Hohenemser, *Verfassungsstreit*, 103–104.

36. See, for example, 51er Protocolla 1726–28, passim, and 1732, 159–162.

This influence of commercial interests within the political leadership of the burgher party was reinforced by the exclusive election of important merchants to the Committee of Nine reestablished in 1717 to oversee city finances (Table 32).[37] Although the militia officers nominated more of their own members for the committee, the council elected only two officers to the original group of Nine. Merchants outside the corps thus gained a firm hold on one of the two most important institutions for burgher participation in Frankfurt's government, and there followed some antagonism between the Nine and the officer corps, which did not want the new committee of merchants to become entirely independent of the old nucleus of the burgher party.[38] Despite minor rivalry and personal jealousies, however, the Committee of Nine and the burgher deputies cooperated to push forward their program of financial and administrative reform.

Opposition to that program arose among a small group of burghers in 1721, when thirty-five artisans and retailers petitioned the emperor

TABLE 32

The Committee of Nine, 1717

Name	Age	Occupation	Origin
Johann Jost Lindheimer	55	Cattle Dealer War Provisioner	Native son
Lt. Seger von der Berg	54	Banker	Denizen, then burgher
Johannes Roth	54	Merchant	Native son
Lt. Mathias Servas Bansa	42	Druggist (Colonial Wares?)	Native son
Georg Schwartz	55	Merchant	Immigrant
Johann Wilhelm Bruder	46	Cattle Dealer	Native son
Christoph Ruprecht	47	Merchant	Native son
Jacob Adami	38	Merchant–Banker	Native son
Johann Paul Pauli	50	Wine Dealer	Native son

37. Hohenemser, *Verfassungsstreit*, 257, lists the original committee, and Ratswahlen B23: "Mitglieder der 9er" is a manuscript listing of all members with some biographical data. Again I have drawn from Mr. Itzerott's files to learn that all 9er chosen before 1740 were merchants.

38. There were several disputes between the 9er and the officers. I cite as an example one over the rotation of positions in late 1732, during which the officers apparently sought to change the social composition of the committee by nominating six men—a lawyer and five retailers, rather than big merchants—to assume positions which the 9er themselves did not consider open yet to new elections; see HHSA Wien: Reichskanzlei: Kleinere Reichsstände, fascicle 109, 237–245, especially 239.

for a speedy end to the conflict between the council and the burgher deputies. Besides charging that the new burgher administrators applied taxes too harshly, the dissatisfied burghers argued that the Ausschuss was prolonging the conflict by extending its demands beyond the original goals of the movement—restoration of the Citizens Agreement and strict enforcement of the Jewish Stättigkeit. Poor burghers consequently suffered from the unsettled economic conditions which prevailed in the city, while their leaders—among them many wealthy citizens who had not even signed the original mandate for the officer corps—misused the authority given them. Though it received some encouragement from the council, this small opposition had little attention from the burgher deputies or from imperial officials.[39] It deserves our attention, however, because its grievances verify my contention that, with the regrouping which occurred from 1713 to 1716, the burgher party moved in a new direction under new leadership.

An alliance of the burgher officers with prominent merchants was responsible for the major constitutional reforms of the early eighteenth century: the two groups forged the representative institutions—the Committee of Nine and the Committee of Fifty-One through which they shared power in Frankfurt. The latter committee was founded in 1732 as a permanent replacement for the burgher deputation which had spearheaded the reform movement, and its members were usually co-opted either from the officer corps or from the merchant community.[40] Frankfurt enjoyed a "mixed" constitution throughout the rest of the eighteenth century, because an elite from the citizenry shared power with the city's aristocracy. That burgher elite drew its members from several elements of the community—first and foremost merchants, but also some wealthy artisans and retailers co-opted as militia officers into the Committee of Fifty-One. While the merchants gained most in the

39. Hohenemser, *Verfassungsstreit*, 289–292, discusses the opposition and dismisses it as of little importance; documentation is found in the HHSA Wien: RHR Decisa 2210 which includes a specification of the thirty-five burghers as well as their petition to the emperor.

40. For the election of the original Committee of Fifty-One, see 51er Protocolla 1732, 210–216; cf. Ratswahlen B23: "Mitglieder der 51er." Helmut Böhme, *Frankfurt und Hamburg*, 103, argues that the Fifty-One were an executive not of the burghers "but of the wealthy Calvinist and Catholic merchants and bankers." The burgher captains elected the original committee, which enlisted its members thereafter. Only one Calvinist was included in 1732, and the membership through 1750 was overwhelmingly Lutheran (though I confess I have not checked every name). Unless the burghers underwent a real change of heart after 1750, Böhme is certainly wrong on this point. And it is not a small point, since he uses it to buttress his argument that the Fifty-One did not constitute a *Zwischeninstanz* between the council and the common citizenry.

new constitutional arrangements, they did not alienate more than a handful of their supporters among the common citizenry. And the bulk of the support for burgher leaders, if measured in numbers and in enthusiasm rather than financial terms, came from Frankfurt's artisans.

Chapter 6

Artisans and Handicraft Workers: the Brewers

The failure of its guilds to gain a strong political position during the late medieval and early modern periods gave Frankfurt one of the most conservative constitutions among the imperial cities. Despite repeated attempts in 1355–1366, 1525, and then 1612–1616, the city's artisans were unable to shake off the firm control exercised by the patrician families over their political and economic affairs. Although the Fettmilch Uprising did bring new aristocratic elements into the ruling elite, it left the artisans completely subject to the authority of the city council. Deprived of their guilds after 1616 yet still organized in handicraft associations (Handwerke) which the council used to control their activities, the craftsmen formed the broad base of citizen opposition to aristocratic government during the late seventeenth and early eighteenth centuries.

Nevertheless, the victory of the burgher party in the constitutional conflict did not benefit the artisans nearly as much as it did commercial elements in the community. The artisans' political influence in city government remained insignificant and their economic importance limited to the local Frankfurt market. Handicraft industry never dominated the city's economy as wholesale commerce did, but we can understand Frankfurt society and the lives of its ordinary citizens only by examining the artisans and their handicraft associations. I will first outline the general legal and economic situation of most craftsmen and then concentrate on the brewers, the council's most bitter opponents among the artisans.

I. Artisans and Handicraft Industry

The conditions which would have permitted artisans to enjoy some degree of self-government or simply to share the council's power over their economic and social activities were missing in seventeenth-century Frankfurt. Artisan representation on the council's third bench had never been more than a formality, and Frankfurt's guilds saw a steady erosion of their corporate autonomy from 1377 to 1616. They emerged from the "troubles" of the mid-fourteenth century with new guild ordinances not made by the masters themselves but forced on the craftsmen by the emperor and his party in the city council. The unlimited authority over their own affairs and the right of free assembly previously enjoyed by the guilds were modified; after 1377 they had to seek council approval of any regulations they made, any convocations they held, and any punishments they inflicted on their own members. The council also initiated its constant surveillance of the guilds by appointing men (*Ratsmänner* or *Ratsfreunde*) to oversee those which did not have representatives on the third bench.[1] Although the magistracy left the organization and administration of social and industrial activities largely in the hands of the master craftsmen themselves, opportunities for the guilds to play an independent political role were greatly reduced.[2] The patricians further extended their control during the fifteenth and especially the sixteenth century, when the council assumed the right to oversee all guild correspondence, the accounting of guild funds, and the verification of the legitimate birth of all apprentices.[3]

The culmination of this long process by which the council exerted ever-increasing authority over the city's artisans was the Transfix of 1616, which abolished Frankfurt's guilds after their last unsuccessful attempt to wrest power from the patricians.[4] Craftsmen no longer belonged to guilds but to Handwerke. The term *Zunft* (guild) was dropped from official records to remove any possible suggestion of corporate autonomy. Official leadership of the artisan groups passed, as we saw in

1. Benno Schmidt, ed., *Frankfurter Zunfturkunden bis zum Jahre 1612* (Frankfurt, 1914), I, 44–46; Eugen Elkan, *Das Frankfurter Gewerberecht von 1617–1631* (Tübingen, 1890), 44–48.

2. Schmidt, I, 47–48; Elkan, *Gewerberecht*, 53.

3. Schmidt, I, 45; cf. Franz Lerner, *Geschichte des Frankfurter Metzger-Handwerks* (Frankfurt, 1959), 178–179.

4. Cf. Mauersberg, 225, who emphasizes the strong control exercised by the council before 1616; the Transfix itself is printed in Bothe, *Entwicklung vor dem 30jK*, 675–679.

Chapter 5, from elected guild masters (*Zunftmeister*) to men who were sworn adherents of the council (*Geschworene*).[5] Guild halls were sold to pay the heavy fines imposed on groups which had participated most actively in the Fettmilch Uprising, and the social convocations of the Handwerke were generally held in taverns and inns—a partial explanation, no doubt, for the high proportion of brewers and tavern keepers in the burgher officer corps.[6] All guild records were removed to the city hall, and the council maintained the handicraft associations as units of social and economic organization through which it could control the bulk of Frankfurt's population as well as the local economy.

Handicraft people were integrated into the larger urban community through the Handwerke, which preserved the heritage of traditional, corporate social organization and resembled modern occupational groupings at the same time. Frankfurt's social corporations had always united men of similar social or occupational standing; there was no attempt like that in Basel to fit the citizenry into a fixed number of guilds, so professional men did not find themselves in the same corporation with smiths or fishermen.[7] As we have seen in Chapter 3, patricians and commercial people formed their own societies in the late fourteenth century as a response to the strong organizations already in existence among the craftsmen.[8] The number of corporations was allowed to increase during the next centuries as new occupational groups settled in the city; the most vigorous expansion occurred in the late sixteenth century, when the influx of religious refugees was accompanied by the formation of twelve new guilds and the reorganization of many older ones.[9] Article 3 of the Citizens Agreement of 1612/13 then ordered every burgher of Frankfurt into a social corporation.[10] Accordingly, by 1614 there were six nonartisan societies and thirty-eight guilds (Table 33).[11] But the

5. Cf. above, 122; Elkan, *Gewerberecht*, 65–69; Römer-Büchner, *Stadtverfassung*, 186–187.

6. See above, 126–128, on the importance of taverns. On the guild halls, see Bothe, *Entwicklung vor dem 30jK*, 676; Wilhelm Lüttecke, *Das Benderhandwerk zu Frankfurt a. Main bis zur Einführung der Gewerbefreiheit* (Borne-Leipzig, 1927), 33, and Bruno Herberger, *Die Organisation des Schuhmacherhandwerks zu Frankfurt a. Main bis zum Ende des 18. Jahrhunderts* (n.p., 1931), 51, both mention the sale of their guild halls by the coopers and shoemakers and their later assemblies in taverns.

7. Mauersberg, 181–183, on Basel's guilds after the "New Reformation" of 1526.

8. See above 74, where I draw from Lerner, *Alten-Limpurg*, 24–27, 33–34.

9. Schmidt, I, 25.

10. Römer-Büchner, *Stadtverfassung*, 184–185, indicates that the council had been considering the dissolution of the guilds in 1612, while its burgher opponents considered guilds as their only defense against patrician authority. The possibility that the citizens' demands for total organization of the community into corporations might have been a reaction to the appearance of small-scale putting-out industries in the late sixteenth century has not been explored anywhere.

11. Table 33 is based on a list found in Ugb A51 Nr. 16, 292r.

TABLE 33
Societies and Guilds in Frankfurt, 1614

The Societies
1. Limpurg
2. Frauenstein
3. The Free Society
4. The Retailers
5. Old Retailers' Society
6. Neuensteiner

The Guilds
1. Woolen Weavers
2. Butchers
3. Smiths
4. Bakers
5. Shoemakers
6. Old Gardeners
7. Furriers
8. Tanners
9. Fishermen
10. Tailors
11. Coopers
12. Masons
13. Joiners (Cabinet Makers)
14. Carpenters and Cartwrights
15. Purse Makers and Saddlers

Guilds (continued)
16. Tile Roofers (*Steindecker*)
17. Barbers and Brewers
18. Fustian and Linen Weavers
19. Bathers (*Bader*)
20. Ropers
21. Book Printers
22. Lace Makers
23. Goldsmiths
24. Diamond and Ruby Cutters
25. Printers
26. Schoolmasters
27. Chandlers (*Fettkrämer*)
28. Hatters
29. *Hecker* in Sachsenhausen
30. *Hecker* in Frankfurt Proper
31. Whitewashers
32. Day Laborers
33. Musicians
34. *Neuschirner* (Butchers)
35. Wine Porters
36. Porters and Packers
37. Carters (*Haintzler*)
38. Wheelers and Drivers

Transfix of 1616 reversed this trend toward tighter corporate organization of the community: the obligation of all citizens to join corporations was lifted, and only the aristocrats were left with their three societies. Until the wholesalers developed their informal exchange into a chamber of commerce at the end of the seventeenth and beginning of the eighteenth century,[12] merchants and retailers had no formal organizations. Between 1617 and 1631, however, the council incorporated the men working in the most important handicraft occupations into the thirty-four Handwerke (Table 34)[13] which replaced the guilds.

These corporations reorganized some handicraft groups, but they did not encompass all occupations important to Frankfurt's economy. Gardeners and wine growers (*Hecker*) were regarded as craftsmen and

12. *Geschichte der Handelskammer*, 16–20.
13. The thirty-four Handwerke are listed in the order in which the council issued their ordinances; see Elkan, 70–71.

TABLE 34
The Handicraft Corporations Formed 1617–1631

1. Tailors	18. Carpenters
2. Shoemakers	19. Cartwrights
3. Saddlers	20. Tile roofers
4. Joiners	21. Whittawers
5. Fishermen	22. Glaziers and Glassmakers
6. Coopers	23. All Smiths (*Feuerhandwerker*)
7. Bakers	24. Bathers (*Bader*)
8. Fustian and Linen Weavers	25. Barbers
9. Goldsmiths	26. Gardeners
10. Purse Makers	27. Turners
11. Butchers	28. Stringmakers
12. Tanners	29. Dressers (*Tuchbereiter*)
13. Ropers	30. Girdlers
14. Lace Makers	31. Brewers
15. Furriers	32. Diamond Cutters
16. Masons	33. Painters
17. Bookbinders	34. Whitewashers

brought together, like the different types of smiths, into one Hand-werk.[14] Other groups previously united by occupational similarities (pursemakers and saddlers, for example, who both worked with leather) or simply by chance (brewers and barbers) were given separate organizations. Printers, schoolmasters, *Fettkrämer* (chandlers or retailers of fatty products), musicians, transportation workers and day laborers—all of whom had formed guilds by 1614—were not included among the corporate groups after 1616. They became free occupations (as most of them had probably been before the Fettmilch Uprising), while the council made more rational the organization of those groups, often more highly skilled, which had traditionally worked within a framework of corporate regulation. The number of corporations and the specific groupings of handicrafts varied somewhat over the next two centuries, but there was no great change—in 1786 there were still thirty-four Handwerke.[15] The importance of free groups like transportation workers (drivers, wheelers, carters, and porters), day laborers, and packers in one of Central Europe's chief centers for the stapling and exchange of wholesale goods is

14. Heinz Lenhardt, *Die Landwirtschaft der Reichsstadt Frankfurt a. M.* (Geln-hausen, 1933), 75.

15. Moritz, *Frankfurt*, II, 287–310; on 311–312, Moritz lists seventeen crafts not organized corporatively, and among them were the hatters, glass cutters, comb makers, basket makers, makers of musical instruments, soap and candle makers, and upholsterers.

evident, and such occupations were also carefully regulated by council ordinances. The difference between the free groups and the corporations lay in the fact that the former were open to anyone who wished to enter the occupation, while traditional restrictions on membership and on industrial production were preserved in the Handwerke. Artisan opposition to the council's economic policy grew over the seventeenth century not because craftsmen wanted less regulation but because they objected to its liberal practices, which tended to weaken their monopoly over the local retail market. They asked the imperial commission in 1713 for greater independence from council surveillance, so that they might enforce more rigidly the regulations already in the city's books.

Although we cannot grasp the full meaning of handicraft corporations for the artisans without understanding the noneconomic values they served, we must concentrate our attention here on the role played by the craftsmen and their Handwerke in Frankfurt's economy. Historians are generally agreed that, by the seventeenth and eighteenth centuries, most guilds had come to function chiefly as instruments of governmental economic regulation, on the one hand, and as occupational interest groups, on the other.[16] Frankfurt's handicraft corporations were no exception. They shared with all handicraft organizations the same three basic concerns: (1) a decent livelihood (*Nahrung*) for all their members, (2) maintenance of their moral standards and code of honor, and (3) regulation of production and of the reception and training of new members.[17] The success of Frankfurt craftsmen in realizing these aspirations depended both on the influence which they as corporate groups could exert on the council's economic policies and on their own control of the local market.

One of the most striking characteristics of Frankfurt industry was its failure to produce goods for export. In the imperial city's long history, only the weavers of the fourteenth and fifteenth centuries managed to attain importance in Central Europe as producers of cloth for wholesale

16. The best general discussion of guilds and handicraft industry in the Empire is Wolfram Fischer, *Handwerksrecht und Handwerkswirtschaft* (Berlin, 1955): this well-balanced synthesis offsets the tendency to consider guilds simply as economic organizations, while it points at the same time to the proper framework within which their economic functions should be investigated. A study of the noneconomic aspects of Frankfurt's handicraft organizations as reflections of premodern corporatism is Heinz Lenhardt, "Feste und Feiern des Frankfurter Handwerks: Ein Betrag zur Brauchtums- und Zunftgeschichte," *AFGK* 5th series, I, ii (1950), 1–120. Though both Fischer's essay and Lenhardt's monograph are conscious efforts to explore the general social significance of guilds, I think both authors would agree with my statement about the role of their economic functions for such handicraft organizations in the seventeenth and eighteenth centuries.

17. Fischer, 29.

export. Frankfurt's prosperity in the early modern period was based almost exclusively on the city's role as a center for exchange of goods produced at widely separated points; it was best known for its commission businesses, which handled the goods of foreign firms in the great fairs, and for its banking interests, which made the city an important financial center.[18] Noticeably absent from the major commercial transactions in the fairs were domestically produced items. Burghers who were not involved in wholesale commerce did, of course, take advantage of the influx of merchants and other fair visitors twice a year: everyone—even patricians—rented any available space to the city's guests, craftsmen sold their wares at the best prices they could get (price regulations lapsed during fair time), and the retailers who supplied food and drink enjoyed a fantastic business. These periodic shots in the city's economic arm strengthened many residents for the less prosperous months of the year.[19] But the city's handicraft industries did not reach out beyond the local market and the windfall it brought them twice a year to serve a larger Central European market. Here we may contrast Frankfurt with Nürnberg, which exported over half of its industrial products during this period.[20] Frankfurt was undoubtedly a more active economic center than Nürnberg after 1648, but its importance remained commercial rather than industrial.

This failure on the part even of industries with export potential—cloth, beer, metal products, tobacco—can be traced to the refusal of the craftsmen to keep up with the technological changes which occurred over the seventeenth century and their inability to tolerate any individual entrepreneurial efforts which threatened their traditional corporate economic arrangements. Production remained small-scale, organized in individual shops by a master craftsman with the aid of his paid apprentices; use of water- or animal-powered machines found little acceptance; and the few domestic or putting-out industries organized by immigrants in the late sixteenth century remained exceptions, limited in both size and productive capacity.[21] "The Alpha and Omega of the

18. Bothe, *Geschichte*, 467; Dietz, *FftHG*, IV, i, 115 ff. On the relationship between industry and commerce generally, see Mauersberg, 184–185.

19. Ibid., 173–174.

20. Ekkehard Wiest, *Die Entwicklung des Nürnberger Gewerbes zwischen 1648 und 1806* (Stuttgart, 1968), 24, estimates that well over 50 percent of Nürnberg's industrial products were exported from the city. Wiest settles on that average figure, despite Nürnberg's relative economic decline after the Thirty Years War and the prevalence of mercantilist trade restrictions within the Empire during the seventeenth and eighteenth centuries.

21. Willy Herforth, "Die Lage des Frankfurter Gewerbes (in ihren Grundzügen) während des 16. und 17. Jahrhunderts" (dissertation in typescript; Johann Wolfgang Goethe University in Frankfurt, 1923), 23–24, 39–40. Nürnberg's industry was, in

council's economic legislation," wrote Friedrich Bothe, "was to prevent the introduction of large capitalistically organized industry into the city." The tobacco industry, for example, was forbidden in Frankfurt presumably because it would have been organized in a manner comparable to the factory system—it would, to quote the law, "bring the poor into the city."[22] Nor did the council accept the petition of the enterprising Daniel Behagel in 1661, and, as a result, one of Germany's most famous porcelain works was established about twenty miles away in the small town of Neu-Hanau instead of in Frankfurt itself.[23]

Hans Mauersberg has noted the antagonism shown by cloth and metal producers toward immigrant and even native-born colleagues who attempted to introduce new industrial techniques,[24] and the domestic silk and ribbon trades provide an excellent example of this attitude, which prevailed throughout the seventeenth century. At their almost violent insistence, the introduction of the mechanical loom—which might have enabled Frankfurt manufacturers to compete with the lower prices of ribbons from Basel and Holland—was forbidden by the council in 1647. It reaffirmed that decision in 1662 against its own better judgment and against the advice of cloth wholesalers in the city. The council decided the issue as the Handwerke demanded, however, because the aristocrats feared that changes which so directly antagonized the economic conceptions of the artisans might lead to another insurrection comparable to the one in 1612–1616.[25] While the story of the mechanical loom does illustrate the ability of artisans to influence the council's economic policy, the absence of large-scale industry from within Frankfurt's walls resulted as much from the hesitation of the aristocrats to allow a large number of dependent workers in the city as from the strong opposition of the crafts.[26] Industries other than the small-scale handicrafts

contrast, much less backward: the domestic system became the prevalent form of organization, and water-powered machines were numerous; Wiest, *Nürnberger Gewerbe*, 88–93, 104–106.

22. Bothe, *Geschichte*, 473.

23. Rudolf Jung, "Die Anfänge der Porzellan-Fabrikation in Frankfurt a. M.," *AFGK* 3rd series, 4 (1893), 368–374. A porcelain works was introduced in the city about forty years later, but little is known about it and its apparent failure. The Behagel family later centered its commercial activities in Frankfurt, but production was in Neu-Hanau. Although the Nürnberg council shared the prejudice of its artisans against *Manufakturen*, it did not prevent the establishment of some tobacco and porcelain works in the city in the seventeenth and early eighteenth centuries; Wiest, *Nürnberger Gewerbe*, 94–102.

24. Mauersberg, 330–335.

25. See Dietz, *FftHG*, IV, i, 76–86, for a discussion of the silk and ribbon industries and their long struggle against the loom first introduced in Holland in 1620 and later used so successfully in Basel.

26. Cf. the general discussion of these industries in Dietz, *FftHG*, IV, ii, 613–619.

were driven from the city itself to such nearby towns as Hanau, Offenbach, and Höchst, while the artisan was left with the local market in which to make his living.

The craftsmen expected that the council's regulation of the local economy would ensure protection of their corporate monopolies, so that every man in the Handwerke would have a decent livelihood. Unfortunately we have little information about the economic condition of Frankfurt's artisans during the seventeenth and eighteenth centuries, and since all tax records were destroyed during World War Two, it seems unlikely that a clear picture of their situation will ever emerge. Such a picture would have to be based on studies of individual occupations in relation to contemporaneous economic changes, and it would undoubtedly show much variety among the crafts over the two-century period.[27] At present, however, some fairly safe generalities reveal the artisans' relationships to the council and to other social groups in Frankfurt. Most artisans naturally lived on a social and economic level inferior to that of the aristocrats in the council and of the great wholesalers who made Frankfurt important in the European economy. There was also great differentiation within individual occupations, as Hussong's study of the tailors has shown.[28] Despite such internal disparities, artisans generally acted together as unified status groups. Like the Limpurger and the Frauensteiner but unlike the Graduates and commercial people, the craftsmen in the major industries in Frankfurt were united by a strong corporate sense. Their tradition was one of corporate monopoly of the local retail market for their goods as well as corporate regulation of production and of occupational training.

Organization of production and distribution varied from one occupation to another, but every master was subject to the same standards set by the council for his craft. The ordinances given the Handwerke after 1616 generally confirmed traditional practices designed to give each producer an equal chance to exploit the raw materials, labor supply, and marketing possibilities available in Frankfurt.[29] Masters were usually forbidden from buying, with an eye to making profit from possible

27. Such is the case with Wiest's quantitative study of Nürnberg industry. Based on various remarkably detailed *Gewerbelisten* from 1621 to 1811, his *Nürnberger Gewerbe* evaluates the relative importance of different industries in the local economy, places them in the social and political order of the city, and even estimates the living standards of the various crafts. A comparable study for Frankfurt is, as far as I can determine, impossible.

28. See Chart III, based on Walter Hussong, *Das Schneiderhandwerk in Frankfurt am Main und das Schneiderhandwerk in Heilbronn: ein Vergleich* (Gelnhausen, 1936), 86–88; for his study Hussong did use the tax records (*Schatzungsbücher*) later destroyed in World War Two.

29. Elkan, *Gewerberecht*, 134; Herforth, "Lage des Gewerbes," 6.

scarcities, a larger supply of raw materials than they themselves could manufacture, but, despite the council's attempts to stop the practice especially by the wealthier craftsmen, violations were frequent.[30] To avoid such problems, several Handwerke—among them the weavers, bakers, butchers, and shoemakers—established group control over supplies; after 1614, for example, a committee of four masters made wholesale purchases of leather which was then distributed to individual shoemakers as they needed it.[31] Most craftsmen produced and sold their wares, as I noted earlier, in their own small shops with the assistance of paid journeymen and apprentices. Only the shoemakers organized distribution through a common shop,[32] but how typical they were of other crafts in producing on order rather than selling ready-made items is unclear. Masters received fixed prices for the wares they produced according to the traditional standards of their craft, and, as we shall see later in the case of the brewers, one of the most important functions of the Handwerke was to provide a collective front of masters who wished to influence the council's decisions on equitable retail prices.

Perhaps an even more important function which corporate organization served for the artisans was the regulation of occupational training or of the relationship between the masters and their workers. The appointed leaders of each Handwerk oversaw the detailed regulations passed by the council on both apprenticeship and the final admission of young men to the full privileges of mastership. While those regulations varied with the occupations concerned, the same general stages of training applied to most crafts—apprenticeship, journeymanship, and final examination (based usually on the execution of a "masterpiece" according to the craft's standards). A boy wishing to apprentice himself to a master had to present proof of his legitimate birth for official registration, and almost all crafts required him to undertake three years of work as a *Lehrjung* with a single master.[33] Presumably he then undertook journeymanship elsewhere, while journeymen from other areas came to Frankfurt for more intensive training; such young men had to present themselves to the supervisors of the Handwerk, who then sought to place them with masters. Masters were generally limited to three workers (two journeymen and one apprentice), though that stipulation was often overlooked when poorer artisans passed up the chance to hire a journeyman and wealthier masters cared to take on another. The new man was first offered to masters who did not yet have the prescribed number,

30. Ibid., 16.
31. Ibid.; Herberger, *Schuhmacherhandwerk*, 88–91, 136.
32. Ibid., 96.
33. See Elkan, *Gewerberecht*, 70–76, for a presentation of the general regulations for masters, journeymen, and apprentices.

however, before a wealthy craftsman might hire him.[34] The journeymen (*Gesellen*) might receive room and board in their masters' houses, or they might be lodged together by their masters in a common house or in an inn—a practice begun in the last half of the sixteenth century.[35] In either case, they also received a standard, small weekly wage; artisans seem to have shunned the idea that handicraft workers might, like them, do piece work.[36] After such arrangements were made inside the Handwerk (according to stipulations laid down by the council), the journeyman registered his papers with the city government and was then subject to its endless, and probably unsuccessful, attempts to tame his rough habits. He became a member of the journeymen's brotherhood for his own craft, participated in its official monthly meetings and informal drinking bouts, and worked in expectation that he himself would soon be a master.

The Handwerke, however, were becoming increasingly closed corporations of privileged artisans, a fact demonstrated clearly by the growing cleavages between masters and journeymen as well as between families already associated with the corporations and foreign Gesellen who wished to enter. While frustration of the journeymen's hopes for advancement was by no means new in the seventeenth century, it was certainly intensified after 1616. To become a master, a young man usually had to be a journeyman for six years and, if he had not worked in the city, to have at least three years' experience in Frankfurt itself. Then he had to pass his final examination or produce a masterpiece before he applied for citizenship and full mastership.[37] Herberger has traced the historical development of such requirements for the shoemakers and has pointed to the increasing difficulties for outsiders to enter that craft. As early as 1377 an initial separation was made between masters' sons and outsiders in the payment of entrance fees, and in 1579 outsiders were required either to produce a masterpiece or have two years' working experience (*Mutzeit*) in Frankfurt. After 1614, however, the outsider had to prove a three-year apprenticeship (as against only two years in 1579) and a four-year journeymanship before he undertook work in Frankfurt for three years and then presented a masterpiece. Should he marry the widow or daughter of a master shoemaker, he would be for-

34. Herberger, *Schuhmacherhandwerk*, 82.

35. Hussong, *Schneiderhandwerk*, 30; Lenhardt, "Feste und Feiern," 27–28.

36. Herberger, *Schuhmacherhandwerk*, 82. Herberger found no evidence on the amount of wages but concluded from the high fines that journeymen often had to pay that their wages must not have been very low. Hussong, *Schneiderhandwerk*, 30, found that tailors paid their workers between 4 and 10 xr. weekly (depending on their experience) but shows that these sums could scarcely have been more than pocket money.

37. Elkan, *Gewerberecht*, 72–75.

given the three-year work experience in the city, but otherwise the old alternatives were erased and both the Mutzeit and the masterpiece were required. Masters' sons, however, enjoyed not only smaller fees but apparently also exemption from *Wanderschaft* (training outside the city) and the three-year "waiting period" in Frankfurt.[38]

This favoritism shown to families already established in the corporation was, of course, typical of most guilds in the early modern period. So, too, were the other measures which increased the difficulty of moving from a worker's position to a mastership. A major obstacle was the rising cost of producing a masterpiece and having it approved by the supervisors; by the late 1660's a council investigation revealed not only some very high fees but also wide variations among the Handwerke and among men entering the same craft (Table 35).[39] Some corporations had

TABLE 35

Some Cost Estimates for Masterpieces, 1668–1671

Handwerk	Estimates Presented to the Council
Coopers	One estimate of 90 fl.; another of 40 fl.
Bookbinders	One estimate of 100 fl.
Saddlers	One estimate of 100–120 fl.
Tailors	One estimate of 100 fl.; another of 70 fl.
Barbers	One estimate of 100 fl.; another of 40 fl.
Blacksmiths	One estimate of 55 fl.; another of 60 fl.
Joiners	One estimate of 100 fl.; another of 150 fl.
Locksmiths	Two estimates of 40 fl.
Cartwrights	One estimate of 40 fl.
Bakers	One estimate of 40 fl.
Shoemakers	Four estimates: 30 fl.; 88 fl.; 94 fl. 56 xr.; 57 fl. 48 xr.
Goldsmiths	Two estimates of 60 fl.
Tile Roofers	One estimate of 20 fl.; another of 25 fl.
Purse Makers	Two estimates of 18 fl.
Stringmakers	No masterpiece but about 15 fl. 30 xr. misc. costs
Brewers	No masterpiece but meal and drink for masters cost 3 fl. 50 xr.
Turners	No masterpiece but meal and drink for masters plus a fee totaled 56 fl.
Painters	No masterpiece and no costs

38. Herberger, *Schuhmacherhandwerk*, 17, 64–66, 81.

39. Table 35 is a representative selection of the estimates to the council in the course of its investigations from 1668 to 1671 and found in Ugb C29 Ggg, 3r–5r. The outcome of the investigations themselves is unclear.

limits set on the number of yearly admissions to their ranks: after 1630, for example, only four new masters were to join the shoemakers each year.[40] The council agreed to admit no more than six new masters (three native sons and three immigrants) to the tailors' Handwerk in 1613, but the corporation finally succeeded in 1707 in having the number of admissions cut to four (two masters' sons, one son-in-law, and one immigrant) yearly.[41] The masters demanded strict enforcement of all such regulations, and they became increasingly bitter over the council's more liberal attitude toward men whom the stipulations were designed to exclude.

The two most frequent complaints of the artisans were that their crafts were becoming too crowded and that the council was not protecting them from competition outside their corporations. The result, according to their petitions to the council, was a declining standard of living (*Abgang der Nahrung*) for craftsmen—the large majority of Frankfurt's burghers. However exaggerated such petitions may have been, they attest to increasing artisan discontent before the constitutional conflict. While the council was investigating the high costs of producing masterpieces in many Handwerke, the aristocrat Jacob Bender von Bienenthal was prompted to write that "one hears almost everywhere in the city a daily complaint about the decline in the standard of living, especially among handicraft people who complain that they get no work and therefore suffer great deprivation . . ."[42] Much as we would like to have statistical evidence on the economic position of individual crafts, little has been uncovered. Hussong's study of the tax assessments for the Frankfurt tailors does indicate changes in relative wealth within the craft between the Thirty Years War and the end of the constitutional conflict (Chart III),[43] and his figures illustrate that in one important Handwerk relative increase in the wealth of most masters before 1701 was followed by relative decline in the first decades of the eighteenth century. That these statistics reflect anything more than fluctuations of the general business cycle or that they reflect a general decline of local handicraft industry would be difficult to argue. In a city with a rapidly increasing population during the last half of the seventeenth century, we would in fact expect demand in its local retail market to grow just

40. Herberger, *Schuhmacherhandwerk*, 104–105.

41. Hussong, *Schneiderhandwerk*, 25, 37. In the same year, the council agreed that only four coopers (two masters' sons and two outsiders who married masters' widows or daughters) should be admitted to masterships each year; see Lüttecke, *Benderhandwerk*, 84.

42. Bender von Bienenthal, "Merckwürdige Aufsäze . . . 1669," 84.

43. Chart III is based on figures presented by Hussong, *Schneiderhandwerk*, 86–88. Hussong regards an assessment of under 300 fl. as an indication of poverty.

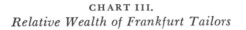

CHART III.

Relative Wealth of Frankfurt Tailors

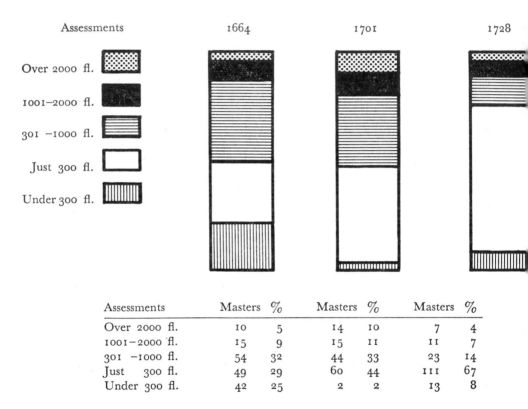

Assessments	Masters	%	Masters	%	Masters	%
Over 2000 fl.	10	5	14	10	7	4
1001–2000 fl.	15	9	15	11	11	7
301 –1000 fl.	54	32	44	33	23	14
Just 300 fl.	49	29	60	44	111	67
Under 300 fl.	42	25	2	2	13	8

as rapidly. As long as they could control such an expanding market, Frankfurt's handicrafts should have flourished.

But here lay their basic problem: the established artisans faced increasing competition inside the city for this lucrative retail business. Although their legal position as burgher artisans traditionally entitled them to share with burgher retailers (*Krämer*) a monopoly over the local market, the ability of outside producers to find retail outlets in the city for their cheaper products could undermine the economic security which the citizens' legal status was supposed to provide. But competition came not only from more technically advanced foreign industries the products of which could enter Frankfurt wholesale at fair time and then be distributed—albeit illegally—especially by Jewish retailers, it came as well from producers inside the city. The masters of most crafts saw a sizable increase in their own numbers as a threat to their prosperity, and they bitterly resented competition from local craftsmen permitted by the council to practice trades without entering the Handwerk.

The artisans' alienation from the aristocratic council resulted, then, from its policies that tended to expose them to the dangers of the open market and the open craft.[44] Master craftsmen argued that their corporations were growing too large, and Table 36 confirms that the Handwerke which Frankfurt historians have examined saw large increases in mem-

TABLE 36

Membership in Four Handwerke

Year	Masters	Year	Masters
Shoemakers		*Tailors*	
1616	60	1581	96
1643	91	1668	140
1663	130	1687	165 and 20 widows
1674	120	1696	150 and 30 widows
1675	129	1706	180
1681	124	1714	183
1717	160	1721	200
1734	180	1737	180–190
Gardeners		*Butchers*	
1601	48 and 9 women	1608	58 (estimate)
1670	67	1661	47
1672	70	1665	79
1718	100	1698	101
		1725	155

44. Cf. Mauersberg, 225–227.

bership by the early eighteenth century.[45] As the masters sought to make admission to the Handwerk more difficult, the council showed a leniency which the artisans considered intolerable. The council's policy on this issue was never spelled out for the craftsmen, and we cannot be entirely certain why the aristocrats were willing to admit so many men to corporations already considered crowded by their members. There were, of course, some financial incentives: we know that the senior burghermaster received gifts from men becoming masters,[46] and the craft entrance fees registered in the Bürgerbücher were another, though not a major, source of revenue for the city government. In any case, the magistrates seem also to have believed that the masters carried their exclusiveness too far when they rejected young men to whom both the Handwerk and the council had some obligation. After a journeyman had already invested many years in his training, the councilmen did not wish to deny him a mastership because of recently discovered illegitimacy (which should have been checked before his training began) or other offenses against the strict moral standards of the craftsmen.[47] A journeyman's failure to pass his final examination (usually on his masterpiece) meant that he had to continue as a dependent worker until permitted to take the test once again; in some cases, however, the council permitted the journeyman to establish an independent trade with the understanding that he had to prepare for a new examination and could not employ apprentices until he became a master.[48] During the constitutional conflict, the established masters sought greater independence from council control and especially the right to select the leaders of the Handwerke, so that they might end the liberal practices forced on them from above through the appointed craft supervisors.

Even more important to the masters was their fight against local competition outside their corporations. This competition, which first became a serious problem in the late sixteenth century, took several forms. Often one craft infringed on the traditional selling rights of another closely related Handwerk; furriers would, for example, also retail articles of clothing which the tailors considered their monopoly.[49] Disputes between corporations could be settled by the council, and they did not

---

45. Table 36 is based on figures from Herberger, *Schuhmacherhandwerk*, 123–124; Hussong, *Schneiderhandwerk*, 81; Lenhardt, *Landwirtschaft*, 74, for the gardeners; and Lerner, *Metzger-Handwerk*, 406. Cf. the figures presented by Mauersberg, 185–188, which show that the number of master craftsmen did not grow as rapidly over the early modern period as did the number of merchants.

46. Cf. above, 109.

47. I shall discuss specific examples provided in Ugb D24 Ll when I deal with the brewers in the next section.

48. Hussong, *Schneiderhandwerk*, 20.

49. Hussong, *Schneiderhandwerk*, 22, 130.

cause the same bitterness among artisans as that aroused by individual intruders in their retail market. These intruders (*Störer, Pfuscher, Stümpler*) were most often journeymen who illegally sold the items they made presumably on their own time; special groups like soldiers or country artisans undersold the tailors and shoemakers with wares they produced during their "off seasons."[50] Most hated of all intruders were the Jewish retailers who, in defiance of the stipulations under which they were permitted to live in the local ghetto, kept little shops in the city or engaged in that most despicable of economic practices—peddling. I cannot overemphasize the deep antagonism which grew up between burgher artisans or retailers and their Jewish competitors after the Thirty Years War.[51] The strong sense of frustration felt by the burghers when the council failed to enforce the law which protected their economic position from its most vigorous rivals was, as I have pointed out earlier and shall discuss in greater detail in Chapter 7, the most important factor bringing popular support to the militia officers' attack on Frankfurt's aristocratic government.

With these individual Störer the council's sin was one of omission—failure to proceed with vigor to eliminate them—but conscious commission was its fault in the case of a third type of competition. Already in the last third of the sixteenth century, the council gave its permission for some masters to practice trades outside the guilds; because of the greater demand for meat as a result of the influx of immigrants, for example, the councilmen allowed free masters to establish their own butcher shops in 1575.[52] These free butchers tended to band together, but permission for free practice of a craft was always granted on an individual basis and with the stipulation that the craftsman could not have any apprentices or journeymen. Examination of the Bürgerbücher for the seventeenth century shows that the council extended the privilege of free mastership to men in most crafts, though the shoemaker trade was certainly exceptional if it had, as Herberger thinks it did, more men outside the Handwerk than inside it by 1646.[53] Once again the practice varied according to occupation, and there seems to have been no special

50. Ibid.; Herberger, *Schuhmacherhandwerk*, 139.

51. See, for example, Herberger, 115, and Hussong, 22.

52. Lerner, *Metzger-Handwerk*, 168–170. These free masters or *Neuschirner*, as they were called, formed a loose community and even a guild by 1614, but they were free again after 1616; constant quarrels between the two groups of butchers led to a long court case in the early eighteenth century, with the result that the RHR ordered them united in 1746. Ibid., 248–262.

53. Herberger, *Schuhmacherhandwerk*, 108–109. Since the Bürgerbücher contain records of registration fees for Handwerke, I hope that my analysis of them will eventually present a relatively accurate picture of the statistical relationship between the corporate and free masters.

concern on the part of the tailors about competition from free masters until the 1690's.[54] In no case did these "loners" outside the corporations arouse the bitterness and fierce demands for their suppression that the illegal Störer and especially the Jews did. But the existence of free masters, like the polarization between big masters and small ones which became greater over the late seventeenth and the eighteenth centuries, does reflect a deterioration of the traditional corporatism, which the council had preserved in weakened form when it maintained the Handwerke after 1616.[55] While keeping some of the social spirit engendered by late medieval corporatism, the Handwerke served their members chiefly as organizations to represent their economic interests to the council and, after the council had failed them, to the imperial commission. Their bitterness toward the council grew sharper before 1713, when they finally laid all their grievances before Count Schönborn. Before turning to the fate of their cause in the early eighteenth century, however, I shall trace in more specific terms the alienation of the council's most vigorous opponents among the craftsmen—the brewers.

II. The Brewers in the Seventeenth Century

The brewers were one of several occupational groups in Frankfurt which were first organized into guilds in the late sixteenth century; in 1594 they joined the barbers' guild, and not until 1630 did they receive their own handicraft association.[56] They seem to have been fairly wealthy compared with other artisans before the Thirty Years War, for even though they were not active in the struggle of guilds against the council, they were quite heavily taxed by the burgher leaders of the Fettmilch Uprising.[57] Statistics published by Emil Wolff give the indirect taxes on beer and wine collected by the city between 1618 and 1713 and indicate, despite great fluctuations, that local consumption of beer probably increased considerably over the seventeenth century.[58] Al-

54. Hussong, *Schneiderhandwerk*, 35. Cf. Lüttecke, *Benderhandwerk*, 82, for free masters among the coopers.

55. On the polarization between masters with large concerns and those with only small ones, see Herberger, *Schuhmacherhandwerk*, 119–120, and Schnapper-Arndt, *Lebenshaltung*, I, 219, note 4.

56. Schnapper-Arndt, *Lebenshaltung*, I, 121; the section on beer and the brewers was written entirely by Schnapper-Arndt's student and editor, Karl Bräuer. Emil Wolff, *Zur Geschichte des Bierbrauergewerbes in Frankfurt a. M. vom Jahre 1288 bis 1904* (Nürnberg, 1904), 9, is incorrect in his view that the brewers were first organized corporatively in 1630.

57. Ibid., 9–10.

58. Ibid., 11, 12, 18.

though Frankfurt beer never became an important export commodity, it was a serious rival of wine in the local market by 1648. Besides stipulating a standard quality for the brew, the city council enacted precise regulations for its production, distribution, and cost to the consumer. The Beer Ordinance of 1630 ordered that each brew of "common beer" consume seven sacks of malt (each sack weighing eight *Simmern*) and a half *Zentner* of hops; these ingredients were combined to make 29 *Ohms* of beer.[59] A lager and a "double" beer could presumably be produced according to more individual standards, and the council occasionally altered the strength of the "common" brew.[60] The city inspected the malt used in the brewing process and also made provisions for its sale in only one market place, where all brewers would have a fair chance to acquire the amount they needed at reasonable prices.

The Brewers' Articles of 24 June 1630 organized their Handwerk and occupational training and further regulated production and distribution.[61] The burghermasters of the city appointed four Geschworene to oversee the enforcement of all regulations and to act as the brewers' spokesmen to the city government. An immigrant who wished to become a master brewer in Frankfurt had to apply for citizenship and present his papers to the council; he and his wife were both to be of legitimate birth, and he had to prove that he had served two years as an apprentice, had traveled two more years as a journeyman, and then had worked three consecutive years under Frankfurt masters. As in other occupations, advantages were given to those who married widows or daughters of masters: an immigrant who did so served two years in the city before admission to a mastership, while a native Frankfurter who married into the Handwerk served only one. The masters' sons naturally received most rapid advancement; they were required to serve only the two-year apprenticeship and a two-year *Wanderschaft* before being admitted without any *Mutzeit* to the corporation. Once he had become a master, the brewer was to hire no more than four workers—two journeymen, an apprentice, and a carter (*Fuhrknecht*). Also associated with each master could be as many as four tapsters (*Zäpfer*) who sold beer over the counter but did not brew it themselves; later a fifth tapster was permitted each brewer, if he wished to have one in the Jewish ghetto.[62] Tapsters could not be located within ten houses of a brewer unless they purchased their

59. The Beer Ordinance (23 February 1630) is printed ibid., 13–14.

60. The most important alteration came on 30 April 1657, when the weight of the sack of malt was dropped from eight to six *Simmern*; ibid., 13. The quantity of beer also seems to have varied between 28 and 30 *Ohms* per batch. Cf. Schnapper-Arndt, *Lebenshaltung*, I, 122.

61. Wolff, *Bierbrauergewerbe*, 14–16, reprints the articles.

62. Both ordinances of 1630 regulated tapsters, and the revised beer ordinance of 1657 provided for a possible fifth man in the ghetto.

beer from him, so each brewery was protected from competition in its immediate vicinity while, at the same time, almost every street in the community enjoyed the possibility of having a neighborhood tap.[63] Only a few wealthy families took advantage of each burgher's right to brew enough beer for his domestic consumption,[64] and the master brewers were the only citizens permitted to sell beer in an expanding local market.

The number of brewers (Table 37)[65] increased steadily over the seventeenth and early eighteenth centuries; from the small group of fourteen masters who joined the barbers' guild in 1593, the brewers expanded to 100 masters by 1704 and 130 masters by the time the imperial commis-

TABLE 37

Master Brewers in Frankfurt

Year	Masters	Source
1593	14	Ugb D24 Hh
1628	15	Ugb C51 F
1630	27	Ugb C51 F
1659	20 and 1 widow	Ugb D24 Gg
1671	36 and 5 masters' sons about to enter	Ugb D24 Mm
1677	51	Ugb D24 Qq Nr. 1
1685	70	Ugb D24 Qq Nr. 4
1688	70	Ugb D24 Pp (Cf. Ugb D24 Tt)
1690	Over 70	Ugb D24 Qq Nr. 3
1701	96	Ugb D24 Yyy
1704	100	Ugb D24 L5
1706	105	Ugb D24 L23
1710	121 plus widows	Ugb D24 L27
1713	130	Ugb C18 G
1728	131 and 8 widows	Ugb C18 Q
1764	186 and 43 widows	Schnapper-Arndt, *Lebenshaltung*, I, 129
1782	209 and 39 widows	Moritz, *Frankfurt*, II, 292

63. Cf. Schnapper-Arndt, *Lebenshaltung*, I, 122.

64. Ibid., 121.

65. Cf. the five figures given by Bräuer, ibid., 129; I disagree with Bräuer only on the number of brewers in 1682—not included in Table 37 because Ugb D24 Ww presents a petition signed by 47 (not 46) brewers instead of an estimate of the total masters for that year. The figures presented by Wolff, *Bierbrauergewerbe*, 19, seem absurdly low at first glance, and only after careful scrutiny of his table on 19 and of a passing remark on 22 does it become clear that he gives estimates not of the total number of masters in the corporation but only of the number of masters actually brewing beer—a distinction to which I must return shortly in the text.

sion opened its hearings in 1713. In those one hundred and twenty years the brewers faced several problems which were typical for all artisans in the city and led to ever-increasing dissatisfaction with the council's regulation of the Frankfurt economy. Among the first problems that confronted the brewers was outside competition. I find no mention of free masters brewing beer in the city, but beer was imported from neighboring villages and towns like Bornheim, Hanau, Bad Vilbel, Bonames, and especially Bad Homburg (famous for its white beer, which was apparently popular among the city's aristocrats).[66] Local brewers petitioned the council as early as 1628 to halt the influx of foreign beer, but the Beer Ordinances of 1630 and 1657 provided only that tapsters should not sell imported ales within ten houses of a Frankfurt brewery.[67] In 1671 the masters finally succeeded in having the importation of beer from surrounding villages prohibited, but the council modified its position in the following year by permitting the sale of any foreign beers drunk for reasons of health. This medicinal loophole probably resulted from the aristocrats' own preference for imported brews, but their caution in moving against importers may also have reflected a desire to avoid conflict with the Hessian Landgrave over the issue.[68] Further complaints from local brewers in 1696 elicited only a token response: all future beer imports were to be approved by the Renthen-Amt.[69] Once again in 1704 the brewers pointed to the inadequate enforcement of the prohibition and demanded that regular importers like the cooper master Fay be punished, and once again the council passed an ordinance forbidding the sale of foreign beers by tapsters but permitting private importation by persons who needed the beer to bolster their health.[70] The brewers became increasingly impatient with the council's inability or unwillingness to halt the flow of beer from the villages into the city, and they added this issue to the score they had to settle with the council before the imperial commission in 1713.

Increasing concern among master brewers over the rapid growth of their own corporation paralleled their fight against competition from outside the city. The high number of men whom the council and the Geschworene admitted became a serious issue for the craft by the 1680's,

66. Ugb C51 F, Nr. 1: brewers' petition of 4 September 1628; cf. Bräuer's discussion in Schnapper-Arndt, *Lebenshaltung*, I, 128–129.

67. Ugb C51 F, Nr. 1; Article 5 of Beer Ordinance in Wolff, *Bierbrauergewerbe*, 13.

68. See Ugb D24 Kkk for both the ordinance of 28 February 1671 and the decree of 26 March 1672; cf. related documents in Ugb D24 Mm and Bräuer's remarks in Schnapper-Arndt, *Lebenshaltung*, I, 128–129.

69. Ugb D24 Kkk for the petition of 30 June 1696; Bgmb 1696–97, 30r (30 June 1696) ordered publication of the edict, which may be found in CLF V, Nr. 80.

70. Ugb D24 L5: petitions of 8 May and 15 July 1704; the edict of 31 July 1704 appears in CLF VI, Nr. 27 as well as in Beyerbach, *Sammlung*, 804–805.

when its seventy masters felt that the saturation point had been reached. Further admissions could only damage the economic position of the established brewers, but their ensuing attempts to tighten admission requirements were frustrated by the council's leniency toward applicants. The failure of the magistracy to respond to the demands of the masters remains rather puzzling, but since the entrance fee charged brewers was much higher than that for other handicraftsmen, a desire for revenue is perhaps a plausible, though certainly only partial, explanation for the council's determination not to close the craft. The city fathers did block the entrance of persons who seemed to undermine the craftsmen's moral standards directly; otherwise, the council seemed to condone a more lax morality than the stern brewers could approve. The authorities denied admission to Johann Adam Nuss in 1675, when he married a bender's widow who had conceived his child before wedlock—neither the benders nor the brewers would have such a couple.[71] But the council was not so harsh with Vincent Haselbach, a child of premarital intercourse, when he sought membership in 1669, nor did the councilmen agree to expel Johann Nicolaus Diehl as a punishment for his elopement with a girl whose parents had been stubborn but who was not pregnant.[72] While this tolerance clearly offended the craftsmen's rigid notions of morality, their concern about an overcrowded Handwerk was probably a more important cause for their inflexibility in moral matters and for their disgust with the city government's more easygoing policies.

In the 1680's masters were attempting to block many journeymen from membership by not providing them with continuous local employment for the three years necessary for completion of their training period. The workers were apparently fired shortly before the Mutzeit should have been finished, and, since the period of continuous employment was to be started over, the journeymen would have remained dependent workers much longer than the prescribed time. The council intervened on behalf of the journeymen, however, and foiled another move by master brewers to halt the influx of so many new men.[73] Nor were the councilmen at all responsive to the brewers' pleas in 1690 for the restriction of future admissions to masters' sons or immigrants who

71. Bgmb 1674–75, 93v, 94r (11 February 1675); the petition for mastership is found in Ugb D24 Ll.

72. Bgmb 1669–70, 80r (26 October 1669) and the petition in Ugb D24 Ll; Ugb D24 Ll, Nr. 3 on Diehl's elopement. Cf. the case of Casper Siegfriedt in Ugb D24 L29 and in Bgmb 1711–12, 91v–92r (15 October 1711).

73. See, for examples, Bgmb 1681–82, 14r (7 June 1681), dealing with the petition of Nicolass Lelong found in Ugb D24 Ll, and Bgmb 1687–88, 141v (26 January 1688), admitting Peter Herzog as a master after his petition which is found also in Ugb D24 Ll, Nr. 2.

married into masters' families.[74] Demands for a longer Mutzeit in Frankfurt for immigrants—one of six rather than only three years—went unheeded in 1706, but when the council realized in 1710 that the burghers were winning imperial support for an investigating commission, it finally passed a similar proposal for lengthening the work period inside the city and for limiting admission to two new masters (one immigrant and one native) per year.[75] The council's generosity in admitting two journeymen named Itter and Kistner, who had applied to the Handwerk for mastership before the new regulations had been enacted and were then refused under the 1710 ordinance, so angered the brewers in 1711, however, that they determined to appeal the matter to the Reichskammergericht in Wetzlar.[76] Their anger had not subsided by 1713, when the master brewers complained to the imperial commission that the council and its supervisors of their Handwerk were still admitting almost anyone who requested mastership. The council's policy of forcing new masters on the craft against its regulations had already led to an expensive court case, and the only satisfactory solution was to permit the brewers to select their own Geschworene, who would be more discriminating about future admissions.[77]

Closely related to the problem of an overcrowded handicraft were an increasingly apparent cleavage between large and small enterprises and the consequent appeals of the smaller masters for protection against the larger masters and their tapsters. By providing for the sale of malt in one regulated marketplace and by limiting the distance around a brewery within which tapsters could sell beer, the ordinances of 1630 had attempted to guarantee each brewer a decent standard of living. The picture that emerges from the brewers' petitions to the council by the 1670's, however, is one of growing disparity between a few masters with active, expanding enterprises and the majority with small-scale operations just holding their own against increased competition.[78] In 1677

74. See the petition of the brewers dated 3 April 1690 in Ugb D24 Qq, Nr. 3; it was denied by the council on the same day: Bgmb 1689–90, 208r.

75. For the petition of 7 September 1706, see Ugb D24 L23 and Bgmb 1706–07, 47v–48r (9 September 1706). Ugb D24 L27 shows that the brewers' proposals of 26 August and 27 November 1710 both led to special council investigations and a rather unclear edict; see also Bgmb 1710–11, 85v–86r (18 December 1710). The documents on the cases of Itter and Kistner in Ugb D24 L27 made it clear, however, that the new regulations were passed.

76. All Frankfurt documents on the case are in Ugb D24 L27.

77. Ugb C18 G, Nr. 1a: "Gegrundete Beschwehrden des sämtl. Bierbrauer Handwerks . . ." signed by the brewers on 6 April 1713 and presented to the commission on 25 April, grievances 9, 10, and 11.

78. A similar picture emerges from two of the better studies of brewing industries in other German cities; cf. Karl Hoyer, "Das Bremer Brauereigewerbe," *Hansische*

the councilmen learned that there was scarcely any street in the city without its brewer, whether or not he had his own brewery, and that the rich masters and their tapsters were ruining the economic prospects of the newer masters.[79] Not all masters were able to afford their own breweries; a vat was apparently very expensive, and several brewers might share the same equipment.[80] Those who could not make arrangements to share a vat were forced, like tapsters, to buy beer wholesale from a master able to produce large quantities. Such dependent masters were thus reduced to the same position as tapsters; although they had completed training as master brewers, they were retailers and probably could neither afford nor train journeymen and apprentices. While many tapsters were also completely dependent for their livelihood on selling beer, a majority of them were craftsmen (especially benders) or general retailers who tapped beer as a secondary source of income and who were probably better off than the nonbrewing masters in the Handwerk.[81] We have only a few figures to indicate the relative numbers of these three groups involved in the production and distribution of Frankfurt beer: in 1701 there were 96 masters in the corporation and 80 tapsters (who, of course, did not join the Handwerk), and nine years later 82 of the master craftsmen actually brewed beer while 41 did not. Few of those 82 brewers could have operated breweries without sharing equipment, for as late as 1782 there were only 26 breweries in the city.[82]

Nevertheless, there were some enterprising brewers whose operations were expanding, not contracting, during the late seventeenth century,

---

Geschichtsblätter 19 (1913), 199–200, 209, 218, and Hans Albrecht, "Das Lübecker Braugewerbe bis zur Aufhebung der Brauerzunft 1865," *Zeitschrift des Vereins für Lübeckische Geshichte und Altertumskunde* 17 (1915), 91, 94.

79. Ugb D24 Qq, Nr. 1: petition signed by 51 brewers (18 October 1677).

80. Ugb C18 G, Nr. 1a: grievance 5 indicates that the tax alone on acquiring a vat was 2000 fl.; Georg Körber's petition in Ugb C51 O for permission to open a new brewery indicates that he and two other masters were using a brewery in the Schäffergasse in 1678. The Lübeck council worked out a complicated system of rotation, in which the all-too-numerous brewers there were supposed to have an equal opportunity to use a limited number of vats. When exceptions were made for special beers, concentration of production in the hands of a few brewers resulted quickly. Strict rotation was then enforced from the late seventeenth century until 1865, despite the complaints of burghers about the low quality of the beer produced according to city regulations. See Albrecht, 77, 92–95.

81. See Ugb D24 Qq, Nr. 4: "Klag und Bittschrifftlein" (22 October 1685) and Ugb D24 Qq. Nr. 1: brewers' petition (18 October 1677) on the tapsters. Albrecht, 108, 252–256, found the same tendency for Lübeck tapsters (or *Krüger* as they were called in the north) to be more prosperous than small brewers without their own vats.

82. Ugb D24 Yyy for the 1701 figures; Wolff, *Bierbrauergewerbe*, 22, for the number of masters brewing and only tapping in 1710; and Moritz, *Frankfurt*, II, 292, on the number of breweries in 1782.

and they were resented by their less prosperous fellow masters. When the council permitted Georg Körber to move in 1678 from a small brewery which he shared with two other masters in the Schäffergasse and to establish his own larger concern, the corporation protested that he would only cause more intensive competition in the Allerheiligengasse.[83] A decade later the brewers sent a major statement to the city fathers which opposed the request of Jost Christoph Hellwig for the right to operate a second brewery. No other craft allowed its masters to operate two concerns, and, besides, the position of smaller masters was already being damaged by men like Hellwig, who employed six or seven journeymen (instead of only two) and was always seeking to expand his operations. But the council was deaf to pleas from the corporation against the more enterprising brewers.[84]

The smaller masters concentrated their efforts on the fight they had already undertaken to reduce the number of tapsters competing with them for the retail market. In 1682 they failed to gain a reduction from five to two outside tapsters permitted each brewer, nor did the council abolish tapsters altogether in 1685 and leave beer-selling to masters alone.[85] The councilmen reversed their stand in 1701, however, and agreed in principle to the abolition of tapsters outside the Handwerk; the problem then became one of finding the best means to implement the decision.[86] Before the Rechney could study the problem, however, a group of twenty-three masters protested against any reduction of the number of tapsters, let alone their total abolition. These masters—and among them were both Dietrich Stein and Johann Wilhelm Fritsch, the two most important burgher leaders during the first years of the constitutional conflict—presented strong counterarguments: the increase of the number of masters was no ground in itself for limiting the number of tapsters, the failure of some masters to compete in a city where credit was so easy to obtain was simply their own fault, and the system of having tapsters did not damage the corporation but benefited the entire citi-

83. Ugb C51 O for Körber's petition of 30 May 1678 and the brewers' protest of 28 July 1678; Bgmb 1678–79, 35v–36r (31 July 1678) shows that the council stood by its original decision and granted permission for the brewery if Körber agreed to contribute 1000 Rtlr. *zum Kirchenbau*, which refers, I assume, to the reconstruction of St. Catherine's church.

84. Ugb D24 Tt: "Memorial und Bittschrift" (18 July 1689); Bgmb 1689–90, 51v (16 July 1689), for the initial approval of Hellwig's request; and ibid., 55r (18 July 1689), for confirmation of the decision after the brewer's memorial and petition.

85. Ugb D24 Ww for the petition of 47 brewers on 15 June 1682 and Bgmb 1682–83, 19r (15 June 1682), for its rejection; for the petition of 22 October 1685, see Ugb D24 Qq, Nr. 4, and the delaying tactics of the council in Bgmb 1685–86, 71v (22 October 1685).

86. Bgmb 1700–01, 167r (22 February 1701).

zenry by providing work for many widows and poor people.[87] The dispute within the Handwerk over the issue meant that no action was taken against the tapsters in 1701,[88] but the disagreement between large and small masters was resolved by 1713. Notwithstanding the disparities between them, the two groups shared enough mutual interests to unite them against the council; among themselves, they were able to reach an apparently satisfactory solution by which outside tapsters were abolished and the Handwerk organized the masters who did not brew beer as tapsters for their more enterprising colleagues.[89] That settlement leads into the constitutional conflict itself.

III. The Brewers in the Constitutional Conflict

In Chapter 5 we saw that the brewers provided important leadership for the entire citizenry during the early years of its struggle against the aristocratic council. Here we can use the history of the handicraft to show the effects of the conflict on the artisan's position in the community. The brewers fought against the council with greater vigor than did most Handwerke: Captains Fritsch and Stein spearheaded the original drive to have an imperial commission appointed; when the commission opened its sessions, the brewers elected a special committee of masters to direct their efforts and then hired their own lawyer instead of relying exclusively on the new burgher deputies and their legal consultants; and, as early as 1713, the brewers sought and obtained special permission from the commission to hold strategy meetings without the presence of the Geschworene appointed by the city council.[90] The master brewers also pressed their case further than most craftsmen; yet their grievances and the eventual settlements reached either through negotiations with the council or by imperial decisions were broadly representative of the situation most artisans faced in the early eighteenth century.

87. See Ugb D24 Yyy: petitions of 10 March and 30 September 1701.

88. Bgmb 1700–01, 175v (10 March 1701) shows that the council was swayed by the arguments of the masters opposing abolition of the tapsters.

89. See Ugb C18 G, Nr. 1a: grievance 4; ibid., Nr. 2a: the council's response; and especially ibid., Nr. 5: "Vollmacht des Bierbrauer Handwerks wegen Abschaffung der Bierzäpfer" (5 September 1713), the settlement presented by the corporation and accepted by the council. While there is no evidence of such a rational corporate decision in Bremen, the same economic shift occurred there. Hoyer, 209, argues that many small producers went out of business and became the *Krüger* for the big brewers. Since brewing and retailing beer were legally separated activities in the coastal cities of the north (except Hamburg), such small brewers would presumably have left the corporation to become Krüger. The solution in Frankfurt was just the opposite; to be even a tapster after 1713, a man was to enter the Handwerk.

90. Ugb C18 G, Nrs. 1a and 1b.

With three different purposes in mind, the burgher deputies asked the individual crafts to present their grievances to the imperial commission during the first two months of its hearings. First the Ausschuss wanted to impress Count Schönborn with the fact that there was no Handwerk without grievances; moreover it hoped to burden the council with a whole series of bothersome problems, while it tied the greatest possible number of citizens to the burgher cause.[91] Some forty-six occupational groups availed themselves of the opportunity during March and April of 1713. They presented common grievances against the council's arbitrary authority over industrial policy, especially against its appointment of craft leaders and its toleration of outside competition; all groups sought tighter regulation of handicraft industry and their own right to nominate the supervisors of the Handwerke. At the same time, each craft raised specific grievances applying to its own economic activities. Basing its legal defense on the Transfix of 1616, the council held firm on the issue of its general authority over the handicraft corporations, but the city fathers proposed that they negotiate with the artisans concerning all grievances—only when no mutually satisfactory settlement was possible were matters to be taken to the imperial commission for its judgment.[92] I shall return at the end of the chapter to the broader issues of council authority and artisan independence; for the present, an examination of the settlement of the brewers' problems will indicate how artisans fared during the conflict.

The brewers' grievances were originally outlined for the commission in thirteen points:

(1) The council's general authority to change (*mehren und mindern* was the detested phrase) handicraft regulations gave no security to the brewers—only arbitrary power to the council.

(2) Although Article 35 of the Citizens Agreement had set the tax on malt at two shillings per sack, a smaller sack of three *Simmern* was now taxed at two Gulden, besides which a tax of two *Kopffstücke* (40 xr.) was now levied on every *Ohm* of beer.

(3) The corporation had protested for a long time against the importation of foreign beers, but the council's decree of 1696 had never been adequately enforced. Not only were foreign beers still imported, but they were charged only 1 fl. 4 xr. duty compared with 1 fl. 12 xr. for a Frankfurt brew.

(4) The sale of beer (*Bierzäpfen*) had to be limited to the 130 master brewers in the city.

(5) Article 35 of the Citizens Agreement had set the tax on a

91. Hohenemser, *Verfassungsstreit*, 174.
92. Ibid., 174–177.

dyeing or a brewing vat at two Gulden, but in fact 2000 fl. were now charged.

(6) The current practice of forcing burghers to have grain or wood that had been acquired outside the city weighed a second time as it was brought into Frankfurt was unfair, especially since the burghers had to pay for the extra weighing.

(7) The old right of brewers to buy the rings for their barrels at the river without giving the coopers first choice ought to be restored.

(8) The price of beer ought to be permitted to fluctuate with the changes in the price of grain and hops.

(9) The corporation ought to choose its own supervisors; the council generally appointed young masters with little experience and thus brought harm to the craft.

(10) The council's supervisors generally granted a mastership to anyone who applied; when they received complaints, their excuse was that if they did not approve the application, the council would create masters without any consultation with the Handwerk at all. This was the real source of disorder in the craft: masters ought to be able to choose supervisors who would be more selective.

(11) New masters had been forced on the craft contrary to its regulations, and long and expensive cases in the imperial courts resulted.

(12) Yet when some masters undertook appeals to the courts, they were degraded (als meineydige Leute gescholten).

(13) The brewers' oath had to be altered, for even the council members who administered it admitted that the masters could not adhere to it.[93]

Several issues raised in the initial presentation were resolved in the negotiations that followed in September 1713 between the council and representatives of the handicraft. The councilmen saw no difficulty in giving brewers an equal chance with coopers at choosing barrel rings, and although they maintained that the measuring of wood and weighing of grain was important to the city, they agreed to cut the fees charged for the service by half.[94] The most significant measure settled by these negotiations was the abolition of tapsters outside the Handwerk: the council argued that the limitation or abolition of tapsters would be a disadvantage to the community at large but consented to decide the issue on the basis of a general memorandum from the master brewers. The

93. I have summarized or more often paraphrased the grievances that appear in Ugb C18 G, Nr. 1a (25 April 1713).
94. Ugb C18 G, Nrs. 4 and 7.

city fathers may have expected the same kind of internal dispute which had stalled action on the question in 1701, but they finally accepted the demand of ninety-three masters that all tapsters except those in the Jewish ghetto be eliminated and that poorer brewers be substituted as tapsters for the big concerns.[95]

There seem to have been no tangible gains for the brewers on three other issues, yet these were not taken to Count Schönborn. Since council investigations of the brewers' appeal to the imperial court at Wetzlar had revealed considerable pressure exerted by several active masters on their more reluctant colleagues, the Handwerk found it diplomatic both to drop any further discussion of its charge that the council was degrading its opponents and to accept the authorities' rather vague statement that they would follow the guidelines set down in the craft's regulations as long as the masters themselves accepted their real spirit.[96] The implication was that the regulations were to establish the standards for occupational training rather than serve as a means of excluding new masters from the craft—a position to which the council consistently adhered. The brewers realized that the issue of admissions to the handicraft was connected with the appointment of Geschworene and would be taken up by the imperial commission later, but why they were so willing to accept similar vague assurances from the council on the importation of foreign beer and the establishment of beer prices is unclear. Without any indication of more effective means of enforcing their good intentions, the councilmen simply reaffirmed their previous bans on foreign beers not imported by individual citizens for reasons of health.[97] For some time the brewers had been submitting expense accounts which usually showed losses when beer was sold at the prices established by the council; we may take an account for 1711 (Table 38) as a typical example.[98] The presentation of such accounts was the craft's only way to influence the council's price policy, and there is some reason to feel the skepticism shown both by the councilmen and later by Frankfurt historians concerning the validity of the brewers' claim that they operated at large losses over the seventeenth and early eighteenth centuries. Karl Bräuer found it highly unlikely that brewers would have refrained from weakening the brew if they lost money making only twenty-eight

95. Ibid., Nr. 5, Nrs. 4 and 7; Nrs. 9 (19 December 1715) and 12 (26 March 1716) show that there were some violations of the 1713 law. It is interesting to note that only nine tapsters protested against the settlement of 1713; see ibid., Nr. 10.

96. On the investigations conducted by the council in 1712, see Ugb D24 L27; otherwise, Ugb C18 G, Nr. 4.

97. Ugb C18 G, Nr. 7.

98. Ugb D24 L28: "Bier Rechnung" of 26 March 1711. I have located some thirty-seven accounts for the period 1629 to 1743—evidence of the active role played by the Handwerk in attempting to influence prices.

TABLE 38

Beer Account, 1711

	fl.	xr.
1. Tax (on 10½ sacks malt at 2 fl. each)	fl. 21	— xr.
2. 15 *Achtel* barley at 3 fl. each	45	—
3. 50 lb. Eisenacher hops at 9 Tlr. per *Zentner*	6	45
4. 7 pieces of wood at 4 *Kopfstücke* each	9	20
5. *Mitter* for weighing barley and malt		26
6. Miller	1	24
7. Brewer's expenses	15	—
Total Cost	fl. 98	55 xr.
Sale of 28 *Ohms* of beer at 3 fl. each	84	—
Loss	fl. 14	55 xr.

Ohms.[99] It is also conceivable that the brewing expenses (item seven) were somewhat inflated, especially for the larger concerns, which did most of the brewing anyway. In any case, the Handwerk did not see fit to present the commission with detailed accounts or to press the council any further than a reaffirmation of the general principle that the price of beer should fluctuate with the price of barley and hops. Instead the brewers questioned the validity and high level of the taxes levied on beer as a means of reducing their costs, and in doing so they raised their sharpest disagreements with the city council.

The legal battle between the senate and the brewers over taxes was bitter and long—it lasted, in fact, from the beginning to the very end of the constitutional conflict. The masters raised three different tax issues in 1713: the very high levy on brewers' vats, the excise on beer introduced in 1664 to support the imperial war against the Turks, and the malt tax. Why there was no dispute over the first impost we cannot be certain, but the Handwerk finally agreed with the council that Article 35 of the Citizens Agreement establishing a yearly tax on the right to brew beer need not be interpreted literally. A one-time levy on each vat seemed preferable to a yearly sum charged to each master. Moreover, the council's hint that a high duty was one of the most effective methods of preventing an overcrowding of the craft by new brewers seems to have been enough to convince the masters to let the matter drop.[100] Such an easy solution was not possible, however, with either the beer excise or the malt tax. The brewers argued that the excise had been introduced without consultation with the burghers and was therefore illegal. Al-

99. Schnapper-Arndt, *Lebenshaltung*, I, 124. Cf. the council's statement on brewers' profits in Ugb C18 K, Nr. 14.

100. See Ugb C18 G, Nr. 6: a general statement on the brewers' taxes presented by the council to the imperial commission on 16 May 1713.

though the senate defended its right to tax the Bürgerschaft and insisted that the excise was valid, the brewers simply stopped paying it.[101] The issue was kept alive for some fifteen years in the many discussions of the malt tax, which was the subject of even sharper disagreements between the council and the handicraft. Eventually the Committee of Nine urged both sides to compromise: the council should eliminate the excise in return for maintenance of the malt tax at 2 fl. per sack. The councilmen agreed to abolish the excise but wanted to increase the malt tax to replace lost revenues—a suggestion unacceptable to the brewers, who now felt somewhat betrayed by their own leaders.[102] As attention became focused on the hotly disputed malt tax, Count Schönborn apparently decided to close the matter of the excise. He abolished the tax and lowered the price of beer accordingly.[103]

On no issue were the master brewers so doggedly tenacious in their opposition to the council as on the malt tax, which they believed had been arbitrarily raised from the two-shilling level established by Article 35 of the Citizens Agreement to a height of two Gulden per sack. From the beginning of the dispute, the senate explained that the brewers were confusing two separate taxes—the *Mahlgeld* or general tax on grinding grain levied on malt and the *Maltzgeld*, a special impost on malt itself. Although the Mahlgeld on malt had been set at two shillings per sack in the Citizens Agreement, the Maltzgeld was not mentioned in that document. After the emperor declared the Agreement the fundamental basis of Frankfurt's constitution, the city council agreed to lower the Mahlgeld to its former level of two shillings per sack. But the senate insisted that the tax on malt itself was important to the city budget and had to be maintained at two Gulden. The brewers, on the other hand, denied the existence of two separate taxes on malt; if I have understood them correctly, the brewers must have regarded the tax on grinding barley as an import duty (it was paid at one of the city gates) and the reference to Mahlgeld in the Agreement of 1612/13 as interchangeable with Maltzgeld—hence only one tax on malt, a tax which was much higher at the beginning of the eighteenth century than the constitution allowed. A thoroughly confusing debate over the number of legal taxes

101. Ugb C18 G, Nr. 4 on the negotiations between the brewers and the council; ibid., Nr. 8 (14 November 1713) shows that the brewers refused as early as 1713 to pay twice as much as other burghers who might brew a little beer; a note at the end of Ugb C18 H explains that during the transition from council to joint burgher-council control of the Renthen-Amt in 1717, they stopped paying altogether.

102. Ugb C18 Q, Nr. 8: summaries of the negotiations of 7, 12, 16, and 23 January 1728 as well as a copy of the council's decree of 16 January 1728.

103. See Müller, *Frankfurt contra Frankfurt*, I, 133–134, for the commission decree of 27 August 1728; Ugb C18 Q: the commission hearing of 24 October makes it clear that the price of beer had to be lowered. Cf. also HHSA Wien: RHR Relationes 37.

on malt lasted exactly twenty years. We cannot follow it in detail here: the recurrent appeals and counterarguments; the threats to withhold either taxes or barley; the presentation of documents and the denial of their validity; and the tendency even to confuse the issue of malt taxes with the beer excise—all make for an almost incomprehensible story.[104] Besides sympathy for Count Schönborn, a present-day reader of the documents involved in the dispute has the impression that the brewers hoped to gain a victory as long as the terminology remained garbled. The breakthrough toward real clarification of the matter occurred in the negotiations of January 1728, during which the council (indeed, Dr. Ochs himself) finally convinced the burgher deputies and the Committee of Nine that Mahlgeld and Maltzgeld had always been separate taxes.[105] After 1728 the brewers were in an impossible position: they stubbornly refused the compromise suggested by the Nine which might have meant an amicable end of their conflict with the councilmen, and burgher leaders could no longer support their case. Even after abolition of the beer excise, the craftsmen remained obstinate about the malt tax.[106] Because the council showed itself willing to compromise on the excise tax, the brewers' victory on that issue was much less impressive than the council's success in obtaining a complete vindication of its position on the malt taxes in 1733.[107]

Thus, by the end of the constitutional conflict, the brewers had gained favorable decisions on only two major grievances specific to their craft. Although the abolition of the beer excise did not benefit them materially, it did represent a victory for their constitutional arguments. The brewers' greatest achievement was the arrangement to eliminate tapsters from outside the handicraft and to substitute masters in their place. The city fathers made no major concessions to the masters, while the brewers suffered ignoble defeat on the tax issue that they pressed most vigorously. A strikingly similar pattern of council success in preserving the status quo has been found by Franz Lerner in his examination of the specific grievances raised by Frankfurt's butchers during the constitutional conflict.[108]

Of much greater significance, however, was the council's victory in the larger issue of handicraft independence from its authority. The princi-

104. The often bewildering narrative from 1713 to 1728 may be constructed from documents in Ugb C18 H, Ugb C18 J, and Ugb C18 K.

105. Ugb C18 Q, Nr. 8: negotiations of 12 January 1728, the lucidity of which saved me from totally misunderstanding the dispute.

106. Ugb C18 Q: commission hearings from October 1729 to January 1730; they are also in HHSA Wien: RHR Decisa 2230, 1r-34v.

107. Müller, *Frankfurt contra Frankfurt*, III, 61–62: RHR decree of 29 January 1733.

108. Lerner, *Metzger-Handwerk*, 234–241.

pal demand of every Handwerk in 1713 was for an end to the council's broad authority to regulate handicraft industry as it saw fit. The crafts sought not only a general abrogation of the council's unlimited power but also a concrete reform: the right to select their own craft supervisors. By choosing their Geschworene, the artisans hoped, above all else, to control admissions to their crafts more effectively. They gained the shadow but not the substance of that power when the imperial government granted them the right to nominate three candidates for each supervisory position to be filled by the council.[109] Although the Geschworene selected by the brewers after 1714 attempted to limit admissions to the handicraft by adhering strictly to regulations that might disqualify applicants, the council continued to intervene on behalf of the journeymen and to force the Handwerk to accept qualified men as new masters.[110] Artisan demands that registration of handicraft workers be handled by the Handwerke themselves rather than by the city government were apparently not even considered by the imperial commission.[111] As late as 1731, when the commission was concluding its work, Captain Notebohm reminded the Reichshofrat that it had not yet guaranteed the independence of artisans from arbitrary regulation by the council.[112] But Notebohm could hardly have expected imperial officials to contradict, in Frankfurt's case, the general policy they set out in the Imperial Handicraft Ordinance of 1731, which attempted to strengthen, rather than weaken, the control of local authorities over craftsmen.[113] The city's artisans were to be as carefully controlled during the eighteenth century as they had been in the seventeenth.

109. See the first imperial resolution of 1725 in Müller, *Frankfurt contra Frankfurt*, I, 12, for confirmation of the right already effectively granted by the commission in a decree of 17 August 1714. Cf. Count Schönborn's final report on the matter, HHSA Wien: RHR Decisa 2205, 95r–95v.

110. See a representative sample of applications for masterships in Ugb C18 A (1724–25) and Ugb C18 C (1726). Herberger, *Schuhmacherhandwerk*, 116–119, confirms these findings for the shoemakers as well.

111. On the demands, see the council's "General-Beantwortung der Handwerker Gravaminum" (5 July 1713) found in HHSA Wien: RHR Decisa 2149, 204–211, and in the Holzhausen Archive (deposited in the Frankfurt City Archive), Kasten 175.

112. "Pro Memoria in Sachen Frankfurt contra Frankfurt Commissionis," a pamphlet printed in Vienna (4 September 1731); a copy is located in the Frankfurt archive: Leonhardi Nachlass, fascicle 12.

113. On the Imperial Handicraft Ordinance, see Fischer, *Handwerksrecht*, 24; cf. the suggestive essay by Georg Fischer, "Absolutistische Handwerkerpolitik und Friedrich Karl von Schönborn," *Jahrbuch für fränkische Landesforschung* 29 (1969), 19–38. The ordinance was promulgated by the council in Frankfurt on 19 November 1731.

PART FOUR

BURGHERS VERSUS OUTSIDERS

... the principles of all well-formulated
[domestic] policies are that burghers be
cherished over immigrants, that natives be
left to make their living and protected
from foreigners.
The Committee of Nine (1729)

Chapter 7

The Frankfurt Jews

The Jewish community in Frankfurt suffered from the unmitigated hatred of almost every other group in the city. Religious and cultural antagonisms between Christians and Jews were reinforced and, indeed, overshadowed by economic competition between the two groups. Jewish moneylenders were the chief object of burgher concern before the Thirty Years War; during the Fettmilch Uprising at the beginning of the century, Christian debtors demanded and obtained stricter regulations on interest rates charged by Jews and their general lending practices. Burgher hatred for the Jews went so deep that the most radical phase of the uprising saw a plundering of the ghetto in 1614 and the expulsion of its inhabitants, but they were restored and placed under special imperial protection during the reaction that followed in 1615–1616.[1] The Stättigkeit of 1616, which subsequently regulated Jewish life in Frankfurt, was drawn up by the imperial commission, and I have already emphasized that the Jews gained many advantages from the ambiguity of their relationships with the emperor and the Frankfurt city council.[2]

After the war period, when moneylending decreased and retailing

1. Isidor Kracauer, "Die Juden Frankfurts im Fettmilch'schen Aufstand 1612–1618," [Geigers] Zeitschrift für die Geschichte der Juden in Deutschland 4 (1890), 347–365; 5 (1891), 1–11.
2. Cf. above, 58–59, and 114–115.

activities emerged as its most important means of livelihood, the community's continued economic success depended on the influence it exerted with the governments in Vienna and in Frankfurt. Since the Jews were a rich source of revenue, the council hesitated to enforce regulations that forbade them from infringing on the burghers' retail market. As the size of the Jewish population grew and its competition with burgher retailers increased during the second half of the seventeenth century, citizens demanded council protection by strict enforcement of the Stättigkeit. Their frustration at council inaction was so intense that the Jewish issue was the immediate cause for the determination of the officer corps to seek imperial intervention and, therefore, for the entire constitutional conflict itself.

Despite the bitterness shown by craftsmen and retailers toward the Jews, however, their violation of the city's economic regulations did not remain the central issue of the reform movement, which was eventually taken over by the big merchants. Although imperial officials generally favored the burgher party over the magistracy, they shared the council's reluctance to damage the economic potential of the Jewish community. Not only were citizens unable to prevent the Jews from expanding their woefully inadequate living quarters, but the dispute over Jewish retail shops dragged on in the imperial courts long after the constitutional conflict itself was concluded. And the Jewish community, despite burgher opposition and the setbacks suffered in the great fires of 1711 and 1721, continued to flourish throughout the eighteenth century.

I. Organization and Regulation of the Jewish Community

Although they were subject to the city of Frankfurt, the Jews constituted a separate corporate community with its own officials responsible to the council for the enforcement of the regulations under which all Jews lived. A group of elders (*Vorgänger* or *Älteste*) had formed apparently during the sixteenth century, and two men from its ranks were elected as official leaders (*Baumeister*) every two years. The elders served for life, enlisted their own members, and by the end of the century were a small oligarchy of ten men who virtually controlled their community. Demands for broader representation led in 1618 to the creation of an additional committee of seven men to participate in communal government, but continued discontent finally caused the council to intervene and reorganize Jewish leadership. After 1623 an executive body of twelve members, selected to serve three-year terms by twenty electors who were chosen by lot from among those Jews with assets of at least one thousand Taler, supervised the community. The Twelve controlled the admission of new people to the ghetto, administered the property of orphans, oversaw money-changing activities, and helped enforce the city council's ordinances. Two Baumeister remained as the chief administrators of the ghetto; they represented the community before the council and were largely responsible for enforcement of city laws in the *Judengasse*. Their duties included administrative tasks, such as collecting taxes and overseeing street-cleaning, as well as limited judicial and even legislative competence. Other community officials included the Rabbi and his assistants, a physician, tax collectors, two hospital supervisors, and two alms administrators.[3] Through these various functionaries drawn from their own ranks, the Jews enjoyed a small degree of self-government within the limits placed on them by the Stättigkeit of 1616 and regular council legislation.

The Stättigkeit was a codification of the regulations on Jewish life in Frankfurt, and although it guaranteed the community imperial protection against plundering and expulsion from the city, the document also maintained the deep social cleavage between Jews and Christian residents.[4] Drawn up by the imperial commissioners and confirmed by Emperor Mathias at the end of the Fettmilch Uprising, the Stättigkeit of 1616 gave the Jewish community greater security than it had known previously. Individual Jews could be expelled for misconduct, but the community itself was granted perpetual privileges to be renewed automatically every three years upon the payment of a "tribute" to the city.[5] Furthermore, the council was ordered to punish severely burghers and especially handicraft workers who harmed the Jews in any way; in traditional fashion, journeymen had to take a special oath in which they promised to leave Jews alone except to help them fight possible fires in the ghetto.[6] Both the wording of the Stättigkeit and the symbolic gesture of having the imperial eagle and the words "Protection of his Imperial Majesty and of the Holy Empire" emblazoned above the three entrances to the ghetto left little doubt that the community could rely on outside help in case of serious trouble with other residents of the city.[7]

Yet the emperor who asserted his role as protector of the Jewish com-

3. I have summarized the detailed discussion by Isidor Kracauer, "Beiträge zur Geschichte der Frankfurter Juden im Dreissigjährigen Krieg," [*Geigers*] *Zeitschrift für die Geschichte der Juden in Deutschland* 3 (1889), 345–352.

4. Ibid., 359. The best edition of the Stättigkeit itself appears in Bothe, *Entwicklung vor dem 30jK*, 247–317.

5. Article 15 of the Stättigkeit. Kracauer, "Juden im 30jK," 337–338, says that the automatic renewal cost each household one Goldgulden. For purposes of collecting the money, households in the ghetto were counted every three years; see ibid., 131–132, for the number of households from 1618 to 1651.

6. Article 118 of the Stättigkeit.

7. Kracauer, "Juden im 30jK," 359.

munity also confirmed the sharp social distinctions that kept the Jew inferior to any Christian living in Frankfurt. Besides the segregation of the community into a crowded and unsanitary ghetto, various specific regulations reminded the Jew of his separation from other residents. Jews were not permitted to assemble outside the Judengasse, and no more than two might by seen together on the public streets. They were not to appear outside the ghetto at night, on Sundays, or on specified feast days; when they did go outside, they were to identify themselves clearly by wearing a large yellow ring on their clothing. Although they might hire "Saturday women" to do special work for the Sabbath, Jews were not to employ Christian servants or wet nurses. They were always to behave modestly in the presence of Christians, especially at market-places, where they dared not touch fruits or vegetables (if they did, they were to pay for the soiled produce).[8] Such regulations, difficult as they undoubtedly were to enforce, were traditional measures to preserve the Christians from contamination.[9] Old prejudices and fears were thus reflected in official legislation, even if more subtly and less irrationally than in the anti-Semitic tracts that warned about the dangers to Christian children whose blood the Jews wished to use in their Passover celebrations.[10]

The major thrust of the Stättigkeit as of later council legislation, however, was to regulate the economic activities of the Jews so that the welfare of Frankfurt citizens would be protected. During the Fettmilch Uprising, burghers convinced the imperial commissioners that the Jewish community had grown too large and that the interest rates charged by Jews were exorbitant. Article 22 of the Citizens Agreement of 1612/13 promised specific legislation on both matters and, in the interim, established a ceiling of 8 percent interest on loans made by Jewish creditors.[11] The Stättigkeit fulfilled that promise just four years later. To keep the ghetto's population from growing larger, the city was to tolerate a maximum of five hundred households. Only six outsiders could be admitted to the community in any one year, and then only on the condi-

8. For all these regulations see Articles 23–35 and Article 40 of the Stättigkeit.

9. In his *Jüdische Merckwürdigkeiten* . . . (Frankfurt and Leipzig, 1714), II, 253, the Frankfurt rector Johann Jacob Schudt explained the contemporaneous degradation of the Jews as the natural result of their own degradation and murder of Christ.

10. Kracauer, *Geschichte der Juden in Frankfurt am Main* (Frankfurt, 1927), II, 103–104, uses the book by the Heidelberg professor Johann Andreas Eisenmenger, *Entdecktes Judentum*, as typical of popular fears about the Jews. The author had spent much time in Frankfurt, and his book was printed there apparently in 1700; with the emperor's help, the Jewish community prevented its distribution until 1751.

11. See Bothe, *Entwicklung vor dem 30jK*, 499–500, for the Citizens Agreement; Kracauer, "Juden im Fettmilch'schen Aufstand," 137–141, 151–154, 161–162, on burgher complaints against the Jews during the uprising.

tion that each man had assets of a thousand gulden and that, if he wished to marry, he would wed a local Jewish girl. As a final measure of population control, only twelve couples were permitted to marry each year.[12]

The Stättigkeit contained many provisions that favored debtors over Jewish moneylenders and protected burgher retailers from Jewish competition. First, no loans to dependent persons were permitted: burgher sons or orphans under twenty-five could not be loaned money without the knowledge and consent of their parents or guardians, while under no circumstances were handicraft workers and household servants to become debtors of the Jews. Borrowers' widows were not held responsible for repayment of loans under thirty gulden, and they could be held liable for larger debts only if they had been officially registered with the city government as cosigners in the original transactions made by their husbands.[13] Most importantly, interest rates that had averaged about 24 percent before 1612/13 were now fixed at 8 percent on loans for which security was given and 10 percent on loans backed only by promissory notes.[14] No interest could be charged on unpaid interest, terms for repayment were written to benefit the debtor, and limitations on the objects which could be offered as collateral were extended[15]—all to protect burghers from falling deeply into the Jews' debt once again.

While Jewish moneylending was a major concern of Frankfurt citizens at the beginning of the seventeenth century, measures to protect burghers from Jewish retail activities were also included in the Stättigkeit. Except for a few men like butchers who provided special services, Jews could not practice handicrafts in Frankfurt. Wholesale commerce and moneylending were open to them, and they were permitted to sell in the local retail market items that had been forfeited for nonpayment of loans. Thus dealing in secondhand goods (called *Trödelhandel*) had become an important yet ancillary means of livelihood for many Jewish merchants.[16] A major restriction was imposed on the practice, however, because only burghers could own regular retail shops in the city; the Stättigkeit confirmed the old prohibition against operating open shops or stands without the council's permission, but it explicitly allowed Jews to peddle their wares in the streets.[17] Jews had long been active in both the cloth and clothing businesses, and again the Stättigkeit maintained

12. Articles 103–109 of the Stättigkeit.

13. Articles 51–57.

14. Article 58. Kracauer, "Juden im 30jK," 142, points out that pre-1612 interest rates averaged 24 percent and that in 1626 the council permitted the Jews to charge outsiders higher rates than those set on loans in Frankfurt.

15. Articles 59–71.

16. Kracauer, "Juden im 30jK," 143.

17. Article 75.

older provisions that the only new clothing they could sell was that produced by Frankfurt craftsmen. Otherwise, they could retail only cloth or clothes that had fallen into their hands as forfeitures on debts.[18] The regulations of 1616 further forbade the peddling of silks, tin products, and spices, and they required Jews who sold precious metals and stones to use official city scales rather than their own.[19] Enforcement of these measures—together with the advantages the citizens received over Jewish creditors—would certainly have given Frankfurt burghers adequate protection from the Jews during the rest of the seventeenth century, had the next few decades not seen an important change in Jewish economic activities.

II. Jewish Competition with Burgher Retailers

The period of the Thirty Years War saw a significant shift in Jewish commercial interests from moneylending and the secondhand dealing associated with it to regular retail trade. The change resulted not only from the fact that interest rates had been scaled down to about one third their previous level but, more importantly, from the heavy losses suffered by Jewish creditors during and immediately after the war itself. Even before the Fettmilch Uprising the Jews had been making more loans to outsiders than to residents of Frankfurt, and in 1626 the council authorized a higher interest rate on such outside loans than could be charged in the city itself. Because of their own setbacks during the war years, however, many borrowers from surrounding areas to whom Frankfurt Jews had made loans were simply unable to repay their debts. The losses suffered in turn by the creditors led many Jews to shift their remaining capital from moneylending to investments in wholesale and retail commerce.[20] This is not to say that moneylending was no longer important to the local Jewish community, but it took second place to their retail activities. The earliest visitation of the ghetto after the war which recorded the occupations of its inhabitants occurred in 1694; in that year, 109 heads of households were engaged in moneylending and Trödelhandel, while 163 devoted themselves to retailing (Table 39).[21]

18. Articles 73 and 74.
19. Articles 76, 77, 79, and 80.
20. Kracauer, "Juden im 30jK," 145; cf. Kracauer, *Geschichte*, II, 25.
21. Table 39 is based on the figures presented by Bücher, *Bevölkerung*, 588–589. Other heads of households were not commercial people; some were professionals—religious leaders, physicians, lawyers, etc.—and there were a few special craftsmen permitted the community. Cf. Table 13, even though Unna's figures used there do not completely agree with Bücher's, which I have used here.

TABLE 39
Jewish Commercial Activities, 1694

Heads of Households	Occupations
109	Moneylenders and peddlers of secondhand goods
106	Retailers of cloth, clothing, ribbons, buttons, stockings, etc.
24	Retailers of spices and groceries
14	Retailers of skins, feathers, fatty products
5	Sellers of fruits, horses, wines
9	Tapsters (both beer and wine)
3	Innkeepers
2	Owners of delicatessens

This invasion of the retail market in large numbers violated the Stättig-keit and was yet another threat to the burgher in that area of the city economy legally reserved for him.

The burghers responded by demanding that the council strictly enforce the Stättigkeit and end all illegal retailing by the Jews. As early as 1623 both spice and cloth retailers complained about competition from Jews, who used several arguments to defend themselves. First they argued that the technical language of the Stättigkeit could be interpreted to allow them the particular cloth retailing in which they were engaged; then they pointed out that most Frankfurt citizens would save money because of the competitive prices Jewish peddlers could offer them. Although the council fined some of the Jews who had been selling spices, its pronouncement on their sale of cloth was too vague to settle the dispute over the materials that Jews could legally peddle.[22] By 1635 new protests were being lodged against Jewish trade in clothing, silks, gold and silver thread, hats, pistols and other firearms, spices and groceries, and even bacon; according to burgher craftsmen and retailers, the Jews were completely ignoring restrictions against their retail activities. They sold their wares on streets outside the ghetto, in public inns, and occasionally even in the shops of some tailor masters who allowed Jews to sell items in return for a share of their profits. In these ways the Jews gained access to the best customers of the 1630's—soldiers passing through the city—and managed to undersell burgher retailers. In April 1636 the magistrates once again ordered the Jews to adhere strictly to the Stättigkeit and to end their retail activities.[23]

Although Christian retailers interpreted the ordinance of 1636 as a great victory (in gratitude for which they contributed a thousand Gul-

22. Kracauer, "Juden im 30jK," 145–146; *Geschichte*, II, 26–27.
23. Kracauer, "Juden im 30jK," 146–147; *Geschichte*, II, 27–28.

den to the city's Hospital for the Poor), the decision avoided a specific rejection of the Jews' literal interpretation of the Stättigkeit as prohibiting only certain types of cloth from their trade. Apparently no action was taken against the thirteen Jewish cloth dealers named by the burghers as serious violators of the law. The Jews argued that since they were not permitted to own land on which to grow food and they could not make money in their usual lending business because of the war, they had no alternative to earning their livelihood by retail commerce.[24] The community was heavily taxed by the city and had to support its own poor; how could it meet these obligations without finding new sources of revenue? The council seems to have been sympathetic to the Jews' plight, because enforcement of the Stättigkeit did not follow the pronouncement of 1636.

Eleven years later the tailor Handwerk complained about Jewish competition and asked the council for more than a simple confirmation of the provisions of the Stättigkeit; the tailors wanted a new ordinance forbidding Jews from selling clothes—or at least permitting only second-hand clothing—and from peddling their wares in the streets. Again the Jews were quick to respond (and the council seems always to have given them opportunities to do so) with their own explanation of the tailors' economic troubles. The craft itself was too large in relation to Frankfurt's population. Most of the masters were unable to produce clothing in the new popular styles. And burgher tailors charged higher prices without making any arrangements for credit or payment in kind from their customers. Naturally, buyers preferred to make purchases from the Jews, who were able, in turn, to provide extra work for about fifty of the 135 masters in the Handwerk. As far as peddling was concerned, the Jews wanted to give up the practice, but they could not do so until the council permitted them either to have regular stands in the markets or to open retail shops. Such open concessions the councilmen were unwilling to make, though they apparently were already tolerating the existence of six shops in the ghetto itself—as long as they remained unmarked and not open to the street. But just as the council refused to allow any stands or shops outside the ghetto, so too it denied the tailors' demands for prohibition of Jewish peddling.[25]

The dispute over Jewish retailing activities intensified during the second half of the century, as it became focused on the questions of their peddling and their operating stands and shops outside the ghetto. Burgher craftsmen and retailers continued to push for legislation that would go beyond the Stättigkeit to outlaw Jewish peddling, while the Jews

24. Kracauer, "Juden im 30jK," 147–148.
25. Ibid., 148; Kracauer, *Geschichte*, II, 28–29.

continued to expand their businesses. The council, caught between the legitimate demands of its citizens and the tacit recognition that the Jewish community had to prosper, was unable to take clear and decisive action. Its legislation was usually based on compromises that suited neither side, and it was often not enforced. As the result of many burgher grievances, a major council pronouncement came in 1670. Instead of completely outlawing peddling, as the burghers wanted, the ordinance imposed a fine of twelve Gulden on a Jew if he took his wares from the street into customers' houses to display them. Jews were not to sell their wares in public inns, and they could deliver goods there only to persons of high station. The councilmen finally decided that the Jews were correct, however, when they argued that the Stättigkeit had prohibited them from selling only the woolen cloths which were no longer used but which had been popular in the sixteenth and early seventeenth century. But their cloth trade was to be limited: the Jews were to have no more than six shops, presumably only in the ghetto, and these were not to be open to the street.[26] We may be fairly certain that the council intended this cloth business to be wholesale only, but the failure to be precise in the edict of 1670 was an invitation to further violations.

Despite the efforts of Jewish community leaders to keep retailing within moderate bounds, increased competition antagonized Frankfurt burghers so much in the 1680's and 90's that they lost patience completely with the moderate policy of the council. In communal statutes drawn up by specially elected committees in 1675 and 1685, Jewish leaders set up rules designed to make the Jews' retailing as inoffensive as possible to the burghers who had been exerting pressure on the council for tighter regulations. The statutes repeated the council's prohibition against the use of rented rooms in public inns or private houses for display and sale of goods; Jews were to retail only remnants of cloth that had been used to make clothes, not whole bolts of material; especially strict observance of laws against commercial activities on Christian holy days was emphasized.[27] But neither the watchful eyes of Jewish leaders nor the threat to bar violators from worship services seems to have curbed the offenses of which burghers complained.

Furthermore, the council's policies could only have confused and angered Christian retailers in these years. In 1681 the Rechney, the city office which oversaw Jewish affairs, granted a Jew the right to retail cloth; then in 1683 the council threatened sharp penalties for violations

26. Ugb D49 Nr. 5: council edict of 3 March 1670; it was also published by Beyerbach, *Sammlung der Verordnungen*, 645–657. Ugb D49 Nr. 6 says that the edict was read in the synagogue each year from 1670 to 1697. Kracauer, *Geschichte*, II, 38, discusses the edict briefly.

27. Kracauer, *Geschichte*, II, 40–43.

of the 1670 ordinance.[28] That edict was renewed in 1688, but in the same year several Jews were permitted to enlarge their houses.[29] Burghers could only ask themselves whether expansion did not mean more Jewish families in the ghetto and thus more competition. In 1689 burgher wholesalers and retailers succeeded in obtaining another council decree to close all Jewish shops in public inns and elsewhere outside the ghetto; peddling was to be regulated according to the Stättigkeit, and the two burghermasters were to check on violations.[30] But complaints about Jewish retail shops outside the ghetto continued unabated. In 1695, for example, Jews selling books in the city had to be ordered to close their shops and remove their books to the ghetto.[31] And the council opened itself at the same time to charges of duplicity by permitting a Jew named Sichel to rent a small shop in a cloister and sell remnants of cloth.[32]

By 1696 complaints about Jewish retail shops outside the ghetto were so frequent and so sharp that the council realized it faced a serious problem of burgher disaffection. The magistrates responded in January 1697 with a strong decree ordering that the burghermasters and the Rechney punish any violations of the Stättigkeit, the Jews close all their retail shops outside the ghetto within two weeks, and all innkeepers prevent the use of their establishments by Jewish retailers.[33] Pleased with this show of strength, burgher retailers pressed for clarification of the whole issue of what retail rights Jews might enjoy. The councilmen turned to their own legal experts for an opinion, and the syndics wrote a memorandum which reviewed the grievances of Christian retailers against their Jewish competition. The legal advisers argued that, although the council decree of 1670 interpreted the prohibitions of Jewish cloth retailing in the Stättigkeit as applying only to the rough woolens of the previous century, the original intention of that document had been to

28. For the decision (8 February 1681) by the Rechney, see Verzeichnis der Rechneiamtsprotokolle 1641–1776, item 253: Prot. C² (1669–1690), 23a; the council decree of 5 June 1683 is located in Verordnungen des Rats, rechtliche and gewerbliche Verhältnisse der Juden in Frankfurt a. M. betr., so weit einzeln vorhanden (a collection in the Frankfurt City and University Library with documents dating from 1683–1805; cited hereafter as Verordnungen des Rats), Nr. 18.

29. Ugb D49 Nr. 6: Nr. 26, renewal of the ordinance of 1670 (22 March 1688); Verzeichnis der Rechneiamtsprotokolle, item 258: Prot. C² (1669–1690), 28–29, for the permission to enlarge several houses in the ghetto.

30. Ugb D49 Nr. 6: Nr. 27, council edict (28 May 1689); cf. Kracauer, Geschichte, II, 39.

31. Ugb D49 Nr. 6: Nr. 93, extracts from Ratsprotocolle for 14 March 1695.

32. Verzeichnis der Rechneiamtsprotokolle, item 264: Prot. E (1695–1706), 5b, for the Rechney decision of 19 July 1695.

33. Verordnungen des Rats, Nr. 24, decree of 21 January 1697. For burgher complaints which preceded the ordinance, see Ugb D49 Nr. 6: Nrs. 28–31.

restrict the Jews to dealing in secondhand cloth that had been forfeited for nonpayment of debts. Although the syndics recognized the council's prerogative to change the Stättigkeit (a right which burgher leaders were to question in the ensuing constitutional conflict), they pointed out that burgher retailers did have reason to believe that the restrictions of 1616 had been meant to apply as well to the finer cloths which were currently popular. In fact, the council ordinances of 1624, 1636, and 1649 also provided a legal basis for the burgher position, so that the magistrates could easily redress grievances arising out of its decision in 1670 by returning to its own previous legislation rather than the Stättigkeit. Granting the Jews six retail shops in 1670 had, in addition, been a gracious gesture by the city fathers—one they might withdraw, should they see fit to do so. Jewish retailers had taken undue advantage of the council's generosity, for they had established over thirty shops since 1670. Finally, the syndics advised that it would be more politic in the future to consult the Jews secretly and allow them to defend their position orally, but permission for them to submit written statements on these issues only offended the burghers.[34]

Although the syndics' memorandum indicated that a skillful reversal of policy in the direction demanded by burgher retailers was advisable, the council continued to waver. Enforcement of the strong decree of 1697 was not effective, and, although the councilmen planned to revise the 1670 ordinance in 1698, they finally renewed that decree rather than strengthening it. This action confirmed both the Jews' interpretation of the Stättigkeit and their operation of six retail shops in the ghetto.[35] In 1699, however, the council ordered enforcement of its ordinances against Jewish shops and storage rooms outside the Judengasse,[36] and the Rechney made a major blunder. In order to show the council's willingness to protect its citizens, Rechney officials permitted the retailers to elect a committee to represent them in a joint inspection of the city for illegal Jewish shops.[37] During the inspection tour, the committee members were informed that the council had given the Jews permission to operate six shops in the ghetto. Remarkable as it may seem, this was the first knowledge burgher retailers had had either of the original ordinance of

34. Ugb D49 Nr. 6: Nr. 35, "Bedenken in der Christilichen Crähmer Sachen contra die Juden, de Mai 1697."

35. Ibid., Nrs. 37 and 38.

36. Ibid., Nr. 68, the edict of 28 March 1699, and Nr. 42, the ordinance of 1 August 1699.

37. Ibid., Nr. 44, "Anzeig und Bitten" from the "sämbtlich der Seiden, Wüllen, Gewand, Specerey, Leinwand und Hutstaffirer Handlungs anverwante Bürger" (19 October 1700), indicates that the Rechney allowed the formation of the Ausschuss on 23 December 1699.

4. An enlarged section of the 1682 Merian Plan of Frankfurt, showing the Jewish ghetto.

(Courtesy of the Frankfurt City Archive)

Albhdeligenport

5. Captain Dietrich Notebohm, a merchant and the most important leader of the burgher party.

(Courtesy of the Frankfurt City Archive)

1670 or of its renewal in 1698.[38] The two decrees had apparently been issued only to the Rechney and to the Jews themselves without being distributed throughout the city; in any case, burghers learned in 1699 that their council had not only failed to enforce laws designed to protect them but had also given commercial concessions to their Jewish competitors. The discovery evoked a strong feeling among the Christian retailers that they had been betrayed; their confidence in the magistracy was at its lowest point.

In October 1700 the council appointed a special committee to negotiate a satisfactory settlement with the representatives of the burgher retailers.[39] Sharp burgher demands for revocation of the ordinance of 1670 and its 1698 renewal were linked to bitter complaints about the council's failure to enforce its own edicts against the Jews. Burgher retailers also sought a much stricter interpretation of the Stättigkeit: instead of the more liberal view of the council that anything not expressly denied was permissible, the citizens demanded that anything not specifically granted Jewish dealers in the Stättigkeit be strictly forbidden.[40] The city fathers gave in to this pressure almost at once, and on 9 December 1700 they revoked their decrees of 1670 and 1698 and asserted that Jews would be forced to adhere strictly to the trade prohibitions of the Stättigkeit.[41] The retailers were pleased by the council's move, though they remained skeptical of its implementation by the councilmen, whose record had been poor over the past century. More important, however, was the immediate reaction of the Jews, who announced six days later that they would appeal the decision of 1700 to the Reichshofrat.[42]

The Jewish appeal to the imperial court removed the dispute from the council's jurisdiction, and, had it not eventually led the burghers to seek a special imperial commission to investigate the situation in Frankfurt, the move would have extricated the council from its difficult position. Caught between the demands of its own citizens and the advantages of having a prosperous Jewish community from which to draw ordinary and extraordinary revenues, the council had vacillated. That lack of decisiveness benefited the Jews, because they continued to expand their retail businesses as long as the council attempted to find a compromise and failed to enforce the legal trade restrictions on the community. When the Jews took the case to Vienna in order to reverse the decree of

38. Ibid., Nr. 68, a statement (31 May 1701) from the retailers to the council deputation investigating their grievances against the Jews indicates that the burghers learned of the ordinances on 31 January 1699.

39. Ibid., Nr. 43 (12 October 1700).

40. Ibid., Nr. 46 (1 November 1700).

41. Ibid., Nr. 51 (9 December 1700).

42. Ibid., Nr. 52 (15 December 1700).

1700 forced on the council by its angry citizens, the city fathers had to defend their action in court. But the responsibility for decision lay with the Reichshofrat, and though always jealous of its own prerogatives, the council may well have appreciated a relief from the direct pressure of its angry burghers. Perhaps steps toward reconciliation could even be taken, as the councilmen hastened to assure the Christian retailers that they would vigorously support the burgher case on retail shops in the imperial court.[43]

The Reichshofrat delayed its decision, however, and only increased burgher frustration; the retailers became so angry about continued Jewish expansion and the council's inaction that they sought the support of leading burgher militia officers for a proposal to request a special imperial commission comparable to that appointed a century earlier to investigate Frankfurt's internal problems. All necessary documents related to the dispute over Jewish retailing seem to have been submitted to the court by April 1701, but the usually efficient Reichshofrat (as opposed to the slow Reichskammergericht in Wetzlar) issued no judgment on the case.[44] The later history of the court case indicates that the imperial government—which was probably influenced by its own Jewish creditors and which, like the city council, had an interest in keeping the financial resources of the Frankfurt Jewish community strong—was willing to allow the matter to be lost from sight. The only way to tolerate Jewish competition in the Frankfurt retail market without ruling openly against the burghers was simply to make no official judgment at all.

Burgher retailers could not have known in 1701 that no definitive solution would be forthcoming from the Reichshofrat, and they grew impatient as they saw the Jews increase their trade while everyone waited for the court's decision. In 1702 the retailers authorized Johann Jacob Böhler to go to Vienna and seek a private audience with the emperor, who would surely protect the burghers' privileges against Jewish infringements.[45] Before Böhler left the city, though, the retailers informed the council of their intentions and demanded in tones which made their request sound like an ultimatum that the city fathers aid the burgher cause not merely with advice and intercession with the emperor but also with active leadership. The first step had to be rigid enforcement of the

43. Ibid., Nr. 60 (1 January 1701).
44. Ibid., Nr. 63, Jewish appeal (undated); Nr. 69, RHR statement (29 April 1701) that the council's *Vorbericht* had been received. A complete report from the council should presumably have followed, though the RHR could have proceeded without it if the court had really cared to do so.
45. Ibid., Nr. 86, *Vollmacht* for Böhler (15 December 1702).

1700 decree until a court decision was handed down.[46] While the council waited two months before it ordered the Rechney once again to close Jewish shops outside the ghetto, burgher leaders proceeded to petition the emperor in the name of the retailers' committee and the officer corps for the appointment of a commission to settle the problem once and for all.[47]

In 1704 the emperor denied the request for a commission, but the council's vigorous investigation of both the retailers and their relationship with the militia officers steeled burgher determination to seek imperial intervention in Frankfurt. Instead of refusing the burghers' request outright, officials in Vienna asked for a full council report that would bring them up to date on the dispute, and they ordered the magistrates to take no punitive action against either the retailers or the officer corps for their extraordinary appeal over the council's head.[48] The councilmen had already sprung into action: they used their agents and money to influence the decision of the Reichshofrat against the burgher request,[49] and they interrogated leaders of the retailers about their association with burgher officers and about the source of the idea for the request to have an imperial commission appointed.[50] The discontented burghers could scarcely have failed to note the unusual vigor with which the council fought their proposal or to contrast its apparent concern over the cooperation between the retailers' committee and some militia officers with the lack of decisive action against the Jews. The city fathers called the request for a commission the project of a few conspirators who had little support among the retailers or the entire officer corps, and the emperor agreed in May 1704 that no special commission was necessary to resolve the dispute between Jewish and Christian retailers. The matter involved a legal appeal which had to be decided in the regular courts, and it involved only retail tradesmen. Other groups were ordered not to meddle in the case.[51]

46. Ibid., Nr. 70, "Anzeig und Bittschrift" presented to the council on 17 July 1703.

47. Ibid., Nr. 72, council decree (10 September 1703); Nr. 73, the retailers' "Anzeig und Bitte" to the emperor (9 October 1703).

48. Ibid., Nr. 80 (18 December 1703).

49. Ibid., Nr. 74, a letter (17 October 1703) from Gudenus, the council's agent in Vienna, to councilman Johann Jacob Müller in Frankfurt which indicates that bribery was to be used; Nrs. 75–78 are also letters which reveal council concern that the burghers might succeed in obtaining a commission; Nr. 75, a letter (17 November 1703) from Gudenus which asserted that the RHR did not really consider the matter very important.

50. Ibid., Nr. 88, council deputation hearing (5 March 1704).

51. For the council's position, see ibid., Nr. 87, a draft of the council's report to the emperor (22 March 1704), and Nr. 92, another report to Vienna (10 May 1704);

While the decision gave the council everything it had requested, burgher opposition did not cease. In fact, the retailers' committee and several militia officers had already met to draft another memorandum to the emperor just about the time Vienna issued the May rescript which denied the request for a commission and ordered an end to collusion between retailers and other groups not directly concerned with the issue of Jewish competition. The council used the rescript to threaten its opposition, as it launched a thorough investigation of continued cooperation between the retailers and the officer corps.[52] The council inquiry—which I cannot treat in detail here—explains the developments which directly preceded the opening of the constitutional conflict in 1705. The hearings of June and July 1704 reveal how tense the political situation had become: while some of the retailers called for questioning were timidly silent about, or conveniently ignorant of, moves taken to gain broader support for imperial intervention, others refused to give specific information to the council, which had done nothing to aid their cause. A few like Böhler and Captain Stein—two of the three most important leaders during the first phase of the constitutional conflict—were openly defiant.

By this time the retailers were looking to the officer corps for leadership, and at least some captains were ready to provide it. They were active in trying to form a burgher *Feuer Cassa* (a pool of funds to be used as insurance against losses due to fire) against the council's wishes, and they continued to press for Böhler's idea of requesting an imperial commission.[53] What the syndics feared would happen was already becoming a reality: the burgher officers were assuming direction of the retailers' cause. They would soon set themselves up as leaders of the entire citizenry and head a burgher party which would fight the council on much broader issues.[54] Because of the bitterness engendered by Jewish retail

---

despite the fact that the purpose of the two documents was to belittle the size of the opposition, they may be cited as clear evidence that no wholesalers—only retailers and artisans—were involved. The emperor's rescript of 26 May 1704 is located in Ugb D49 Nr. 7.

52. Ugb D49 Nr. 7 is the fascicle of documents on the investigations of the summer of 1704.

53. The retailers had admitted earlier that the idea of requesting an imperial commission was Böhler's; Ugb D49 Nr. 6: Nr. 88, hearing of council deputation (5 March 1704). On the *Feuer Cassa*, see Bgmb 1704–05, 21r (19 June 1704).

54. Ugb D49 Nr. 7 contains the syndics' memorandum of 5–6 June 1704 which indicated their fear "... dass die Burger Officers sich vor andern der Direction anmassen und leicht geschehen könte, dass Sie unter diesem vorwandt sich in andere in das Polizey-wesen und Statum publicum einläuffendte negotia einmischen, als vorsteher der Bürgerschafft sich auffwerffen, mithin eine Parthie wieder den Magistrat formiren ..."

activities, the stage was set for action. All that was necessary was the right occasion for another bold move, and it came in 1705.

III. The Jewish Issue in the Constitutional Conflict

Since the council's failure to protect its own citizens against Jewish competition was the immediate cause of the constitutional conflict launched by the officers in 1705, it seems puzzling that burgher grievances against the Jews did not remain the central issue of the long fight which followed. Strict enforcement of a narrow interpretation of the Stättigkeit and restoration of the Citizens Agreement of 1612/13 were declared the twin goals of the burgher party, both in 1705 and again in 1713 when the second Ausschuss was formed. As I pointed out earlier, hatred of the Jews was clearly the strongest motivation behind the efforts of the first group of burgher leaders who fought against strong odds in the years from 1705 to 1712 for the appointment of an imperial commission. Fritsch, Stein, and Böhler represented the economic interests and narrow prejudices of wealthy craftsmen and retailers, and the perseverance the three men exhibited was closely related to their passionate conviction that Frankfurt Jews were not only ruining their retail trade but also corrupting the entire city government.[55]

The wholesale merchants who gained control of the burgher party after 1713, however, felt the Jewish threat much less directly than Böhler, Fritsch, and Stein. Although the Ausschuss under Notebohm and Hoppe showed signs of antagonism toward the Jews and did not entirely neglect its obligation to work for enforcement of the Stättigkeit, it became engrossed in other issues, such as electoral reform for the council, financial and administrative reorganization, and greater burgher participation in the city government.[56] As far as dealing with outsiders was concerned, this second group of leaders was much more responsive to the wholesale merchants' demand for action to exclude Calvinist denizens from the citizenry than to the retailers' fight against the Jews. The history of the two issues followed different paths before and during the constitutional conflict: as the denizen problem became increasingly important and finally overshadowed most other concerns of the burgher party by the late 1720's, that of Jewish violations of the Stättigkeit, initially foremost, gradually faded from prominence.

55. See my discussion in Chapter 5, 131, and the references there in note 25.

56. These were certainly the issues given priority by top leaders like Notebohm, Hoppe, and the Klotz brothers. When Notebohm returned to Frankfurt in 1729 to discuss the denizen issue with the entire officer corps, one of the charges against him was that he had not acted vigorously enough against the Jews; 51er Protocolla 1729, 171: meeting of deputies and officer corps with Notebohm (10 October 1729).

The chief explanation for the diminished importance of the Jewish issue during the conflict, however, lay not so much in the change of burgher leadership as in the fact that the imperial government treated the dispute over retail shops outside the ghetto as a separate problem. Since the Jews' appeal against the council decision in December of 1700 was already before the Reichshofrat, the question was not considered by the imperial commission under Count Schönborn. The most important source of burgher-Jewish antagonism was diverted from the regular channel through which burgher leaders worked and then ignored by the imperial court. The subsequent failure of the Reichshofrat to make a definitive pronouncement on Jewish retailing was not simply an oversight or the result of too heavy a schedule; it was a decision by officials in Vienna to tolerate the illegal shops so that the prosperity of the Jewish community would continue. Since the Jews were such a convenient source of extraordinary revenue, the imperial government chose to favor them over burgher retailers.

As long as no pronouncement came from Vienna, the council decrees against the shops were not enforced and Christian retailers continued to face sharp Jewish competition. The Frankfurt rector Johann Jacob Schudt described the situation in 1714:

> Our Jews do not abide by the ordinance; instead they interfere in all kinds of trade and barter whatever and wherever they can. The merchant has to consider himself lucky if Jews do not mix in his trade, and because of this, the Christian merchant community faces ruin (*aufs ausserste ruiniret wird*). The Jew can always sell his wares a bit cheaper than the Christian, for he contents himself with poor living conditions, threadbare clothes, and little food and drink. He delivers everything himself and lugs his wares around in a knapsack or under his arm as a cat carries its young; only seldom does he keep hired help. In contrast the Christians are weighted down with high house and shop taxes, expensive hired hands, clean clothing, and an upright style of life [*honnête Lebens-Art*]—not to mention the deceitful advantages many Jews use, so that they can sell cheaper than Christians.[57]

Since Christians would not agree to buy items only from their coreligionists, Schudt argued that they had only themselves to blame for the hard plight of the burgher retailers.[58] But the rector's argument did not take the edge off the bitterness felt by many craftsmen and retailers. De-

57. Schudt, *Jüdische Merckwürdigkeiten*, II, 163.
58. Ibid., 165; Schudt pointed to the example of the Calvinists, who generally bought goods from other people only if members of their own Reformed religion could not provide them.

pendent on the emperor's good will yet unable to evoke a final legal decision from the Reichshofrat, frustrated burghers probably watched with some satisfaction as their apprentices occasionally got into scuffles with Jews.[59] But they were unable to curb the very practice that had led them to seek imperial intervention in Frankfurt.[60]

Leaders of the burgher party did seek redress of various other grievances which involved what they called council favoritism toward the Jews, but the results were disappointing. A long pamphlet campaign as well as several petitions to the imperial commission raised many issues that were finally dealt with in a resolution of 1 June 1728.[61] In contrast to most of the charges levied against the council, complaints about its favoritism toward the Jewish community were lightly dismissed. The imperial decree announced that the council had denied the charges (presumably in the same way it had denied all burgher accusations) and that, in any case, both the council and the community Baumeister had promised to be responsible for future enforcement of the Stättigkeit. No blame was assigned and no fines levied. Burghers were to be satisfied with a simple confirmation of all articles of the Stättigkeit except those involved in the current legal dispute before the Reichshofrat and those amended by the resolution itself. The eleven specific provisions of the decree did give the citizens a few concessions. Debtor-creditor relationships were more closely regulated, and all Jewish loans to burghers, denizens, or dependent subjects of the city had to be registered in court to

59. Various council decrees indicate that scuffles took place: the decree of 17 March 1711, which publicized an imperial rescript of 11 February 1711, was published ibid., 128–130; a decree dated 19 September 1713 is found in Verordnungen des Rats, Nr. 30; another dated 30 January 1721, ibid., Nr. 33; the edict of 16 July 1730, ibid., Nr. 40; that of 18 January 1731, ibid., Nr. 42. Finally two decrees of 1 May and 16 October 1738 were much more strongly worded than previous warnings against molesting Jews: ibid., Nrs. 45 and 48.

60. Even after the constitutional conflict, burgher leaders tried to have Jewish shops and storage rooms outside the ghetto closed. In 1738 the leaders bought the aid of the Committee of Fifty-One in persuading the council to close the shops; see Ugb D49 Nr. 8: Nr. 168, "Klag und Bluschrift" of the Committee (8 July 1798), and Beyerbach, Sammlung der Verordnungen, 659, for the council decree (16 October 1738) which granted the request. The Jews appealed once more to the RHR, which ordered that the shops be tolerated until a definitive pronouncement was made: Johann Jacob Moser, Alte und neue Reichs-Hof-Raths Conclusa (Frankfurt and Ebersdorff, 1743-1745), IV, 274–277: RHR decree of 18 March 1740. For summaries of the events after the conflict, see Moritz, Frankfurt, I, 248–250; Johann Heinrich Bender, Der frühere und jetzige Zustand der Israeliten zu Frankfurt am Main (Frankfurt, 1833), 35–36; and Kracauer, Geschichte, II, 400–401.

61. The resolution was published by J. J. Moser, Von der Reich-Stättischen Regiments-Verfassung (Frankfurt and Leipzig, 1772), 114–120. I shall not even attempt to trace the pamphlet campaign or the petitions here, for the effort would produce only repetitious results.

be valid. The old burgher charge that local courts were generally bribed to give Jews favorable decisions led to a prohibition of any moneylending by Jews to judges in Frankfurt. On the other hand, the decree issued a sharp warning to burghers and especially to their apprentices against fighting Jews, and it further explained that vague charges of council favoritism would not be accepted in the future, only specific charges against individual Jews. Citizens had complained for some time about Jewish violations of the regulations on their clothing and their Sunday and holiday activities, but while the decree of 1728 ordered strict adherence to the old regulations against Jews' appearing outside the ghetto on Christian holy days, it abolished the symbol of Jewish degradation— the wearing of yellow rings on their clothing.

Two provisions of the 1728 resolution dashed once and for all burgher hopes to cut down the size of the Jewish community in Frankfurt and limit its living quarters to even less bearable dimensions. The decree confirmed earlier imperial approval of the purchase of two gardens outside the ghetto by Jews, whose use of the newly acquired space as a bleaching grounds and even for a few small houses had aroused sharp burgher opposition.[62] Parallel with the fight over Jewish acquisition of land outside the ghetto (which belonged, we must remember, to the city and was rented to the Jews) ran burgher efforts during the constitutional conflict to halt the expansion of houses inside the Judengasse. A 67-percent increase in the ghetto's population over the second half of the seventeenth century had naturally caused a housing crisis, which the Jews had attempted to solve by dividing apartments, adding higher stories to buildings, and transforming almost all buildings into living quarters. In 1711, however, the ghetto suffered a terrible fire which destroyed all housing facilities; the poor were forced to find lodgings in surrounding villages, while wealthier Jews rented rooms from Christians in the city itself. The destruction of the ghetto signaled a move by burgher leaders to have the Jews expelled from Frankfurt; failing that, burghers sought a building ordinance (Bauordnung) which would limit the size of houses and hence the number of Jews who could be accommodated. Burgher demands were so strong that in April 1713 the council replaced with harsher regulations the original construction plans, which were favorable to the Jews. When the Jewish community appealed this decision to Vienna, burgher tempers were hard to control, and fighting between citizens and Jews broke out in September. The emperor not only ordered

62. On the purchase of the gardens, see Kracauer, "Die Geschichte der Judengasse in Frankfurt am Main," *Festschrift zur Jahrhundertfeier der Realschule der israelitischen Gemeinde (Philanthropin) zu Frankfurt am Main 1804–1904* (Frankfurt, 1904), 332–333, 356; Bender, *Zustand der Israeliten*, 33.

the council to protect Jewish residents from injury by Christians, but in May 1714 he also restored the original plans for a larger ghetto.[63]

Burgher leaders were bitterly disappointed by the decision, which had been obtained through the assistance of the emperor's Jewish creditor, Samson Wertheimer, but they apparently made no similar move to discourage rebuilding the ghetto after a second conflagration in 1721.[64] Both fires severely weakened the Frankfurt Jewish community, and in response to its plea, the imperial resolution of 1728 guaranteed that the limitation of five hundred households in the ghetto would include only independent families. Poor or dependent people would not be figured in the total, so that the community could count on a high number of prosperous men to help restore its former affluence. Although burgher leaders were again deeply disappointed, they soon gave up their initial impulse to appeal to Vienna once more. Both the council (which was cooperating with burgher leaders against the denizens by 1728) and the imperial commissioner in Frankfurt, Count Schönborn, refused to support any further burgher moves against the Jews.[65]

Since the Jewish community exerted strong influence in Vienna, burgher appeals for protection against the outsiders—based as usual on the citizens' special legal status in the Empire and in Frankfurt—were to no avail. The struggle of the burgher party against the Jews shows how dependent the citizens of Frankfurt were on their emperor during the constitutional conflict. When he favored their cause, it won over the council and over the wealthy denizens, but when he found that his interest lay in supporting the Jews, the burghers suffered defeat at the hands of their most resented enemies.

63. The conflict over the rebuilding of the ghetto is fully discussed in Kracauer, "Judengasse," 334–355, and in his *Geschichte*, II, 101–198.
    64. Kracauer, "Judengasse," 361–366.
    65. Kracauer, *Geschichte*, II, 154–155.

Chapter 8

The Denizens

The growing number of denizens in Frankfurt during the seventeenth century aroused bitter animosity between burghers and the outsiders, whose economic competition and religious views were not welcome in the predominantly Lutheran commercial center. Though other groups also felt the effects of denizen competition, Frankfurt's merchants led a movement to limit the commercial activities of Beisassen and to prevent their gaining the economic benefits of citizenship by marrying burgher widows or daughters. The Denizen Ordinance of 1708 granted the burghers' demands; it prohibited denizens from stapling goods in Frankfurt, forming partnerships with citizens, or operating the businesses of burgher women whom they might marry. The legislation created a basis for cooperation between burgher leaders and the city council against the outsiders but at the same time caused sharp religious disputes between Lutherans and Calvinists within the Bürgerschaft. Marriage into a burgher family was the easiest method for any denizen to attain citizenship, and it was most important for the religious minorities to whom the council hesitated to grant citizens' privileges.[1] Religious issues became entangled with commercial rivalry, as the admission of denizens to citizenship became the principal point of contention. While the Calvinists pressed for free public worship in the city, revocation of the Denizen

---

1. See above, 41–44.

Ordinance, and access to Frankfurt citizenship, most burghers opposed them vigorously. The Calvinist argument that Frankfurt's commercial prosperity depended on its willingness to receive outside merchants as new citizens found support only in Captain Notebohm himself; other burghers and their leaders believed that their city had to be protected against the dangers of economic competition and religious penetration from outside.

I. Denizen Competition with Burgher Retailers

In Chapter 2 I cited evidence for a sizable increase in the denizen population over the seventeenth century until it reached at least 1212 heads of households in 1714. Examination of their occupations in that year revealed that denizens could generally be divided into two groups—a large number of men in low-caliber or wage-earning occupations and an elite which enjoyed high economic and social positions.[2] Now we must look more closely at the economic privileges of Beisassen to see which groups of burghers were threatened by their competition. In contrast to transient foreigners, a denizen who was registered with the Office of Inquisition could earn his living under the general protection of the city's laws. But his means of earning a livelihood were much more restricted than were those of burghers: after 1570 only a citizen could acquire fixed assets (liegende Güter) in Frankfurt, and a man had to be a burgher before he could become a master craftsman in a Handwerk.[3] Although denizens could not legally be independent artisans, they clearly did serve as wage-earning workers in many crafts; they were especially numerous in clothing industries, where they usually worked as seamsters instead of tailors or as shoe repairmen rather than shoemakers.[4] Most of the Beisassen, however, were in free occupations as day laborers; transportation workers; scholars, artists, and publishers; and, most important, wholesale merchants.[5] Unfortunately there is very little information on laborers or on the scholarly and artistic groups in the city before and during the constitutional conflict. Denizen wholesale and retail merchants, however, had become a major concern of the burghers by the late seventeenth century.

2. Cf. above, 39, 56–57.

3. Moritz, Frankfurt, I, 206, says that denizens could also acquire fixed assets until 1570, when the Reformation or codification of city laws limited the privilege to burghers; in effect, Article 8 of the Citizens Agreement of 1612/13 and the imperial rescript of 26 July 1732 confirmed the change of 1570. Lerner, Metzger-Handwerk, 179, reports that the council required a man to become a burgher before entering a guild in 1604, but a mastership had probably always depended on citizenship.

4. Above, 57.

5. See Table 12.

Although wholesalers and retailers generally moved in separate economic and social spheres in Frankfurt, their interests did coincide in several respects, and we should not draw an absolute distinction between them. It was common practice for many wholesale merchants to retail their own wares inside the city, and the different terms for merchants (*Kaufleute, Händler, Krämer*) were often used interchangeably.[6] The economic differences between large-scale commerce and small-scale marketing were obvious, of course, and a social gap always separated the men who were no more than retailers from the wholesalers engaged in long-distance trading. The cleavage had found concrete expression in their separate social corporations during the late medieval period and into the early seventeenth century; although the two groups were not organized corporatively after 1616, the division between them received fresh confirmation in the police ordinances of the seventeenth century and, by the early eighteenth century, in separate organizations to represent their economic interests—a retailers' committee and the chamber of commerce for wholesalers.[7] In 1713 specially formed committees presented separate briefs to the imperial commission. Though the two groups generally moved in different worlds, they shared many grievances. I hope to indicate some of their differences in the course of this chapter, but my immediate task is to explore their common opposition to the commercial activities of the denizens in the city.

Denizens could engage in wholesale commerce quite freely until 1708, when burgher merchants finally succeeded in having legal restrictions placed on their stapling activities and commission businesses.[8] But

6. Cf. the remarks of Friedrich Bothe in a manuscript which was to have been a fourth edition of his general history of Frankfurt and is now in the Bothe Nachlass deposited in the city archive. Bothe was discussing commerce in the sixteenth century when he made this general observation.

7. Cf. Table 33 for the corporate societies and Table 14 for the legal orders established in the police ordinances. The retailers had formed a *Crämer Ausschuss* by 1701 primarily to fight the Jews; see Ugb D49 Nr. 6: Nr. 57, a power of attorney for its lawyer (24 January 1701). The council apparently suppressed it, but a *Handlungs Ausschuss* was reorganized on 23 January 1713 to present the retailers' case to the imperial commission; see HHSA Wien: RHR Decisa 2152. On the development of the chamber of commerce—which I shall discuss below—see *Geschichte der Handelskammer* (Frankfurt, 1908), passim. The chamber itself did not lobby during the constitutional conflict; I shall also discuss below the wholesalers' committee formed in 1713.

8. I use the word "stapling" as the best English equivalent for the German *Spedition*, which involved not only the receiving and forwarding of goods—for which the term "forwarding agency" currently used would be quite satisfactory—but also storage and expediting the necessary legal operations of weighing, inspecting, and sealing goods required in the big commercial centers during the premodern period; see *Oxford English Dictionary* (Oxford, 1933), X, 827, for the historical use of "stapling,"

burghers had always regarded the retail market in Frankfurt as their special preserve—one which might be shared with outsiders only during the annual fairs or by special concessions which permitted the sale of specified products at specific times (usually semi-weekly) and in specific marketplaces. A burgher retailer received permission to sell certain types of goods, and the grocer was not to infringe on the baker's market, even though clear divisions between similar products were undoubtedly difficult to define and maintain even in the closely regulated economy of early modern Frankfurt. Most important for my present purposes was the stipulation that only a burgher could have an open retail shop in the city.[9] Flagrant violations of this law by Jewish retailers was the main topic of the preceding chapter, but denizens were also guilty to a lesser extent of the same illegal practices. Although there were scattered complaints from other areas of trade during the seventeenth century,[10] the most important confrontation was between local spice dealers and a group of Italian denizens who brought fruits and spices from their homeland to the retail market in Frankfurt.

In 1628 a few Italian merchants received a concession to import lemons and oranges from the South. Most of their sales were to have been wholesale, but they were also permitted to vend their wares over the counter in the open markets held twice a week in Frankfurt. These Catholic families were accepted only as denizens, not burghers, but their businesses prospered by gradually expanding beyond the terms of the original concession into the spice trade.[11] By 1671 twenty-six burgher spice dealers and confectioners demanded that the city council curb the enterprising Italians, who were now retailing as well as wholesaling spices. These denizens did not hesitate to use open shops forbidden them by Frankfurt law, and they even hired boys to peddle their wares in the

---

which has now become rare. Commission businesses were, of course, enterprises that handled the sale of goods for the owner in return for a fee.

9. Cf. Moritz, *Frankfurt*, I, 207, 232; I am not certain when the council first passed a legal prohibition against denizen retail shops, though my guess would be that it was during the second half of the sixteenth century.

10. See, for example, Ugb C32 R, Nr. 10: two petitions from 1649 and Nr. 7: a memorial dated 17 April 1651—both of which concern denizen retail competition with burgher cloth dealers. They are cited by Mauersberg, 137, but they are the only grievances of the many he lists which were aimed specifically at denizens.

11. Ugb D10 D includes a nine-page report (19/20 February 1742) by a Syndic Burgk, who summarized the whole history of the conflict between Italian denizens and the burghers; his report was undoubtedly the major source for Dietz's account in *FftHG*, IV, i, 241–246. Another shorter account (3 December 1749) by a "hiesiger Registrator" found in Ugb D10 I2 gives the best indication of the original concession of 1628. The major documents used to trace the controversy are found in Ugb D10 I: "Acta der samptlichen mit Specerey Fisch und Fettwahren traffiquirenden Kauff- und Handelssleuthe, 1671–1736."

streets and local inns.[12] Four denizens—Martin and Anton Brentano, Martin Belin (Bellino), and Inocencio Guaita—argued that not one Italian sold more than 20 Rtlr. worth of spices outside the annual fairs, so they could not be doing any great damage to burgher merchants. Besides, their taxes had increased considerably since 1628, and, in order to meet their obligations to the city treasury, they had had to expand their operations. Their assertion that each of them paid as much into the treasury as five or six of the burgher complainants seems to have had little immediate effect on the council: the denizens were ordered to stop all traffic in spices and to limit their business to the importation of goods from Italy.[13] Just a month later, however—in October 1671—the council decided to initiate the negotiations between burgher spice dealers and the Italians which led to a partial agreement in April 1672. The burghers were willing to extend the list of southern fruits which the Italians might import, but they remained adamant about any dealing in spices. The council failed to make a definitive statement resolving the conflict, so burgher spice dealers became discontented with the city government as their antagonism toward the denizens increased.[14]

The retailers were undoubtedly outraged in 1681 when the council reversed an order from the Rechney which would have prevented Carlo Donato Guilino from operating a small shop in the Schnurgasse.[15] The city government's permission for the Italian to sell goods through an open door, yet not a fully open shop, was followed in 1682 by a strong burgher demand for rigid enforcement of the law: the denizens' illegal commerce had increased during the last decade, and their goods should be confiscated.[16] The council's response that its decrees would be enforced *so viel möglich* was simply not satisfactory,[17] and another confrontation between the spice dealers and the denizens came in 1683. The tone of the burgher demands for curbing Italian trade in sugar, dyes, and fish had become bitter; the Italians were second only to the Jews as a threat to the burgher's *Nahrung*.[18] The response of the denizens, on the other hand, was a rational argument for the continuation of their activities: their prosperity depended on their ability to provide fresh fruit cheaply instead of forcing up prices by dealing through other re-

12. Ugb D10 I, 6–8: "Bittschriftlein allhiesiger samptlicher Würz-Crämer und Zückerbäcker" (7 September 1671).

13. Ibid., 17.

14. There are several copies of the agreement, ibid., 55–62, which only confuse the issue because of what may have been false statements later added to the protocolls; see ibid., 172r–173r.

15. Ibid., 18v.

16. Ibid., 34–35.

17. Ibid., 19.

18. Ibid., 36–40.

tailers; they were not simply removing money from the community, for they paid high taxes into the city treasury; and, since they had been active in the city for thirty years, they should have the same right to trade that citizens enjoyed. The Italians then went to the heart of the matter: most of them had lived in Frankfurt since childhood, yet they had not been granted privileges as full citizens. If citizenship was to be denied them, should they not enjoy at least the right to earn a good living?[19] The council was unmoved, and it preferred to ignore the question of admission to the citizenry. The Italians' confession that they were retailing spices was excuse enough for confirmation of the old prohibitions and, in 1685, for an order to confiscate goods imported in violation of the government's decrees.[20]

The council's failure to enforce its legislation was the source of mounting frustration for burgher retailers. An inventory of the holdings of three Italian merchants in 1692 proved that they were still selling prohibited items.[21] Wholesalers now joined the spice retailers in asking the magistrates to curb Italian commerce (centered in the Nürnberg and Swiss *Höfe* in the heart of the city), and they sparked a quick reaction from the denizens. Anyone could engage in wholesale commerce in Frankfurt; how could burghers ask that theirs be curbed, especially when Italian denizens had been resident in the city for sixty years and were paying very high taxes?[22] Five years later the spice dealers, fishmongers, and chandlers were still demanding action against Jewish and Italian retailing. In 1699 Anton Brentano and Innocent and Matthew Guaita were fined 300 fl. for their violations of city ordinances; their appeal against the fine, though unsuccessful, revealed their situation clearly. They argued that Italian denizens had enjoyed almost free wholesale and retail trade in Frankfurt for more than six decades and had shared the ever-increasing tax burden without complaint, now the burgher spice dealers—acting neither for the good of the community nor as good Christians—were pressuring the council to alter traditional practice. Once again, the council ordered the Italians to pay the fine and to dispose of all goods not specifically listed as items they could retail.[23]

But the city government did not act consistently or vigorously to enforce its orders. Syndic Glock's report on the Italian denizens in December 1705—only two months after the burgher captains had requested imperial intervention in Frankfurt—admitted that the ordinance of 1699

19. Ibid., 47–52.
20. Ibid., 43: council decree of 17 April 1683 and 44: order of the Rechney dated 10 August 1683; ibid., 45: council decree of 15 January 1685.
21. Ibid., 75–77.
22. Ibid., 80–82 and 91–94.
23. Ibid., 154–159.

had never been enforced and that the number of Italian merchants had increased during the intervening six years. The syndic argued that the council had to enforce its prohibitions against Jewish and denizen retailing in order to protect the burghers, and he also insisted that, contrary to the previous arguments of the Italians, there was no reason why the council could not also restrict their wholesale enterprises.[24] The council decided to allow the Italians three months in which to dispose of restricted goods; then men found with such items would lose their denizenship in Frankfurt.[25]

The Italians immediately sought repeal of the decision: they now argued for the principle of free retail and wholesale commerce (*Handlung und Commercien*) as the only foundation for a prosperous republic. They pointed to Holland's example of free trade and toleration of all nations and religions and reminded the city fathers of the prosperity created in the sixteenth century by Frankfurt's tolerant policy toward the Calvinists.[26] Syndic Glock's memorandum in reply to the denizens regretted that the argument had introduced fundamental principles. He was not so concerned about having to refute notions about the value of free trade; the difficult issue was toleration of Catholics and the possibility of granting them citizenship. Admitting the Italians to the Bürgerschaft would raise even more difficulties than their commercial activities had, so Glock urged the council to stick to the practical issue of enforcing its edict of 1705. This memorandum by the syndic is doubly interesting: it reveals that the council and its legal advisers had become convinced by 1705 that they simply had to still burgher discontent by moving against the denizens. Yet, on the very day he signed his report, Glock received the news that the Italians themselves were threatening to appeal to the emperor against the council's decree. He appended a hasty note to his memorandum urging the council to undertake negotiations for a settlement that would satisfy both sides.[27]

The council was clearly caught between the competing burgher and Italian merchants with no positive solution of its own. The Catholic denizens had, in fact, already appealed to the imperial government, and they obtained from Joseph I permission to continue their previous commercial activities until the imperial courts had given a final ruling on the issue.[28] There was no further imperial pronouncement before the council reacted to pressure from the entire burgher merchant com-

24. Ibid., 179–183: Glock's memorandum of 11 December 1705.
25. Ibid., 185v: decree of 29 December 1705.
26. Ibid., 186.
27. Ibid., 215–219: Glock's memorandum of 28/29 January 1706.
28. Ibid., 253: imperial rescript (22 January 1706), which was not yet known in Frankfurt when Glock signed his memorandum.

munity by passing the Denizen Ordinance of 5 June 1708. Article 10 of the ordinance limited the importation of Italian wares to a specific list of goods to be published separately.[29] Burgher spice dealers sought council action against the Italians' retailing in 1709 and 1710, and the Catholic denizens decided that the real solution to their problem was to obtain from the emperor an order for the council to admit them as full citizens of Frankfurt. On 9 April 1711 seven Italians petitioned the emperor for citizenship and obtained the order they sought.[30] Had the council implemented Joseph I's rescript, the Italians' quarrel with the burgher spice dealers would have ended in their victory.

But a more important issue than commercial rights was now at stake, and the council resolved to fight for its own prerogative to determine who could be admitted to the citizenry. Despite the fact that the city government had alienated burgher retailers by not enforcing legislation against the denizens earlier, the aristocrats could count on burgher support for any future moves which might protect the retailers from Italian competition. The spice dealers continued over the next years to remind the council and imperial officials of their right to such protection, but the emperor guaranteed the Italians free wholesale and retail trade until a decision on their admission to the Bürgerschaft was reached.[31] The issue of Italian spice trading was, in fact, never resolved, since it was subsumed in the larger and even more complicated problem of the denizens' admission to full citizenship.

The council then successfully delayed the implementation of the imperial order to grant the Italians immediate citizenship. Each time the order to grant Italians citizenship was renewed—once in 1711 and twice in 1712—the councilmen appealed for reversal of the decision.[32] The senate argued that the Italians had basically distorted their commercial situation when they claimed a long tradition of free trade in Frankfurt; in fact, their trade had been carefully limited by law but illegally extended by the denizens themselves. The fundamental assertion of the

29. Müller, *Frankfurt contra Frankfurt*, III, 91.

30. Ugb D10 I, 261–263: appeal (9 April 1711) and imperial rescript (14 April 1711). The seven men and the years of their registration as denizens were: Matthias Guaita (1678), Joseph Brentano (1694), Innocentius Guaita (1679), Dominico Brentano (1699), Anton Brentano (1680), Andreas Carone (1697), and Joseph del Angelo (1684). Cf. ibid., 414.

31. See ibid., 339–342: a burgher appeal to the council (17 December 1711) signed by 26 men including two burgher captains—Christian Klauer and Gerhard Seegar; HHSA Wien: RHR Decisa 2148, 121r–122r: the grievances of the spice dealers presented to the imperial commission on 25 April 1713. The commercial privileges of the Italians were affirmed by Charles VI on 18 July 1712; see Ugb D10 I, 390. Dietz, *FftHG*, IV, i, 245, asserts that the prohibition against Italian spice trade was never implemented.

32. Ugb D10 I, 271, 318, 326–328, and 391.

liberties of individual imperial territories against arbitrary decisions by the emperor used in the council's brief to the imperial vicar in 1711 was subsequently dropped in its appeals to Charles VI. Instead the city fathers emphasized the practical economic necessity to protect the native population from outside competition and denied that religion had anything to do with the exclusion of the Italians from citizenship. The council praised its own generosity in tolerating non-Lutheran groups as perpetual denizens, but it assured the emperor that no city could tolerate a group which brought economic ruin to its own burghers.[33] Although a special commission of the Reichshofrat met in January 1718 to study the denizens' request for citizenship, it was mysteriously dissolved less than a month after its first session. The dispute over the Denizen Ordinance itself probably seemed more important to imperial authorities; its eventual resolution would presumably provide guidelines for settlement of the Italians' claims to the privilege of citizenship.[34]

II. The Wholesalers and the Denizen Ordinance of 1708

While burgher retailers led the attack on the Italian Beisassen, the city's wholesalers were responsible for securing from the magistracy in 1708 a comprehensive Denizen Ordinance that reaffirmed council legislation against denizen retail trade and also instituted restrictions on their wholesale activities. The last three decades of the seventeenth century had seen a noticeable increase in the number of important merchants who settled in Frankfurt as denizens, either because their religious confession made the attainment of citizenship difficult or because they chose a loose attachment to the city for business reasons. Quite often they were the younger sons of families which centered their wholesale firms in other cities.[35] They came to Frankfurt from many different commercial centers in the Empire, the Netherlands, Switzerland, Italy, and France. Most seem to have been Calvinists; there were fewer Lutherans and only a handful of Catholics.[36] Many denizens, usually acting as permanent representatives of their home firms rather than as inde-

33. Ibid., 274–280: report to the imperial vicar (24 September 1711) and 418–434: "Bericht in der Italiener Sachen" (2 November 1715).

34. Ibid., 478, for the initial appointment of the committee on 27 January 1717; 485, its first sessions a year later; 487–488, for its dissolution on 20 January 1718. The author of the summary of these events in Ugb D10 I2 was uncertain why the commission was dissolved, and he did not make the connection with the general issue of the Denizen Ordinance, which seems to me to be the most convincing explanation of the RHR's action.

35. Cf. Mauersberg, 137; Dietz, FftHG, IV, i, 157, 165–167.

36. Cf. Mangon's figures for 1719, above, 57.

pendent merchants, served as stapling agents and undertook commission businesses in which they sold other merchants' goods. They began as well to retail products within the city between the two fairs—an intrusion into the local market which not only damaged the small retailers but also removed the major competitive advantage inside the city which Frankfurt law gave a burgher wholesaler over his denizen counterpart.

In December 1706 sixty-nine burgher merchants—among them twelve militia officers and twenty-two Calvinists—petitioned the city council for protection against the denizens, whose illegal practices were spelling ruin for many citizens. The Frankfurt merchants argued that the denizen generally came to the city only to make a fortune and then leave once again, while the burgher had cast his lot with the city itself; come good or hard times, the citizen remained, and the magistracy should act to keep the Bürgerschaft as strong economically as was possible. Although they were willing to be somewhat more lenient with denizens who had been in Frankfurt for many years, the merchants insisted that all Beisassen remain within the bounds of the specific business which they could operate independently (*mit Ihren eigenen Mitteln*) and for which they were officially registered with the city government. The petition repeated the old demand of the retailers: the council simply had to end all denizen retail activities, especially those in open shops belonging either to the denizen himself or to a burgher acting as his front. Most significantly, the petition demanded that denizens be prevented from engaging in any commission or stapling businesses. The burghers argued that Beisassen had never been permitted to undertake those enterprises; they had always been reserved for established burghers, just as Swiss cities still reserved for their own burghers the sole right to staple or sell goods on commission.[37] I find no record of previous restrictions on denizens' wholesaling or even of concerted burgher attempts to impose them, however, and it appears that the petition of 1706 marked the first major move by citizen wholesalers to eliminate competition from their economic sphere. The document was signed by all the most important burgher merchants the men who figure prominently in Alexander

37. Ugb B76 Mm for the petition of 21 December 1706 and the sixty-eight (probably sixty-nine) signatories; it is printed as well in *Franckfurtische Religions-Handlungen* (Frankfurt, 1735; cited hereafter as *FftRH*), I, "Magistratus Bericht" (8 January 1735), Beilage F, Adjunctus 2, Sub. Lit. A, 44–47. Dietz, *FftHG*, IV, i, 159, counts only fifty-seven signatures (he probably counted lines rather than the individual signatures), and Mauersberg, 137, gets sixty-one; actually there are sixty-eight individual names on the document, and, since Mexler Söhne probably means at least two men, we may safely say sixty-nine men or their widows signed the petition. Mangon informs us in *Französische Gemeinde*, v 170, 5–6, which men were Calvinists, and I have checked the signers against the lists of militia officers which I cite in Chapter 5, note 15.

Dietz's commercial history of Frankfurt. Dietz's observation about the leading merchants in this fight against the outsiders is striking: they were almost all the descendents of men who immigrated to the city only two or three generations earlier, but they were now eager to block the path that had led to their own commercial success and social prominence.[38]

The big wholesalers had greater influence than retailers on government policy, and their petition produced immediate results. The council appointed a deputation to hear specific charges against individual denizens presented by a committee of merchants (six Lutherans and two Calvinists); their sessions began just a week after the petition was received, and investigations continued into March 1707. Several Beisassen were ordered to cease their commercial activities, and a determined effort was made to fashion legislation that would guarantee proper registration and heavier taxation of the outsiders.[39] The Office of Inquisition's official list of 104 denizens engaged in commerce was nevertheless far lower than the actual number active in Frankfurt, or so the burghers argued in a second general petition to the council in December 1707.[40] This time even greater concern was expressed about the denizens' stapling and commission businesses and about their avoiding detection by changing the names of their enterprises. This second document also gives us our first hint of a possible difference of opinion between Lutheran and Calvinist burghers: it was signed by only forty-seven men—and only one of them was a Calvinist. It seems that the investigations of the preceding months had concentrated largely on Calvinist denizens. Reformed burghers became somewhat concerned about this fact, while most of the Lutherans were eager to put even more Beisassen out of business. The Calvinists became increasingly suspicious of Lutheran intentions, and as a result all but one refused to sign the second petition of 1707.[41] The Lutheran signatories attempted to smooth things over by insisting that they did not wish to abolish the institution of denizenship itself—only to end infringements on burgher economic privileges; their demands to the council were for a sharp renewal of all commercial restrictions on the Beisassen.

Once again the wholesalers got all they wanted from the council—and more. The Denizen Ordinance passed in June 1708 was so important in

38. Dietz, *FftHG*, IV, i, 157.

39. Ugb B76 Mm, passim; see esp. council decrees of 20 January 1707 and 26 October 1707.

40. Both the list of "Handels Beysassen" registered with the Inquisition and the petition of 22 December 1707 are found in Ugb B76 Mm; the petition is printed as well in *FftRH*, I, "Magistratus Bericht" (8 January 1735), Beilage F, Adjunctus 2, Sub. Lit. B., 47–52.

41. See Mangon in Französisch-Reformirte Gemeinde, v 170, 6, 18.

defining the relations between burghers and outsiders that its provisions deserve careful reading:

(1) All foreigners—including those living in private houses or public inns, those working for citizens or denizens, and even those whose parents had resided in Frankfurt as denizens for many years —were expressly forbidden from undertaking a trade (*Handlung*) of their own or from participating in that of a citizen or denizen.

(2) Those who intended to settle and make a living in the city, however, had first to seek permission from the authorities.

(3) If they received permission, they had to register with the Office of Inquisition.

(4) Their commercial dealings could not include open shops or any retailing.

(5) Their wholesale activities could take place only in closed shops; specific regulations determined the minimum amounts of goods they might sell.

(6) Only those denizens already established in the city for ten years were permitted to continue commission businesses; all denizens, however, were forbidden from stapling goods.

(7) Denizens were forbidden from associating in any commercial partnerships with burghers.

(8) Denizens who married burgher widows or daughters were no longer permitted to continue operating open shops or pursuing any other burgher occupations for which the wife might otherwise have had a privilege; in all such economic matters, such men were to be treated just like all other denizens.

(9) No denizen or other foreigner was to violate this ordinance by using a burgher's name to cover his business; any citizen who assisted such a violation was himself to be severely punished.

(10) Denizens who dealt in Italian wares were to abide strictly by a list of permitted goods which was to be provided later.

(11) The Office of Inquisition was charged with supervision of denizens and enforcement of this ordinance.

(12) Not only the regular but also special officials were to keep an eye on the denizens; if any violation of the law were proved, the denizen stood to lose the protection of the city as well as have his goods confiscated.[42]

Most of these twelve articles simply codified legislation already passed by the council; numbers 6, 7, and 8, however, were new restrictions

42. Müller, *Frankfurt contra Frankfurt*, III, 88–91, prints the ordinance which I have paraphrased here.

which resulted either directly or indirectly from the wholesalers' drive against their denizen competitors. We have already seen that the burgher merchants wanted a prohibition of denizen commission and stapling enterprises; they had even made the distinction between new Beisassen and those who had been resident in Frankfurt for many years which Article 6 of the ordinance incorporated.[43] While the burghers had not requested the specific remedies provided by Articles 7 and 8, they had complained that the denizens were avoiding many of the restrictions on their trade by associating with burghers. The city council seems to have taken the initiative, however, to pass the two articles that not only restricted Beisassen but also limited the economic rights of burghers themselves.[44] No longer could a burgher form a business partnership with a denizen or a burgher widow or daughter marry a denizen with the expectation that he could take over a business which she inherited. All three innovations in the ordinance of 1708 were aimed at limiting the economic privileges of Beisassen, but Article 8 touched the more delicate matter of moving from denizenship to citizenship by marrying into a burgher family. In fact, a general tightening of the regulations on denizen economic activities made the attainment of full citizenship all the more desirable to the outsider. The patent intention of the council, however, was to withdraw one of the incentives—the right to take over a woman's business enterprise—which had made marriage the most attractive means of entering the Bürgerschaft.

Despite the strong alienation of burghers from their aristocratic government during the constitutional conflict, the council won the support of almost all citizens for its measures to curb denizen competition and to discourage the influx of new burghers. Opposition to the Denizen Ordinance came only from the religious minorities—particularly from the Calvinists—whose coreligionists were most adversely affected by the legislation. Those groups regularly excluded from direct admission to the citizenry by the council were dependent on the relatively broad commercial privileges they had enjoyed before 1708 and on the possibility of gaining the privileges of full citizenship through marriage. Calvinist demands for free trade and elimination of Articles 7 and 8 of the Denizen Ordinance widened the already apparent rift between Lutheran and Reformed burghers, until it became a major feature of the last years of the constitutional conflict. By the late 1720's the Lutheran citizenry and

43. Above, 207, for my discussion of the petition of 21 December 1706.

44. Captain Notebohm later argued that the council had enacted its own law in 1708 rather than working in close collaboration with the merchants after their petitions of 1706 and 1707; the magistracy's purpose was to divide its burgher opposition along religious lines, according to Notebohm's statement to the RHR in HHSA Wien: RHR Decisa 2174, 73r–73v.

all its important leaders except Captain Notebohm found themselves united with the city council in a struggle against the Calvinists.

III. The Controversy over the Ordinance, 1713–1726

The first phase of the controversy over the Denizen Ordinance lasted from 1713 to 1726 and was not so bitter as the final years of the dispute. The open break between Calvinist and Lutheran merchants did not become apparent until 1713, because the two groups shared so many common business interests that religious differences could often be played down. The chief concerns of the merchants lay in long-distance commerce and the local arrangements that facilitated such trade—fixing exchange rates, regularizing banking procedures, and expediting the stapling and the transportation of goods. On such matters Frankfurt merchants had cooperated at first sporadically during the seventeenth century then more and more frequently, until by the early eighteenth century they had a standing committee of overseers and a regular *Börse*.[45] Table 40 shows that, despite strong Lutheran control of most institutions in Frankfurt, the two confessions were almost equally represented among the overseers of the exchange.[46] The strength of the Calvinists within the merchant community was further demonstrated by the fact that not until 1768 did a Lutheran serve as senior member and treasurer of the board of overseers.[47]

The presentation of the merchants' grievances to the imperial commission in June 1713 was the first occasion for an open disagreement. Though all members of the merchants' committee could work together for solutions to technical problems involved in their commercial enterprises, the Calvinists and Lutherans were so divided on the issue of denizen privileges that they finally had to present separate statements to Count Schönborn. The entire committee sought careful enforcement of

45. *Handelskammer*, 7–21; the editors of this work considered the committee of wholesalers formed in 1706 to discuss the denizen issue with the council as the first standing executive of the *Börse*. Different terms were used for the various executive committees, until the term *Börsevorsteher* was employed regularly in the *Raths und Stadt-Calender* after 1734.

46. Table 40 is based on information in *Handelskammer*, 104–106; here I follow the view of the editors that we should not start a real list of *Vorsteher* until 1713, though I have added the Catholic member of the Merchants' Committee of 1713 not included in *Handelskammer*; see Archiv der französisch-reformirten Gemeinde, v 168, 225, for the list of members in 1713. The next record of the leaders of the wholesalers was their signatures on the financial records of the *Börse* beginning in 1718. Men whose names are preceded by § served as senior member and treasurer of the board of overseers.

47. *Handelskammer*, 107.

TABLE 40
Overseers of the Börse, *1713–1750*

Johann Martin de Ron	Reformed	1713–1718
Isaak Behagel	Reformed	1713–1718
David de Neuville	Reformed	1713–1718
Abraham Mangon	Reformed	1713–1718
Peter Münch	Lutheran	1713–1718
Joh. Nicolas Ohlenschlager	Lutheran	1713–1718
Nicolaus Claus	Lutheran	1713–1727
Joh. Georg Henrici	Lutheran	1713–1714
Gerhard de Poulles	Catholic	1713– ?
§ Joh. Christian Ziegler	Reformed	1718–1729
Seger von der Berghen	Lutheran	1718–1728
§ Jacob de Neuville	Reformed	1718–1730
Remy Heinrich Barthels	Lutheran	1718–1727
§ Abraham von der Lahr	Reformed	1718–1745
Joh. Gerhard Münch	Lutheran	1718–1745
Joh. Martin de Ron d. Jüngere	Reformed	1718–1753
§ Joh. de Bary	Reformed	1730–1758
Joh. Matthias Bansa	Lutheran	1730–1742
§ Joh. David von Neufville	Reformed	1730–1767
Henrich von Uchlen	Lutheran	1730–1746
Remigius von der Berghen	Lutheran	1730–1746
Joh. Peter Cramer	Reformed	1732–1754
Nicolaus Ohlenschlager	Lutheran	1734–1764
Johannes Frank	Lutheran	1745–1756
Joh. Nöe Gogel	Reformed	1746–1753
Joh. Friedrich Firnhaber	Lutheran	1747–1759

existing regulations on monetary exchanges and the payment of debts, new legislation which would make transportation workers personally responsible for "lost" goods, an end to the arbitrary levying of tolls by city officials, rigid enforcement of trade restrictions on the Jews, and a halt to the council's practice of having merchants declare their total assets for tax purposes (merchants, they argued, should be permitted instead to keep their total worth secret and to simply declare themselves liable to the highest level of taxation, i.e. to *grosse* or *volle Schatzung*, a fixed tax of 50 fl. on all assets exceeding 15,000 fl. in value). The committee also requested that companies which were still partnerships between burghers and denizens be forced to pay at least half the amount on tolls and tariffs usually levied on outsiders, a fact which indicates that the council had not yet been able to implement Article 7 of the Denizen Ordinance.[48]

Further agreement on the ordinance was impossible for the confessionally mixed committee. The four Calvinists insisted on presenting the imperial commission with a protest against the council's policy toward outsiders:

> All great lords, republics, and especially commercial cities take great pain over how they may—through different privileges, grants, and freedoms—bring trade into their territories and acquire many citizens and inhabitants. Here, however, the council has been attempting for several years and contrary to older customs not only to make naturalization more difficult but also to make several thousand Gulden out of it; to drive trade and people out of the city; even to take away the inherent rights of burgher daughters and widows who have their own trades but who marry upright and honorable merchants or handicraftsmen who are not burghers—to forbid their trade just as though they had committed a great crime by not marrying a burgher.[49]

Those outsiders who had lived in the city sometimes ten, twenty, or thirty years, who had willingly and faithfully helped bear the burdens of ordinary and extraordinary taxation, and who desired citizenship should receive that privilege; certainly burgher women should not be penalized for marriages outside the Bürgerschaft. With these views of the Calvinist burghers their Lutheran colleagues were in complete disagreement: they refused to sign the grievances as drafted by the Calvinists and instead submitted their own statement, which urged the strongest adherence to the Denizen Ordinance as the only means of preventing great damage to both the city's commercial people and its craftsmen.[50] The battle lines were thus drawn at the beginning of the commission's hearings, though major campaigns were to be delayed for another decade.

We must examine the strategy of each group involved in the fight over the Denizen Ordinance carefully, however, for even this first stage of the conflict reveals much about the mentality of the people involved—not only how they justified their own interests but also how they conceived the workings of the economy and their own social roles within the community. The first development was the intervention of the burgher

---

48. See the Archiv der französisch-reformirten Gemeinde, v 168, 225–232, for all the grievances as presented by the Calvinists on the committee to the commission (9 June 1713); they are also located in HHSA Wien: RHR Decisa 2149, 83–88.

49. Französisch-reformirte Gemeinde, v 168, 228–229.

50. Ibid., v 170, 73.

Ausschuss, which was solidly Lutheran in composition, on the side of the Calvinist merchants. In May 1714 the burgher leaders asked the commission to redress the merchants' grievances, despite their disagreement on the denizen issue. Then the deputies raised the dispute over Article 8 of the Denizen Ordinance to a constitutional plane, because they understood their authority from the citizenry as a mandate to restore the Citizens Agreement as the foundation of Frankfurt's constitution. Article 7 of that agreement had limited the applicability of council legislation against the marriage of burgher women outside the citizenry to poor persons who might cause an increased burden on public charities; since wealthy men were explicitly exempted from such regulations, the council should not now be permitted to extend its legislation discouraging outside marriages to include all denizens, rich or poor.[51] We may be somewhat surprised that burgher leadership, dominated as it was by commercial elements, emphasized constitutional principle over the economic demands of Lutheran merchants in 1713. Indeed, the position of the burgher deputies was later to change, as the wholesalers exerted more pressure for adherence to the ordinance and the Calvinists tied religious demands to their constitutional pleas. But at the beginning of the controversy, the Ausschuss concentrated its efforts on keeping the Calvinists inside the burgher party and attacking the council with the strongest legal arguments.

In response to the commission's request, the city council then submitted a statement of its position on the question of admitting to the citizenry wealthy men who married burgher women. The magistrates argued, first of all, that they had always enjoyed the indisputable right to decide who could and who could not be admitted as citizens of Frankfurt; Article 7 of the Citizens Agreement could not be construed to mean that the council had to admit any man who married a burgher woman as long as he was not poor. The councilmen had to be guided by specific circumstances, and they left no doubt about the danger they were trying to avert. Since the Thirty Years War, the number of Calvinists (both citizens and denizens) in the community as well as their share of the city's wealth had increased rapidly. Already they owned the best houses and controlled the largest part of the city's commerce, and their ambition was to capture all commerce from the Lutherans, gain the right of public worship, and completely control the city's religious and political life as well.[52]

51. Ibid., v 170, 148–149: the deputies' report to the commission (16 May 1714).
52. "Ursachen und Motiven, Warumb die aussländische und frembde durch heyrath der Franckfurther bürgers Töchter das Bürger Recht allein nicht erlangen, sondern Ihre Reception der Obrigkeitlichen Verordnung billich zu überlassen seye," a council statement to the commission (29 June 1714) which may be found in the

Within this frame of reference, the council's policies toward Calvinists become entirely clear: it refused to grant them public worship inside the city walls (an issue to which I shall turn later in this chapter), and it used every method to prevent an increase in the number of Calvinists in the community. The most effective means of striking at the Calvinist danger to the Bürgerschaft was to admit them as denizens with reduced economic privileges and then to prevent their use of marriage as an entree into full citizenship. The council's statement of June 1714 is the best proof that all its legislation which curbed the privileges of denizens and of burghers who married denizens was aimed specifically at the Calvinists.[53] And the council did not wait long to strike another blow. In August 1714 the city fathers passed an ordinance to protect local gardeners from denizen—but certainly not Calvinist—competition; to the same law, however, they appended stricter regulation on burgher women who married Beisassen. Denizen husbands were to have no right to exploit their wives' property in the city, and, to prevent the possibility, female burghers who married denizens were ordered to sell their property to Frankfurt citizens within a year of the marriage.[54] This ordinance was not only a clear indication that the council would not automatically make the burgher's husband a citizen; it was a sharp penalization of outside marriages.

The imperial commissioners were unable to submit a unanimous opinion on the disputed issue of granting citizenship to men who married burgher widows or daughters. This was, in fact, the only important issue on which the commissioners were unable to reach an agreement among themselves. In October 1715 the subdelegates for Lutheran Hesse-Darmstadt supported the council's right to grant or refuse citizenship as it saw fit, while Count Schönborn—a Catholic acting on behalf of the Elector of Mainz—set fundamental limitations on the magistracy's power to exclude outsiders who married burghers.[55] He argued that both Article 8 of the Denizen Ordinance and the later edict of August 1714 were invalid. As long as a burgher married an honorable outsider who met the wealth requirements set up on 6 May 1613 (assets worth 200 fl. for handicraftsmen and 300 fl. for others), was a subject of the

Bavarian State Archive in Würzburg: Mainzer Regierungsakten: Kaiserliche Kommissionen, fascicle 142; a copy was made by Mangon in Französisch-reformirte Gemeinde, v 170, 151–155.

53. Cf. Mangon, ibid., 111.

54. CLF, IV, Nr. 124: council ordinance (9 August 1714). On 29 September 1714, the council denied that the law was designed to hinder marriage with outsiders; its only purpose was to protect gardeners and to see that denizens did not own land. See Ugb C18 J, 8.

55. Hohenemser, *Verfassungsstreit*, 212–218; copies of the separate reports submitted to Vienna in HHSA Wien: RHR Decisa 2175, 2r–47r.

Empire, and belonged to a confession that had enjoyed free public worship in 1624, the council had to grant such a spouse citizenship.[56] Since Calvinists did not enjoy public worship in Frankfurt in 1624, Schönborn's argument did not aid them very much. His major concern seems to have been to guarantee Catholic access to the privileges of citizenship. The lack of consensus on the commission meant that the decision to be made by the Reichshofrat or the emperor would be delayed, and the next years of the constitutional conflict found burgher leaders, the council, and imperial officials engrossed in working out the reforms which ultimately gave burghers joint control of the city administration.

The years from 1715 until 1722, when burgher merchants pressed the issue once again, saw no action on the question of outsiders as Frankfurt citizens. Later events showed, however, that the Calvinists themselves used these years of calm before the bitter fight of the following decade to develop their arguments against the Denizen Ordinance and against the burghers' conception of Frankfurt as a closed community. The Netherlandish and the French Reformed groups selected a joint committee headed by Christian Ziegler and Abraham Mangon to consider what action Calvinist burghers should take to defend their position.[57] The first step—undertaken largely by Mangon himself—was to write clear statements expressing Calvinist opposition to the edict of 1714 and the Denizen Ordinance of 1708; a direct refutation of the council's explanation of its policy toward outside marriages as well as the "Reflections on the Denizen Ordinance" were composed for later use.[58]

The Calvinists' critique of the edict of 1714 did not question the basic right of the council to decide on admissions to the citizenry, but it did deny the council members an arbitrary power to implement a one-sided

56. Ibid., 26r–26v; the ordinance of 6 May 1613 to which Schönborn referred is located in CLF, I, Nr. 82.

57. Mangon explained in Französisch-reformirte Gemeinde, v 170, 23–24, that such a committee was formed, but he did not give the date of its establishment. It was undoubtedly sometime during the years before 1722, when the committee contacted Captain Notebohm for his help.

58. Mangon's reply to the council statement (29 June 1714) on marriage with outsiders was contained in his "Pro Informatione" sent to Notebohm on 6 April 1723; it was, as far as I know, never published and is located in Französisch-reformirte Gemeinde, v 170, 111–122. The statement was submitted by Notebohm to the RHR (17 September 1723); see ibid., 286–299. The "Reflexiones auff die Anno 1708 den 5. Junii errichtete Beysassen-Ordnung" was submitted to Notebohm in April 1723 for his use; see ibid., 166–201. Hohenemser, Verfassungsstreit, 341, says that the "Reflexiones" was published first in 1723 and then reprinted several times before the famous edition of 1731, copies of which are now located in FftRH, I, "Magistratus Bericht," Beilage F, Adjunctus 1, as well as in the Leonhardi Nachlass (Frankfurt City Archive), Kistchen 24, i. The printed version was slightly changed from the original manuscript copy.

policy of exclusion. If the magistracy's power were unlimited, then previous constitutional guidelines were of no significance. Why had property qualifications been set up in 1613 or Article 7 been written into the Citizens Agreement? In fact, the council was now making it more difficult for many wealthy merchants to become citizens than for less wealthy craftsmen. Such a policy, the Calvinists argued, could only be explained in terms of religious bigotry; yet the public good demanded toleration of all three major religions in Frankfurt, just as they were now tolerated in the Empire. Could the council really consider the fact that Calvinists owned the largest and best located houses in the city a justification for its attempts to prevent them from marrying outside the Bürgerschaft? While it was true that Calvinists controlled most of the important commerce in Frankfurt, the council was very wrong to believe that Reformed merchants had "taken" trade away from the Lutherans. On the contrary, the volume of trade had greatly increased over the past few decades; if they had done anything, Calvinists had attracted more and more business to the city. Unlike overpopulated Switzerland, whose exclusionist policies the council often used to justify its own, Frankfurt's commercial community (though perhaps not its handicraft population) could expand much more than it already had. But the government's unreasonable policies toward outsiders its reluctance to admit Calvinists and now its penalization of burghers who married denizens—were sure to drive commerce away.

The "Reflections on the Denizen Ordinance" expanded this last theme: by placing so many obstacles on their commerce, the council had given denizens the harsh alternatives of obeying stringent trade restrictions or leaving the city rather than the reasonable and customary alternatives of either becoming a burgher after a period of time or giving up residence in Frankfurt. Those articles of the ordinance designed to distinguish sharply the denizens' economic privileges from those of burghers were not disastrous for the outsiders; they were only bothersome hindrances that showed how unwelcome the denizens were. Large wholesalers were not dependent on their retail activities inside the city, nor did they usually make a living from commission or stapling operations alone. Of course, all merchants were concerned about proper storage and movement of their goods, yet Article 9 left some doubt whether burgher merchants could handle such problems for denizens. Articles 7 and 8, however, damaged not only Beisassen but burghers as well. How could the council justify its prohibition of partnerships between burghers and denizens inside Frankfurt when such associations with merchants in other cities were permitted? Article 8, the most objectionable of all the law's provisions, deprived burgher widows and daughters not only of their Bürgerrecht but also of the privileges essential to their sustenance. It ignored the guidelines set down in the early seventeenth century for admitting outsiders to the citizenry, and it made an unjustified distinction between male and female citizens. The council had been willing to damage its own citizens while pretending to protect them from the denizens.

The council, so went the Calvinist argument, had placed itself in an impossible constitutional position, while it failed to justify its exclusionist policy with convincing economic reasoning. We should note that the council, not the Lutheran citizenry, bore the brunt of this sharp Calvinist logic. In order to prevent the growth of antagonisms which might split the burgher party and make it unable to fight the council effectively, Mangon and his committee played down the fact that Lutheran burghers fully approved the Denizen Ordinance. The Calvinists attacked the council for passing the law without drafting it in consultation with the merchants who had requested protection from the denizens. This was the weakest of the arguments put forward, since such consultation would certainly have produced results equally unsatisfactory to the Reformed committee. While this strategy of attacking only the council appeared to ignore the widespread opposition to Calvinism in the Bürgerschaft, it was actually the best political tactic to adopt at a time when burgher leaders were pushing for administrative reforms. Mangon could concentrate on exposing the irrational economic views and the religious bigotry of the aristocrats who controlled the city government and who ruled the city so poorly. The councilmen should have known that it was Frankfurt's open door to religious refugees that had made the city a commercial center of European importance in the late sixteenth century. Other flourishing commercial cities, like Amsterdam (*die hohe Schule des Commercii*), Hamburg, Lübeck, and Lyon, were adequate proof that toleration of different nationalities and religions meant increase in population and economic prosperity. No amount of economic reasoning could possibly justify the council's policy of restriction and exclusion; it was motivated by a blind jealousy of merchants and a religious bigotry inconsonant with the welfare of a great commercial center. Having refuted the council's argument that its policy was based on the economic necessity of protecting burghers from outsiders, the Calvinists placed the root of the problem exactly where Catholic imperial officials would understand it best—Lutheran unwillingness to tolerate other confessions.

When burgher merchants demanded an even more forceful law against outsiders in 1722, the Calvinists were prepared to defend themselves by appealing to the authorities in Vienna. Fifty-three Lutheran firms petitioned the council in June 1722 for stiffer provisions for the exclusion of outsiders from both citizenship and denizenship, an open

declaration depriving burgher widows and daughters who married outsiders of their citizenship, and a renewal with strict enforcement of the
prohibition of business partnerships between denizens and burghers.[59]
The city fathers appointed a committee to revise the Denizen Ordinance, and although no legislation followed immediately, they initiated
proceedings to bar several Calvinist denizens from acquiring the assets
of their burgher wives. The Reformed committee became increasingly
concerned about the pressure being exerted on the council, and it decided to write Captain Notebohm in Vienna for his advice and aid. Fear-
ing on one hand a sharp split that would harm the general cause of the
burgher party and anxious on the other about the possibility that the
burgher Ausschuss might reverse its stand and allow a change in Article
7 of the Citizens Agreement to accommodate the merchants' demands
for action against the denizens, the Calvinists laid their problems before
the burgher leader in whose political skill and high sense of fairness
they placed absolute trust.[60] Notebohm agreed to assist the Calvinist
burghers in their fight against Articles 7 and 8 of the Denizen Ordinance, and he advised them to avoid any direct confrontation with their
fellow burghers in the sessions of the imperial commission meeting in
Frankfurt.[61]

A series of test cases involving Calvinist merchants married to burgher women was taken first for reconsideration by the council and then
appealed directly to the Reichshofrat in Vienna. We shall look at only a
few examples of the cases involved. One concerned a Herr Vigny, whose
wife was informed that, by marrying outside the Bürgerschaft, she had
lost her citizenship and had to pay the Tenth-Penny Tax on her assets.

59. Ugb D10 I, 591a–591h; the petition was signed 4 June 1722 and read in the
senate 16 June 1722. Mangon, in the Französisch-reformirte Gemeinde, v 168, 414,
points out that all the signers were Lutherans, since Calvinists refused to cooperate;
three drafts had to be written by the young Dr. Ochs—son of the council's leader—
before the petition was sufficiently strong in its attitude toward the council to satisfy
the merchants. See ibid., v 170, 49–57, for another copy of the petition as well as the
two drafts which preceded it.

60. Ibid., v 170, 25–35: Mangon's first letter to Notebohm (21 November 1722).

61. Ibid., 75–77: Mangon's letter of 15 December 1722 makes it clear that Notebohm
wished to work only through imperial officials in Vienna. There is some question
about Notebohm's motives for supporting the Calvinists against the Lutheran majority in his party: some burgher leaders later charged that he had been bribed, but
the sums sent by the Calvinists to Vienna appear to have been only enough to defray
Notebohm's expenses for acting on their behalf; there are scattered references to the
influence of the Captain's wife, but I have been unable to learn if she herself was
Reformed; finally, I would not write off the view that Notebohm was the least self-
interested and most fair-minded and cosmopolitan of the burgher leaders—he seems
to have been honestly convinced that the Calvinist constitutional and economic arguments were correct and served Frankfurt's best interests.

Vigny appealed to the council in January 1723, and his wife was permitted to remain a citizen. But the senate refused either to produce an edict that ordered the loss of citizenship for women who married outsiders or to grant Vigny himself the privileges of a full citizen. After he was refused a second time in February of that year without any explanation for his failure to qualify for citizenship, the Calvinist denizen determined to appeal to the high court at Vienna. Three other denizens who had resided in Frankfurt for thirty years as husbands of burgher women decided to join Vigny in requesting an imperial order for their admission to the citizenry.[62] The appeal to the Reichshofrat infuriated burgher merchants and the council alike; sentiment grew strong for an ordinance denying citizenship or denizenship to any immigrants from Switzerland (a measure that would not affect subjects of the Empire but would discriminate against the principal source of Calvinist migrants).[63] Burgher leaders were shocked to learn of Notebohm's support for the Calvinist appellants, especially when he succeeded in obtaining from the court an order forbidding any further council legislation or action against denizen-burgher marriages until the emperor had made a decisive pronouncement on Article 7 of the Citizens Agreement.[64] As they waited for the decision, Calvinists rushed several more cases into court, so that they would be settled in conjunction with the general pronouncement to come from the Reichshofrat.[65] Although it passed no new legislation, the council continued to deny the property rights claimed by denizens and their burgher wives, and in May and June of 1725 council members and burgher merchants worked together to strengthen the Inquisition Office's enforcement of existing legislation on denizens and other outsiders.[66]

62. These cases were discussed in Mangon's letters to Notebohm (9 January and 13 March 1723); ibid., 78–86.

63. Ibid., 91: letter of 16 March 1723.

64. Ibid., 244–307, for Mangon's copies of the documents involved in the appeals from April to October 1723; ibid., 318–320: RHR Conclusum (22 October 1723). For indications of discontent among other burgher leaders over Notebohm's actions taken without any consultation with them, see ibid., 254–256, 222–224: Mangon's letter of 14 August 1723; cf. 237–238: letter of 1 January 1724. The bitter and indefatigable Johann Jacob Böhler—also residing in Vienna at the time—wrote the burgher deputies that Notebohm had become the "Cardinal of the Calvinists"; though most members of the Ausschuss and officer corps were disturbed, only a few demanded his withdrawal from Vienna at this point. Even Hoppe made it clear, however, that Notebohm had acted alone on this issue.

65. The four most important—those of Elisabeth Geyssel, Anna Bassompierre, Andreas Heusler, and Johannes Otto—are summarized by Mangon, ibid., 357–391, 408–410, and passim.

66. Ibid., 454–460, for Notebohm's complaint to the RHR (7 January 1726) that the council was continuing to violate Article 7 of the Citizens Agreement; Ugb B76 Tt for the documents on improving enforcement by the Office of Inquisition.

The first of the nine imperial resolutions issued in November 1725 marked a victory for the Calvinists' interpretation of the Denizen Ordinance. It declared that the intention of Article 7 of the Citizens Agreement had been to limit the council's power of excluding outsiders; if a foreigner married a burgher widow or daughter, he could be denied citizenship only if he were so poor that he might need public relief. Article 8 of the Denizen Ordinance and the council decree of 9 August 1714 were therefore invalid, and the councilmen were ordered to admit honorable and wealthy men who married burgher women, provided that they paid a modest percentage of their assets as an entrance fee.[67] Although the council sent a delegation to Vienna to appeal various decisions contained in the resolutions, the two jurors Ochs and Kaib had little success; on 16 April 1726 the Reichshofrat repeated its stand of the previous December and further ordered the council to expedite the pending Calvinist cases by granting the denizens citizenship within two months.[68] After many delays caused by disputes over the amount of *Bürgergeld* to be paid, in October 1726 most of the Beisassen who had taken their cases to court received the privileges of citizenship.[69]

IV. Lutherans versus Calvinists, 1727–1732

The council and its Lutheran citizens were not willing, however, to concede victory to the Calvinists. As burgher leaders worked with the council to restore Article 8 of the Denizen Ordinance and to prevent Calvinists from gaining free public worship in Frankfurt, the struggle reached its most bitter stage during the years 1727 to 1732. The blow dealt the Lutheran burghers in 1725 and 1726 was somewhat softened by two reversals the Calvinists suffered in 1727. Under the protection of the Reichshofrat rulings, Reformed denizens continued to apply to the council for citizenship, and the city fathers tried to block their acceptance as long as possible. One means was to charge 5 percent of their assets as *Bürgergeld*, an amount all the denizens considered too high and some refused to pay. The council also demanded that denizens who had partnerships with burghers in violation of Article 7 of the Denizen Ordinance had to dissolve those partnerships before their applications for citizenship would be accepted.[70] An appeal to Count Schönborn, who

67. Müller, *Frankfurt contra Frankfurt*, I, 13. The resolution was published in Frankfurt on 24 January 1726.
68. Ibid., I, 129; cf. Französisch-reformirte Gemeinde, v 170, 486–502.
69. Ibid., 505b–582, passim.
70. That these were two of the council's most effective methods becomes clear in the appeal of the Calvinists to the RHR (9 April 1728) in HHSA Wien: RHR Decisa

had been given responsibility to oversee implementation of the decisions of 1725–1726, produced disappointing results: the commissioner upheld both the prohibition against denizen-burgher business partnerships and the council's assessment of the Bürgergeld at 5 percent of the denizen's assets.[71]

The Calvinists' request for free public worship in 1727 brought them a second, more important setback. Not only did the council refuse their petition, but it was able to rouse the burgher Ausschuss and the Committee of Nine to join actively in a common struggle against the Calvinist threat to their Lutheran community. The Reformed petition of 2 October 1727 reopened an old issue, for the Calvinists had not enjoyed free public worship in Frankfurt since 1561.[72] At different times private services were held under the auspices of Calvinist nobles residing in the city, and for a short time at the beginning of the seventeenth century (1601–1608) Calvinists used a small wooden church just outside the city wall. Most Reformed worshipers, however, had to ride a few miles outside Frankfurt to the village of Bockenheim, where the Count of Hesse-Hanau permitted them to hold their religious rites. Between 1608 and 1674 the council, despite many intercessions by Calvinist princes, denied at least seventeen petitions for permission to build a Reformed church in the city, and then, in 1686, it flatly refused to accept any more requests for the privilege of public worship either from the city's Reformed population or on its behalf. The Calvinists had no success in using the accessions to the imperial throne in 1705 and 1711 as occasions for renewed appeals over the council's head, and the years from 1711 to 1727 were relatively quiet for the issue. Another appeal to Vienna in 1719 came to nothing,[73] but Frau Rau, Gräfin von Pfalz, lived in the Schomburger

---

22 24. For the individual cases, see Mangon's summaries in Französisch-reformirte Gemeinde, v 170, 583–593.

71. Müller, *Frankfurt contra Frankfurt*, III, 89: commission decree (18 July 1727); the date 8 July 1727 given on page 89 is a mistake, and it is corrected on 90.

72. The issue is very thoroughly chronicled in the *Kirchen-Geschichte von denen Reformirten in Frankfurt am Mayn* (Frankfurt and Leipzig, 1751), which also gives reference to the original documents, most of which were published in *Franckfurtische Religions-Handlungen* (FftRH) in 1735. My discussion here is a very brief summary of the account in *Kirchen-Geschichte*, 248–272. Perhaps the best general essay on Frankfurt's Calvinists is Friedrich Scharff, "Die Niederländischen und die Französische Gemeinde in Frankfurt a. M.," *AFGK* 2nd series, 2 (1862), 245–317; Hermann Dechent, *Kirchengeschichte von Frankfurt am Main seit der Reformation* 2v (Leipzig and Frankfurt, 1913–1921) treats the Calvinists along with the few Catholics and the large Lutheran majority in the city.

73. *Kirchen-Geschichte*, 271, indicates that there was probably only a rumor of a Calvinist appeal to the RHR in 1719, but documents in the Archiv der Französisch-reformirten Gemeinde, v 168, 393–398, 248–249, indicate that such an appeal was in fact submitted. No outcome is recorded anywhere.

Hof in Frankfurt from 1717 until 1733 and held Reformed services which the city's Calvinists also attended regularly. Why they raised the issue of free public worship once again in October 1727 is not entirely clear, although the Calvinists seem to have believed that officials in Vienna were favorably disposed toward them and that they could gain religious privileges at the same time they pressed for enforcement of the Reichshofrat decisions of 1725–1726. In any case they appealed first to the city council and unwittingly played into the hands of the aristocrats.

The council consulted burgher leaders about the Calvinist appeal for the privilege of free worship, and as a result the officer corps, its Ausschuss, and the Committee of Nine all determined to join the magistrates in an active campaign against Calvinist attempts to enter the Bürgerschaft and win freedom of worship. Burgher leaders were pleased both by the council's refusal to consider the Reformed petition and by the fact that the councilmen, who had become concerned that the Calvinists might win imperial favor for their religious demands, turned to the Ausschuss and the Nine for advice and support. A plenary session of burgher leaders decided that the burgher deputies—who had not intervened in the matter since 1714—and the Nine should do whatever was necessary to block Calvinist moves for greater economic or religious privileges in Frankfurt. That the two groups were to assume an active and regular role in opposing the Calvinists is shown by the fact that they were to report to the entire officer corps on their efforts every month.[74]

The merchants' fight against Calvinist commercial competition now became an official campaign of the entire burgher party, working in cooperation with the council, against economic and religious penetration of the community by adherents of the Reformed faith. Since commercial elements completely monopolized the Committee of Nine and tended to dominate the Ausschuss as well, it seems only natural that economic interest would eventually cause official burgher leadership to abandon its initial defense of the Calvinist constitutional argument that Article 7 of the Citizens Agreement invalidated the Denizen Ordinance.[75] But it was the religious issue, raised by the Calvinists just after their victory in the matter of burgher-denizen marriages and used by the council to prove the extent of Calvinist designs, which served as the catalyst to activate burgher leaders in the struggle of natives against outsiders and of

74. 51er Protocolla 1726–28, 227–233: meeting (10 October 1727) of the deputies and the Nine with the officer corps.
75. For the initial position of the Ausschuss, see above, 214. Mangon mentions in a letter to Notebohm dated 16 May 1723, in the Französisch-reformirte Gemeinde, v 170, 90, that Johann Gerhard Münch, a member of the Committee of Nine, was most vociferous in his opposition to Calvinist denizens. On the predominance of commercial elements in the burgher party, cf. Chapter 5, 133–138.

Lutheranism against Calvinism. The denial of free worship had always been considered the best method to discourage Calvinist immigration and economic competition, and this economic motive was reinforced in 1727 by the genuine antipathy toward the Reformed religion shared by most Lutherans in every social group in the city. Nor should we forget the political advantage reaped by the aristocratic council, which took the first step to arouse burgher leaders in 1727. While Dr. Johann Christoph Ochs and his fellow councilmen worked over the next years for several modifications of imperial decisions which would benefit the aristocrats, the attention of burgher leaders was diverted from the fight against the council and concentrated on their efforts to combat the Calvinist threat. A division within the citizenry between Lutherans and Calvinists—so feared by Reformed leaders like Abraham Mangon in 1722—did weaken the general cause of the burgher party after 1727, and the irony of the situation is that the Calvinists themselves provided the council with both the occasion and the issue necessary to turn burgher leadership against Reformed citizens and denizens.

The next four years saw a bitter war of appeals and counterappeals to the imperial court in Vienna. While the Calvinists continued to rely on the arguments they had developed earlier and on Captain Notebohm's aid, they did extend their economic demands. Their petition of 9 April 1728 to the Reichshofrat outlined clearly what steps Reformed leaders felt were necessary to make Frankfurt the open community they hoped it would become. The most important request was for the granting of citizenship to any outsider, whether he married a burgher or not, strictly on the basis of his honorable birth and conduct and his ability to prove that he held assets worth at least 200 fl. as a craftsman or 300 fl. in any other occupation. But there was to be no discrimination based on religion, national background, or even the occupation of the immigrant. Only a nominal charge for men and none at all for women was suggested to replace the 5-percent Bürgergeld being levied by the council on wealthy immigrants. There could be no unexplained rejections of applicants for citizenship, no limitations against joint burgher-denizen business enterprises, and no oaths to bind denizens to the old ordinance of 1708 which had been nullified by imperial decrees. Finally, Reformed leaders requested an end to any kind of exclusion from either handicraft or commercial occupations—all should become open to any burgher.[76] Such a program combined with free public worship for all three reli-

76. HHSA Wien: RHR Decisa 2224: petition presented 9 April 1728 by Reformed leaders to the RHR; the petition was summarized for burgher leaders in 51er Protocolla 1726–28, insert between 169 and 170. The rescript issued by the RHR on 20 April 1728 essentially affirmed the decisions of 1725–26 but did not deal with the more far-reaching requests of the Calvinists; Müller, *Frankfurt contra Frankfurt*, I, 132–133.

gions officially tolerated in the Empire would have completely altered Frankfurt society, and the Lutheran citizenry—no matter how hard it worked for reforms—fought vigorously to preserve the established social order.

During the last years of the constitutional conflict, burgher leaders, working in conjunction with a Committee of Fourteen formed in 1728 to serve as special spokesmen for the Lutheran citizens against the Calvinists, articulated defensive arguments to counter those advanced in Reformed petitions and pamphlets.[77] I shall not discuss each of the principal documents involved in the controversy; instead a summary of the burgher position as it emerged from some of them is sufficient to show how the Lutherans defended an exclusive religious and economic community.[78] First the burghers made clear their agreement with the council's view that the Calvinists intended to take over the city of Frankfurt completely. Established citizens had already felt the economic effects of admitting wealthy Calvinists as new burghers: Reformed merchants controlled all English wares traded in the city as well as most stapling, exchange, and commission enterprises; although they did provide work for local craftsmen and laborers, their usual practice was to give their work to their coreligionists or even to outsiders. The council had acted at the request of the majority of Frankfurters when it sought to discourage Calvinist immigration. Fees levied at 5 percent of the immigrant's assets, strict enforcement of the Denizen Ordinance, and a more exclusive, not more liberal, policy toward denizens and their admissions to the citizenry were necessary to save Frankfurt from ruin.

Burgher leaders rejected the Calvinists' dynamic and optimistic picture of the city's economy; they argued that Frankfurt's economic potential was already fully developed and that further population increase would only mean a decline in the living standard for the individual burgher. The prosperity of the great commercial centers of Europe depended not on the number of merchants who resided in them but on their favorable geographical locations. Frankfurt had developed as much commerce as was possible in its particular region in the center of the continent, and comparisons with Amsterdam, Hamburg, Lübeck, or

77. On the formation of the Committee of Fourteen—one representative for each quarter—under the auspices of the officer corps, see 51er Protocolla 1726–28, 259–268: meetings of 2, 3, and 12 July 1728.

78. For the summary which follows, I have drawn chiefly from HHSA Wien: RHR Decisa 2224: the petition of the Committee of Fourteen submitted to the RHR on 7 October 1728 and once again on 20 June 1729 and from two tracts written to refute the Calvinist "Reflections on the Denizen Ordinance"—"Gründliche Widerleg- und Abfertigung der neulich in Druck gekommenen sogenannten Reflexionum . . ." and the "Gegen-Reflexiones," both of which were later published in FftRH, I, "Magistratus Bericht," Beilage F, Adjunctus 2, 32–52, and Adjunctus 3, 53–56.

Bremen were not relevant. No matter how many immigrants might come to the city, Frankfurt could never become another Amsterdam, as the Calvinists liked to maintain, for the Main was not an ocean and local merchants could never launch ships to the West Indies. The city's great commercial boom at the end of the seventeenth and beginning of the eighteenth century had resulted from the war, not from the large number of immigrants; in fact, the war had led to an increase in the number of merchants, and when the war ended, Frankfurt's prosperity diminished even though its merchant population continued to increase. Wholesalers who seemed to be bringing money into the city were, in fact, bringing more goods than could be sold; the flooded wholesale market led to many bankruptcies among the older firms and great difficulty for only moderately wealthy young burghers who wished to establish new firms. Meanwhile, Frankfurt faced high rents and living costs which were the real causes for the movement of the silk industry and other manufactures from the city to surrounding villages.

Given this view of a more static local economy, the Lutheran burghers argued that the council had to protect established citizens against an influx of new people. The duty of constituted authority was to see that a city had neither too few nor too many inhabitants, and, as the Committee of Nine put it,

> the principles of all well-formulated [domestic] policies are that burghers be cherished and preferred over immigrants, that natives be left to make their living and protected from foreigners; if, however, . . . the petition of the Reformed leaders were followed, if the magistracy had to accept as burghers all persons regardless of their sex, religion, national background, trade, skill, or handicraft, and if a denizen could live without any regulation or responsibility and could therefore be in a better situation than the burgher himself, then the exact opposite would result.[79]

If a city or an individual handicraft was too crowded, outsiders simply could not be taken in. Just as craftsmen were worried about too many masters in Frankfurt, so merchants were also concerned that their ranks were overfull. The slogan that "freedom is the very essence of commerce" was correct when understood to mean that merchants could not be burdened with heavy imposts, but to interpret the saying as license for denizens to ruin the trade of burgher merchants was without any rational basis. If outsiders were to have an open door into the Bürgerschaft by

79. A rather free translation of two magnificent baroque sentences found in 51er Protocolla 1729, 217–218: statement of Committee of Nine read in a meeting (28 October 1729) with the officer corps and Captain Notebohm.

marrying burghers, there was no need to tolerate them as denizens any longer. Surely large fees should be paid for admission to burgher privileges, and the council should exercise great care in admitting foreigners. The wealth requirements set up in 1613 and advocated now by the Calvinists, for example, were far too low for current circumstances. Burgher leaders argued as well that those old requirements and even Article 7 of the Citizens Agreement should not apply to the Reformed, since the ordinance of 1628 against the admission of Calvinists to the citizenry as well as the prohibition of their public worship inside the city were valid measures passed by the council to provide economic security and to preserve the Lutheran religion from outsiders who, if they were in power, would not concern themselves about the prosperity of others or tolerate Lutheranism. While religious arguments were mustered to strengthen their case, the Lutheran citizens worked chiefly to restore the council's argument that economic necessity was the real motivation behind careful regulation of denizens and their exclusion from citizenship.

The burgher Ausschuss and the Committees of Nine and Fourteen not only waged a bitter pamphlet war against the Calvinists, but they also attempted, without success, to end Captain Notebohm's active support for the Reformed position on the Denizen Ordinance and free trade. The burgher leaders were convinced, and with good reason, that Reformed success in challenging the Denizen Ordinance in 1725–1726 had been due to the captain's influence in Vienna. The general displeasure with Notebohm's tendency to act on his own initiative without keeping other leaders informed of his moves was compounded by his siding with the Calvinist minority against the most powerful interests in the burgher party on the issue of denizen-burgher marriages. Notebohm did not petition for specific religious privileges for the Calvinists, but he did accept and use their argument that free trade, a liberal immigration policy, and religious toleration were the real foundations for commercial prosperity and expansion. Burgher alarm that their own representative was working for the Calvinists against them led many to demand the captain's recall from Vienna, and in 1729 he was summoned to Frankfurt to explain why he did not communicate fully with leaders there, why he had become a representative for the Calvinists in matters that lay outside his authority, and why he had not worked more vigorously against the Jews.[80] Notebohm acquitted himself well: after affirming that he had done everything possible to have the regulations on the Jews enforced, he went on to explain that only the provision of more funds

80. Notebohm was asked to return to explain himself on 27 May 1729; 51er Protocolla 1729, 64. He arrived on 3 September and met with the officer corps and Ausschuss on 10 September 1729, during which meeting the issues mentioned were raised; ibid., 167–172.

THE DENIZENS

227

to hire copyists would enable him to keep Frankfurt leaders apprised of all his dealings with imperial officials.

The captain asserted that his original authorization from the officer corps and burghers had charged him with two tasks—the complete restoration of the Citizens Agreement and strict enforcement of the Judenstättigkeit. In conformity with that mandate and having no second *Vollmacht* from the corps changing his instructions, Notebohm had simply supported Article 7 of the Citizens Agreement against the council's unconstitutional penalities on burgher women who married denizens.[81] The captain agreed that if a formal change of mandate were presented to him, he would then consider what steps he should take.[82] The officers did not revise the mandate in 1729 or ask Notebohm to step down as their representative, for they recognized the high favor he enjoyed with the Schönborns and other imperial officials. After his return to Vienna, Notebohm acted consistently with his previous views and continued to aid the Calvinists.[83] The Ausschuss insisted that on this one issue Notebohm no longer represented *its* views. As the time of decision neared, however, burgher leaders became more and more angry with the captain's stubborn insistence on supporting both the constitutional position and the economic views of the Calvinists. The relations between him and other burgher leaders, especially the Committee of Nine, degenerated in 1730–1731 into a bitter quarrel, with both the captain and the Nine maintaining that the other had no authority to speak for the entire citizenry on the Calvinist question.[84] Mutual recriminations grew so sharp before the imperial decision that the embittered Notebohm chose to remain in Vienna after 1732 rather than return to live out his days among his fellow burghers in Frankfurt.[85]

81. Ibid.

82. Ibid., 220: meeting of 28 October 1729.

83. His most important statement was the "Allerunterthänigste Anzeig ad Resolutiones Caesareas de 22. November 1725 . . . in specie die Beisassen-Ordnung betreffend," presented to the RHR 13 August 1731 and including another printing of the "Reflections on the Denizen Ordinance."

84. Deteriorating relations between Notebohm and the officers' Ausschuss may be traced in the 51er Protocolla 1730 and 1731, passim; Protocolla 1732, 176–177, shows that the officers finally voted to recall him as their representative in Vienna. See also HHSA Wien: RHR Decisa 2200: Memorial presented by the Committee of Fourteen to the RHR 29 May 1730; RHR Decisa 2232: the "Declaration" on the denizen issue presented by the Nine to the RHR 22 November 1731, which contained a copy of a statement from the officer corps that Notebohm no longer represented their views on the Calvinists as well as a copy of the "Grundliche Widerleg- und Abfertigung . . ." See finally Notebohm's Memorial (8 November 1732?) in RHR Decisa 2174 for his views of the Committee of Nine; he refers there to a "Nothdringliche Vorstellung" presented by the Nine to the RHR on 18 October 1731, but I have not seen its very sharp attack on Notebohm.

85. Hohenemser, *Verfassungsstreit*, 368.

Of the three imperial resolutions issued in 1732 which ended Frankfurt's constitutional conflict, the second addressed itself to the issue of granting citizenship to outsiders.[86] The resolution brought several setbacks to the Calvinists. Outsiders who married burgher widows or daughters were to be admitted to the Bürgerschaft as long as they were willing to pay a Bürgergeld that amounted to 5 percent of their assets[87] and only if they could produce an official statement from authorities in their former residences that Frankfurt burghers could, under similar circumstances, obtain citizenship there. Not only did the Calvinists fail to gain almost unrestricted admission and a lower fee, but the clause about the possibility of reciprocal arrangements between Frankfurt and the immigrant's homeland was intentionally added to cut down the number of Reformed merchants who would qualify for citizenship. Burgher leaders and imperial officials were certain that Calvinists coming from France, Switzerland, and even Holland would not be able to produce evidence of reciprocity; burgher economic arguments had been effective enough to influence the Reichshofrat to place obstacles in the path of immigrant merchants, while it formally adhered to its previous decision on burgher-denizen marriages.[88] Moreover, Article 7 of the Denizen Ordinance, which had outlawed business partnerships between Beisassen and citizens, was confirmed. The success of burgher efforts during the last years of the conflict was further demonstrated by the imperial government's order that the council not accept any more immigrants as denizens unless it had special reasons. Despite the influence so often exerted by Captain Notebohm, the Reichshofrat accepted the view that citizens had to be protected from outside economic penetration. And a final disappointment for the Calvinists came with the decision of the court that religious privileges had to be dealt with separately from the economic issues raised by the Denizen Ordinance; Reformed leaders were advised to petition the council once again and then, if necessary, to appeal to the imperial courts for free public worship. The Calvinists followed this advice, but they had to fight burgher opposition until 1787 before they enjoyed the same religious privileges as Catholics and Lutherans in Frankfurt.

The burgher victory in 1732 led to the publication of a revised Denizen Ordinance in 1735. The only change from the original ordinance of 1708, however, was the deletion of Article 8, in accordance with the imperial decision that a female citizen's economic privileges could not be

86. Müller, *Frankfurt contra Frankfurt*, III, 20–21.

87. Wealthy female immigrants who married burghers were to pay only 2.5 percent of their assets; ibid., 20.

88. HHSA Wien: RHR Vota 15, 231r–260v: votum of 8 March 1732, on which the resolution itself was based.

abridged because she married a denizen.[89] Although some of the council's advisers espoused more liberal economic views,[90] most Frankfurters clearly rejected the open society proposed by the city's Calvinist minority. The Lutheran majority, which predominated both in the city council and in the leadership of the burgher party, was determined to preserve its spiritual control of the city. The council's political strategy and the merchants' economic demands found strong support in the deep-seated religious animosity that united most citizens against the Calvinists. Religion might be a cause of conflict in the city, but it was also a basis for communal solidarity for the large majority of Frankfurt burghers. Similarly, the notion of the community as a protected economic sphere united not only the city's craftsmen but also its retailers and wholesalers. The comparison, found in the pamphlet literature of the denizen controversy, between merchants already established in the city and artisans organized in handicraft corporations is a suggestive one, for it points to their common response to their economic situations. As a class, merchants faced open market competition which threatened their security, and they used their legal status as burghers to appeal for protection against the outsiders. Just as the artisan fought to restrict the number of masters in his craft and struck out at illegal intrusion into his market, so Frankfurt's big merchants attacked the economic privileges of their denizen competitors and moved to exclude them from the Bürgerschaft. Both groups sought protection from their class situations in the safety of a closed social order based on their legal privileges as citizens.

89. Müller, *Frankfurt contra Frankfurt*, III, 20–21, also makes clear the revisions in the renewed ordinance of 1735.

90. See the opinions of the syndics on the Denizen Ordinance presented to the council in May 1733; Ugb B78 Mm or, for more readable copies, Samlung vors Schatzungs Amt, ed. Johann Matthäus Hoppe (collection in the city archive, 1781 ff.), X, 155–249.

Conclusion

Conflict and Community

Examination of the various social groups living in Frankfurt has revealed the particulars of a society in conflict. Rather than summarizing here the problems faced by different residents or the specific rivalries among them, we must now consider the more general nature of these conflicts and their effects on the community as a whole. We can distinguish two kinds of conflict in the city: the first was a struggle for power within the corporate body of citizens, and the second pitted burghers against the outsiders permitted to reside in Frankfurt under conditions of inferiority.

The first conflict threatened to tear the community apart. Over the last decades of the seventeenth century there was a steady accumulation of grievances and disputes within the Bürgerschaft. Rather than canceling one another out, as Coser argues is often the case with multiple conflicts in modern or open societies,[1] these quarrels reinforced one another and could all be directed finally against the magistracy. The council was so unresponsive to the demands of most burghers that a party of opposition gained cohesive strength while the polarity between the council and its citizenry became acute. Burgher groups resolved their internal quarrels in an effort to strengthen their resistance to the city government. The more enterprising brewers settled their differences

1. Lewis Coser, *The Functions of Social Conflict* (New York, 1956), 78–79.

with poorer masters over the employment of outside tapsters, for example, so that the entire craft could fight the council more effectively. At the same time, citizen groups as diverse as small craftsmen and big wholesale merchants, with rather different grievances and economic interests, were able to form a common party under the leadership of the militia officers in order to present a strong, united front against the council. As this party of opposition gained internal cohesion, the traditional polity seemed to be torn apart in the constitutional conflict known in the imperial courts as "Frankfurt contra Frankfurt."

Yet the constitutional changes of the early eighteenth century did not sever but only modified the traditional relationship between the aristocracy and the "common" citizens. The second type of conflict in Frankfurt—between burghers and outsiders—stayed the disruptive potential of the first. The fight against the magistrates seldom evoked the degree of bitterness that conflicts with the Jews or with the wealthy denizens did. In the end the clashes with outsiders mitigated the antagonism between the aristocratic council and its burgher opposition and reminded all Frankfurt citizens of the privileges, interests, and values they shared. The Jews were the pariah group: Frankfurters loathed them. The council's willingness to tolerate Jewish retail activities for political and financial reasons outraged burgher artisans and retailers, yet no one accused the aristocrats of any affection for Jews. Hatred of the Jew was one important element in the deep-seated religious unity which became clearer as the council and its opponents found themselves joint defenders of their city against Calvinist penetration. Determination to preserve the essentially Lutheran character of the community united the magistrates, the burgher officer corps, and the overwhelming majority of citizens against the denizens. The same prejudice inspired the exclusion of native Catholics from city offices and foreign Catholics from admission to the Bürgerschaft. These religious conflicts with outsiders (intensified by economic rivalries) promoted integration of the Frankfurt citizenry. By underscoring the legal distinctions between burghers and outsiders, the clashes reinforced the traditional group identity and solidarity of the citizens.

The constitutional conflict laid bare all the tensions in Frankfurt society, but it also reawakened in the citizenry an awareness of its corporate traditions and a profound sense of its existence as a privileged community. The conflict impeded radical structural changes in government and society because it restored unity and cohesion to the Bürgerschaft. Frankfurt's history thus provides ample empirical support for the emphasis, found in the theoretical writings of Georg Simmel, Emile Durkheim, and especially Lewis Coser, on the positive and integrative as opposed to the disruptive functions of social conflict. But we must examine the situation from yet another point of view to understand why the disorder in the city should have led to this conservative result. "Whether social conflict is beneficial to internal adaptation or not depends," according to Coser, ". . . on the type of social structure within which it occurs."[2] My final task is to present a general characterization of Frankfurt's social structure.

Despite tendencies toward a modern or rationalistic social order, Frankfurt society remained essentially traditional in the seventeenth and eighteenth centuries. Significant changes should not be underestimated: the development of a larger fulltime bureaucracy; administrative reorganization which made government more efficient and less arbitrary; the expansion of the ruling elite to make it responsive to a wider segment of the Bürgerschaft; closer integration of the city's commercial and financial enterprises with the international nexus centered in Amsterdam; the relative decline of corporatively organized handicraft industry in the urban economy; the tendency within the crafts for larger, more entrepreneurial masters to leave their fellows behind; a blurring of the previously clearer distinctions in the official social hierarchy by the complex changes of the century following the Thirty Years War—all combined to make the Frankfurt of the early eighteenth century substantially different from that of the sixteenth century. Yet these changes were accomplished within traditional political and social patterns which left the community with a decidedly conservative tone. I refer to such phenomena as the moderate character of burgher political demands, which allowed the aristocratic party to maintain a strong hold on city government. Though the constitutional conflict did bring the most capable individuals to the fore, a clear pattern of kinship relations—so typical of traditional polities—characterized the burgher officer corps as well as the aristocratic council. Seldom did the opposition present a radical alternative to the old order in Frankfurt. Most burgher merchants and artisans firmly opposed the commercial and industrial liberalization that might have benefited entrepreneurs. The burghers chose to rely on their traditional legal position, the special economic privileges derived from their status as citizens, rather than on their ability to compete in an open market.

We are therefore justified in arguing that while class analysis is important to our study of social groups in Frankfurt, considerations of status are even more useful in explaining burgher thought and action in the early modern period. Various disputes in the city can be seen as class conflicts: the concern of burgher artisans and retailers for their market situation led them to demand tighter control over the admission of immigrants into crafts as well as an end to Jewish and Italian retail-

2. Ibid., 151.

ing. Burgher wholesalers sought to limit the economic activities of deni-zens, so that they themselves could take over all the commission and sta-pling business in the city. These groups of citizens found their class positions threatened by powerful outside interests, and they bitterly attacked the aristocratic government for its failure to maintain their privileges.

The Frankfurt burghers acted not only within such class units having clearly defined economic goals but also—and more importantly—within status groups concerned primarily with the preservation of their own social security, their values, and their corporate community. Artisans and retailers, as a class, were directly affected by the retail trade of Jews and the Italian denizens, but other citizens supported these burghers not out of economic motives but from a desire to keep the community Lutheran. And the community was not defined merely in terms of its religious values. It also encompassed a corporate social order, which as-signed groups of men a certain rank in Frankfurt society and was sup-posed to guarantee them enough security to maintain a "respectable" style of life. The first criteria for citizenship, we must remember, were legitimate birth, honorable conduct, and economic independence. The burgher craftsman did not expect to be wealthy, but he demanded a corporate regulation of production which would give all artisans an op-portunity for an "honorable" livelihood. Rector Schudt's vivid descrip-tion of Jewish competition in the city epitomized the burgher's disdain for the peddler and concern for his own *honnête Lebens-Art*, which in-cluded a house, some hired help, cleanliness, and upright conduct.[3]

This sense of social station—even among the lower orders in Frank-furt—was the base on which the community of burghers rested. The twin pillars reinforcing the whole structure were the legal privileges enjoyed by citizens alone and the strong residues of corporatism which continued to influence burgher thought and action. A sense of corporate identity was especially strong in the aristocratic lodges and among the artisans, but it was also evident even among wholesale and retail merchants. Furthermore, the existence of conflict in Frankfurt society was not in-compatible with the persistence of corporative arrangements. The no-tion that the corporatively organized societies of medieval or early mod-ern Europe enjoyed inherently more harmonious group relationships than modern societies is unrealistic; only a thoroughly unromanticized approach to the study of corporatism will enable us to assess its concrete meaning. In Frankfurt we have seen that corporate loyalties and inter-ests could determine both the direction that conflict took and its effects on the entire community. Corporative social arrangements were surely weaker in the seventeenth century than they had been in the fifteenth,

3. See above, 194.

but the constitutional conflict did more to strengthen old social bonds than to loosen them.

Frankfurt's corporative social order was further reinforced by the peculiar balance of social forces within the citizenry. My previous emphasis on the exclusionist character of the Bürgerschaft must not blur our perspective on the community. Immigrants were still admitted to the citizen body in large numbers, even after the burghers gained joint administrative power with the council. Qualifications for admission were more carefully checked, but Frankfurt never adopted a policy that would have made citizenship, like freemanship in the larger English cities, the preserve of only a small percentage of its population. The citizenry always included diverse elements—aristocratic, mercantile, and artisanal—with strong competing claims and influences on the community. The vitality of all three constituents gave the city its conservative stamp and explains the balance of political forces that emerged from the constitutional changes of the early eighteenth century.

Perhaps most impressive was the staying power of the aristocracy in this important commercial center. The demand of the merchants and wealthy artisans who led the burgher officer corps was to share power with the aristocrats, not to take all authority from them. While the reforms of 1725 broke the tight control over the magistracy exercised by the two aristocratic lodges, the Limpurger and Frauensteiner continued to enjoy a special place in the constitution. Of the three nominees for each upper-bench position on the council, one was to be a Limpurger, the second a Frauensteiner, and the third a "distinguished burgher"—preferably a Graduate but perhaps a merchant. The composition of the senate changed gradually, and the most significant gains over the next generation were those of the Graduates. Indeed, the two most prominent political figures in eighteenth-century Frankfurt were holders of doctorates: Johann Christoph Ochs von Ochsenstein, leader of the council during the constitutional conflict, and Johann Wolfgang Textor, Goethe's grandfather. The full integration of the educated elite at the highest levels of authority strengthened the council vis-à-vis the newly established burgher committees, and the aristocratic tone of Frankfurt government was maintained. While the aristocrats were less wealthy than the big merchants, they managed to hold a substantial share of civic power. Their superior social station was simply unquestioned.

Important merchants of the seventeenth and early eighteenth centuries, unlike their late medieval predecessors, were only rarely accepted into the aristocratic societies. As distinguished burghers they held some posts in the magistracy, but their real achievement during the constitutional conflict was the establishment of burgher committees through which they could have effective sway over those areas of government which concerned commercial people most. Exclusive control of the Committee of Nine and preponderant influence in the Fifty-One (or *Bürgerausschuss*) gave merchants joint authority with the council over the city's finances and administrative machinery. Although they remained dissatisfied with the infrequent nomination of commercial leaders for council seats, merchants knew that theirs was real power, not merely a token voice, in Frankfurt politics. Their proposals for the city's commercial and financial policies would continue, of course, to get the favorable hearing they had always received from the council.

In contrast to the merchants, Frankfurt artisans enjoyed a guaranteed but largely ineffectual representation in the magistracy itself. Moreover, they gained little leverage in municipal decision-making as the result of the constitutional changes of the early eighteenth century. Their craft supervisors remained dependent on the aristocratic council, and they had few spokesmen in the Burgher Committee of Fifty-One. The Handwerke were not permitted as exclusive a membership policy as they wanted, but artisan influence on industrial organization did remain sufficiently strong to resist any changes that might have created a labor force available for exploitation by eighteenth-century entrepreneurs.[4] The crafts exercised subtle influence rather than direct power in Frankfurt, but their basic claims on the community were respected. This seems only fitting, since they epitomized the corporate spirit which, although somewhat weakened, was still vital enough in the seventeenth and early eighteenth centuries to shape Frankfurt politics and society.

4. Cf. the discussion by Max Barkhausen, "Der Aufstieg der rheinischen Industrie im 18. Jahrhundert und die Entstehung eines industriellen Grossbürgertums," *Rheinische Vierteljahrsblätter* 19 (1954), 135–177, passim, where Frankfurt provides a prime example of the traditional social arrangements and attitudes which protected privileged artisans and thus obliged new industries to develop outside the major cities.

Bibliography

I. Manuscript Sources

Haus-, Hof- und Staatsarchiv Wien

RHR Decisa: 2075, 2146, 2148, 2149, 2152, 2169, 2174, 2175, 2190, 2192, 2198, 2201, 2203, 2205, 2219, 2224, 2230, 2234.

RHR Vota: 15.

RHR Relationes: 37.

Bayerisches Staatsarchiv Würzburg

Mainzer Regierungsakten: Kaiserliche Kommissionen: 138, 143.

Stadtarchiv Frankfurt am Main

Nota bene: Most of the documents I have used in Frankfurt are classified by "Ugb" number; rather than listing all these items individually here, I have identified each one where it first appears in the footnotes to the text. The following are materials that do not fall into the original "Ugb" classification system.

Archiv der französisch reformirten Gemeinde: 5, 150, 167, 168, 170, 171, 171a, 171b, 172.

[Bender von Bienenthal, Jacob,] "Merckwurdige Aufsäze und Bemerckungen die Stadt Franckfurt betreffend von Jacob Bender von Bienenthal 1669." A bound manuscript, apparently incomplete, dated 20 August 1669 and found in the Leonhardi Nachlass, Kistchen 27.

Bothe Nachlass.

Bürgerbücher.

Bürgermeisterbücher.

Concepta Edictorum. 12v.

Corpus Legum Francofurtensium oder Neue Sammlung derer Raths-Schöffen und Aembter Verordnungen . . . 12v.

Extractus aus Kommissions Akten zur Geschichte des 51er Kollegs.

Frauenstein Protokolle 1598–1717.

Geheime Deputation und Correspondenz: 3, 4, 5, 6.

"Geschriebene Franckforther Chronick." Dated 4 April 1718 on the title page but has entries to 1732.

Holzhausen Archiv: 165, 175.

Index realis Chronologicus Corporis Legum Francofurtensium oder nach der Materie und Zeit verfertigtes Register, über die Raths-Schöffen auch Aembter Verordnungen der Stadt Frankfurt am Main vom Jahr 1345 bis auf das Jahr 1784 inclusive verfertigt von Herrn G. L. v. Rücker JVD^re et Archivario.

Leonhardi Nachlass: Faszikel 12; Kistchen 2, 8, 24, 26, 27, 28, 29, 30.

Neuener-Amts Protocoll: A (1727–1736).

Ochs, Johann Georg, "Chronik über die Jahren 1699–1713."

Protocolla gehalten bey Versammlung Bürgerlichen Herren Ober-Officiers und Deputirten. 1726–1732.

Protocolle so bey Einleitung des neuen Löbl. Bürger-Ausschusses und derselben Berathschlagungen angefangen und fortgeführet worden. 1733 ff.

Räthe und Residenten: III.

Ratswahlen: B23, B24, B26.

Samlung vors Schatzungs Amt, ed. Johann Matthäus Hoppe, JUL und Senator. 15v and 2v indices.

Verzeichnis der Rechneiamtsprotokolle 1641–1776.

[Waldschmidt, Johann Martin,] "Joh. Mart. Waldschmidts Chronicon der Stadt Frankfurt am Main." c. 1704.

[Walther, Johann Friederich,] "Aufzeichnungen des Johann Friederich Walther meist aus 1719–1733."

II. Printed Sources

. . . allerunterthänigst-Rechts begründete Additional-Anzeig ad exhibitum de . . . Intervenientischer Bürgerschaft in Sachen Judenschafft zu Franckfurth contra E. L. Magistrat daselbst . . . das Bau-Wesen betreffend. Pamphlet presented by the burgher representative in Vienna to the RHR 28 September 1714.

Beyerbach, Johann Conradin, *Sammlung der Verordnungen der Reichs-stadt Frankfurt 1530–1806.* 11v in 5. Frankfurt, 1798–1818.

Böhler, Johann Jacob, *Wahr-gegründte Demonstration* . . . N. p., 1711.

Bothe, Friedrich, ed., *Frankfurts wirtschaftlich-soziale Entwicklung vor dem dreissigjährigen Kriege und der Fettmilchaufstand (1612–1616)* v2: *Statistische Bearbeitungen und urkundliche Belege.* Frankfurt, 1920. Volume 1 never appeared.

Brown, Edward, *Account of Several Travels through a great part of Germany.* London, 1677.

Bücher, Karl, ed., *Frankfurter Amtsurkunden.* Frankfurt, 1901.

Deductio Dass E. E. Rath nach dem Burger-Vertrag ohne der Burger-schafft / oder dero Deputirten Einwilligung Extraordinar-Anlagen nicht machen / noch die alte Imposten erhöhen könne: Auch von denen Einkünfften der Stadt Rechnung zu geben gehalten sey. Bey Kayserl. erster Commission den 23. Febr. 1714 übergeben.

Auff das am 26. Januar ergangene Decretum anbefohlene gehorsame Erklärungs-Deduction, auss welchen Ursachen die an die Judenschafft beschehene Uberlassung des völkerischen Gartens . . . ohngültig und solche Stück wiederum der Bürgerschafft einzuraumen. Pamphlet submitted to the imperial commission in February 1714.

Franckfurtische Religions-Handlungen . . . 2v. Frankfurt, 1735. A collection of many important documents, among them Notebohm's "Reflectiones auff die Anno 1708. den 5. Junii errichtete Beysassen-Ordnung"; the "Grundliche Widerleg- und Abfertigung . . ."; and the "Gegen-Reflexiones."

alleruntertänigsten-gründliche Gegen-Information und Exceptiones Sub & Obreptionis auff das . . . kayserl. Rescript . . . in Sachen Judenschafft zu Franckfurth am Mayn contra den Magistrat daselbsten . . . das Bau-Wesen betreffend. Submitted to the RHR 23 July 1714.

Gehorsame Vorstellung betreffend die Judenschafft und dero Stättigkeit . . . Submitted to the imperial commission on 14 May 1714.

Historische Nachrichten, Über die in des Heil. Reichs-Stadt Franckfurth am Mayn zwischen dem damaligen Edlen Rath, und Ehrbahren Bürgerschafft vor 100. Jahren fürgewesene Strittigkeiten, und darbey, vorgekommene Fata funestra, und wie weit auff die jetzige Bürgerschafft darab Application zu machen. N.p., 1715.

Lehnemann, Johannes, *Historische Nachricht von der vormahls in sachzehenden Jahrhundert berühmten evangelisch-lutherischen Kirche in Antorff und der daraus entstandenen niederländischen Gemeinde Augspurgischer Confession in Franckfurt am Mayn, aus beglaubten Urkunden mitgeteilt.* Frankfurt, 1725.

Lersner, Achilles Augustus, *Der weit-berühmten freyen reichs- wahl- und handels-stadt Franckfurt am Mayn Chronica, oder Ordentliche Beschreibung der Stadt Franckfurt.* 2v. Frankfurt, 1706–1734.

Allerunterthänigst gründliche Vorstellung und allergehorsamster Bitten kurtzgefaste Marginal-Ammerckungen des impetratischen Magistrats . . . die vor zwey Kayserl. Commissionen verwiesene und seithero untersuchte anmassliche Gravamina betreffend. Frankfurt, 1715.

Moser, Johann Jacob, *Alte und neue Reichs-Hof-Raths Conclusa.* Frankfurt and Ebersdorff, 1743–1745.

————, *Von der Reichs-Stättischen Regiments-Verfassung.* Frankfurt and Leipzig, 1772.

Müller, Christoph Sigismund, ed., *Vollständige Sammlung der Kaiserlichen in Sachen Frankfurt contra Frankfurt ergangenen Resolutionen und anderer dahin einschlagender Stadt-Verwaltungs-Grund-Gezzen.* Three parts in one volume. Frankfurt, 1776–1779.

Notebohm, Johann Dieterich, *Allerunterthänigste Anzeig ad Resolutiones Caesareas de 22. November 1725 . . . in specie die Beisassen-Ordnung betreffend.* Presented to the RHR 13 August 1731.

Orth, Johann Philipp, *Nöthig- und nützlich-erachtete Anmerckungen über die . . . so genannten erneuerten Reformation der Stadt Franckfurth am Mayn.* 6v (Hauptband; 4 Fortsetzungen; 1 Zusätze). Frankfurt, 1731–1775.

Privilegia et Pacta des H. Römischen Reichsstadt Franckfurt am Mayn sammt der Goldenen Bulla Caroli IV. Frankfurt, 1728. A collection printed in accordance with the first imperial resolution of 22 November 1725.

Des H. R. Reichs Freyen Wahl- und Handels-Stadt Franckfurt am Mayn allgemeiner Raths- und Stadt-Calender. Frankfurt, 1734 ff.

Schmidt, Benno, ed., *Frankfurter Zunfturkunden bis zum Jahre 1612.* 2v. Frankfurt, 1914.

Schudt, Johann Jacob, *Jüdische Merckwürdigkeiten . . . sammt einer vollständigen Franckfurter Juden-Chronick . . .* 3v. Frankfurt and

Leipzig, 1714. *Continuation.* 4v (three parts and a supplement). Frankfurt, 1717–1718.

"Sincerus," *Unparteyische Meynung und Gedancken über die so titulirte Re- und Gegen-Reflexiones auf die in Franckfurth anno 1708. den 5. Junii Obrigkeitlich errichtete so genannte Beysassen-Ordnung.* N.p., 1732.

Species Facti in Sachen der christlichen Handels-Leuthen zu Franckfurth contra die Judenschafft daselbsten in Puncto übertrettener Stättigkeit. Frankfurt, 1726.

Verordnungen des Rats, rechtliche und gewerbliche Verhältnisse der Juden in Frankfurt a. M. betr., soweit einzeln vorhanden. Frankfurt, 1683–1805. A collection of printed ordinances, now in the City and University Library.

Vorstellung einiger Ursachen, warumb denen Hand-Werckern zu gestatten / ihre eigene Vorsteher zu erwehlen / auch Lehr-Brieffe ausszufertigen und in Handwercks-Strittigkeiten dero erforderte Bedencken / an ausswärtige Meister ausszustellen / und bey anderen wiederumb zu erfordern. Presented to the imperial commission 17 May 1714.

Wichtige Gründe, welche bewehren und erläutern, dass die in dem Bürger Vertrag §22 zum Vergleich zwischen E. E. Rath und der Bürgerschaft in Frankfurth biss zu Kays. . . . Ratification aussgesetzte Reduction der übermässigen Mänge jüdischer Innwohner . . . keineswegs finaliter auffgehoben, sondern dieses bloss eine Interims-Verordnung gewesen, folglich solche Reduction annoch gesucht werden dürffte . . . N.p., 1714.

III. Secondary Works on Frankfurt

Behrends, Johann Adolph, *Der Einwohner in Frankfurt am Mayn in Absicht auf seine Fruchtbarkeit, Mortalität und Gesundheit.* Frankfurt, 1771.

Bender, Johann Heinrich, *Der frühere und jetzige Zustand der Israeliten zu Frankfurt am Main.* Frankfurt, 1833.

————, *Handbuch des Frankfurter Privatrechts.* Frankfurt, 1848.

Beyer, Peter, "Leipzig und Frankfurt am Main: Leipzigs Aufstieg zur ersten deutschen Messestadt," *Jahrbuch für Regionalgeschichte* 2 (1967), 62–86.

Bleicher, Heinrich, ed., *Statistische Beschreibung der Stadt Frankfurt am Main und ihrer Bevölkerung. II. Theil: Die innere Gliederung der Bevölkerung.* Frankfurt, 1895.

Böhme, Helmut, *Frankfurt und Hamburg: Des deutschen Reichs Silber- und Goldloch und die allerenglischste Stadt des Kontinents.* Frankfurt, 1968.

————, "Stadtregiment, Repräsentativverfassung und Wirtschaftskonjunktur in Frankfurt am Main und Hamburg im 19. Jahrhundert," *Jahrbuch für Geschichte der oberdeutschen Reichsstädte* 15 (1969), 75–146.

Bothe, Friedrich, *Beiträge zur Wirtschafts- und Sozialgeschichte der Reichsstadt Frankfurt.* Leipzig, 1906.

————, *Die Entwicklung der direkten Besteuerung in der Reichsstadt Frankfurt bis zur Revolution 1612–1614.* Leipzig, 1906.

————, "Der Frankfurter Fettmilchaufstand 1612–14 im Rahmen der deutschen Politik," Typescript in the Frankfurt City Archive. c. 1925.

————, *Geschichte der Stadt Frankfurt am Main.* Frankfurt, 1913.

Braubach, Max, "Eine Wirtschaftsenquête am Rhein im 17. Jahrhundert," *Rheinische Vierteljahrsblätter* 13 (1948), 51–86.

Bräuer, Karl, "Frankfurter Polizeiordnungen im 17. Jahrhundert," *Alt-Frankfurt* 1 (1909), 58–61.

————, "Das Gesindewesen im alten Frankfurt," *Alt-Frankfurt* 4 (1912), 97–104.

Bücher, Karl, *Die Berufe der Stadt Frankfurt a. M. im Mittelalter.* Leipzig, 1914.

————, *Die Bevölkerung von Frankfurt am Main im XIV. und XV. Jahrhundert.* Tübingen, 1886.

Darmstaedter, Paul, *Das Grossherzogtum Frankfurt.* Frankfurt, 1901.

Dechent, Hermann, *Kirchengeschichte von Frankfurt am Main seit der Reformation.* 2v. Leipzig and Frankfurt, 1913–1921.

Diehl, Robert, *Frankfurt am Main im Spiegel alter Reisebeschreibungen vom 15. bis zum 19. Jahrhundert.* Frankfurt, 1939.

————, "Verzeichnis des in den Jahren 1938 bis 1956 neu erschienenen Frankfurter Schrifttums," *AFGK* Heft 45 (1957), 49–146.

————, "Verzeichnis des seit 1928 neu erschienenen Frankfurter Schrifttums," *AFGK* 4. Folge 5 (1938), 115–164.

Dietz, Alexander, *Frankfurter Bürgerbuch*. Frankfurt, 1897.

————, *Frankfurter Handelsgeschichte*. 4v in 5. Frankfurt, 1910–1925.

Elkan, Eugen, *Das Frankfurter Gewerberecht von 1617–1631*. Tübingen, 1890.

Faber, Johann Heinrich, *Topographische, politische und historische Beschreibung der Reichs- Wahl- und Handelsstadt Frankfurt am Mayn*. 2v. Frankfurt, 1788–1789.

Feine, Hans Erich, review of Paul Hohenemser's *Verfassungsstreit*, *ZRG GA* 44 (1924), 449–455.

Friedrichs, Heinz F., "Sippe und Amt in der Reichsstadt Frankfurt," *Familie und Volk: Zeitschrift für Genealogie und Bevölkerungskunde* 5 (1956), 99–103, 146–150, 180–183; *Genealogie* 13 (1964), 49–62.

Gerber, Harry, Otto Ruppersberg, and Louis Vogel, *Der allgemeine Almosenkasten zu Frankfurt am Main 1531–1931*. Frankfurt, 1931.

Gercken, Philipp Wilhelm, *Historisch-statistische Beschreibung der freien Reichsstadt Frankfurt am Main*. Worms, 1788.

Geschichte der Handelskammer zu Frankfurt a. M. (1707–1908): Beiträge zur Frankfurter Handelsgeschichte, ed. Handelskammer zu Frankfurt a.M. Frankfurt, 1908.

Gley, Werner, "Grundriss und Wachstum der Stadt Frankfurt am Main: Eine stadtgeographische und statistische Untersuchung," *Festschrift zur Hundertjahrfeier des Vereins für Geographie und Statistik zu Frankfurt am Main*, ed. Wolfgang Hartke (Frankfurt, 1936), 53–100.

Greuner, Hans, *Rangverhältnisse im städtischen Bürgertum der Barockzeit unter besonderer Berücksichtigung der Freien Reichsstadt Frankfurt am Main*. Frankfurt, 1957.

Habich, Wolfgang, *Das Weinungeld der Reichsstadt Frankfurt am Main: Die Entwicklungsgeschichte einer Getränkesteuer in Mittelalter und Neuzeit im Zusammenhang mit dem sogenannten Kingenheimer-Prozess*. Aalen, 1967.

Hanauer, W[ilhelm], "Historisch-statistische Untersuchungen über uneheliche Geburten," *Zeitschrift für Hygiene und Infektionskrankheiten* 108 (1928), 656–684.

————, "Der Gang der Sterblichkeit in Frankfurt am Main vom Mittelalter bis zur Mitte des 19. Jahrhunderts," *Soziale Medizin und Hygiene* 2 (1907), 237–246.

————, "Geschichte der Sterblichkeit und der öffentlichen Gesundheitspflege in Frankfurt a. M.," *Deutsche Vierteljahrschrift für öffentliche Gesundheitspflege* 39 (1907), 498–518; 40 (1908), 651–678.

————, "Zur Statistik der jüdischen Bevölkerung in Frankfurt am Main," *Zeitschrift für Demographie und Statistik der Juden* 6 (1910), 137–145, 153–159.

Herberger, Bruno, *Die Organisation des Schuhmacherhandwerks zu Frankfurt a. Main bis zum Ende des 18. Jahrhunderts.* N.p., 1931.

Herforth, Willy, "Die Lage des Frankfurter Gewerbes (in ihren Grundzügen) während des 16. und 17. Jahrhunderts." Dissertation. Frankfurt, 1923.

Herr, Jacob, ed., *Bilder aus dem katholischen Leben der Stadt Frankfurt a. M. im Lichte der Domweihe.* Frankfurt, 1939.

Hohenemser, Paul, "Beamtenwesen in Frankfurt a. M. um 1700," *Alt-Frankfurt* 3 (1911), 65–72.

————, "Bürgerkapitän Fritsch und der Beginn des Frankfurter Verfassungskampfes 1705–1712," *Alt-Frankfurt* 2 (1910), 1–13.

————, *Der Frankfurter Verfassungsstreit 1705–1732 und die kaiserlichen Kommissionen.* Frankfurt am Main, 1920.

Horne, Anton, *Geschichte von Frankfurt am Main in gedrängter Darstellung.* Frankfurt, 1882.

Hussong, Walter, *Das Schneiderhandwerk in Frankfurt am Main und das Schneiderhandwerk in Heilbronn: Ein Vergleich.* Gelnhausen, 1936.

Jung, Rudolf, "Die Anfänge der Porzellan-Fabrikation in Frankfurt a. M.," *AFGK* 3. Folge 4 (1893), 368–374.

————, "Das Frankfurter Bürgermilitär im XVIII. Jahrhundert," *Alt-Frankfurt* 4 (1912), 40–50.

————, "Die Frankfurter Prozellanfabrik im Prozellanhofe 1666–1773," *AFGK* 3. Folge 7 (1901), 221–241.

————, *Das Frankfurter Stadtarchiv: seine Bestände und seine Geschichte.* Frankfurt, 1909.

————, "Der Grosse Kurfürst und die Frankfurter Reformierten," *Festschrift für Friedrich Clemens Ebrard* (Frankfurt, 1920), 3–16.

Kirchen-Geschichte von denen Reformirten in Frankfurt am Mayn . . . Frankfurt and Leipzig, 1751.

Körner, Hans, *Frankfurter Patrizier: Historisch-Genealogisches Handbuch der Adeligen Ganerbschaft des Hauses Alten-Limpurg zu Frankfurt am Main.* Munich, 1971.

Kracauer, Isidor, "Beiträge zur Geschichte der Frankfurter Juden im Dreissigjährigen Krieg," [*Geigers*] *Zeitschrift für die Geschichte der Juden in Deutschland* 3 (1889), 130–158, 337–372; 4 (1890), 18–28.

————, *Geschichte der Juden in Frankfurt am Main.* 2v. Frankfurt, 1927.

————, "Die Geschichte der Judengasse in Frankfurt am Main," *Festschrift zur Jahrhundertfeier der Realschule der israelitischen Gemeinde (Philanthropin) zu Frankfurt am Main 1804–1904* (Frankfurt, 1904), 303–451.

————, "Die Juden Frankfurts im Fettmilch'schen Aufstand 1612–1618," [*Geigers*] *Zeitschrift für die Geschichte der Juden in Deutschland* 4 (1890), 127–169, 319–365; 5 (1891), 1–26.

————, "Das Militärwesen der Reichsstadt Frankfurt a. M. im XVIII. Jahrhundert," *AFGK* 3. Folge 12 (1920), 1–180.

Kriegk, Georg Ludwig, *Deutsche Kulturbilder aus dem achtzehnten Jahrhundert.* Leipzig, 1874.

————, *Deutsches Bürgerthum im Mittelalter nach urkundlichen Forschungen und mit besonderer Beziehung auf Frankfurt a. M.* 2v. Frankfurt, 1868–1871.

————, *Geschichte von Frankfurt am Main in ausgewählten Darstellung.* Frankfurt, 1871.

Krug, Friedrich, *Diarium der Frankfurter Raths-Wahlen . . . oder Chronologisches Verzeichniss aller Raths-Glieder vom 11. März 1717 an* . . . Frankfurt, 1846.

Lenhardt, Heinz, "Feste und Feiern des Frankfurter Handwerks: Ein Beitrag zur Brauchtums- und Zunftgeschichte," *AFGK* 5. Folge 1. Band 2. Heft (1950), 1–120.

————, *Die Landwirtschaft der Reichsstadt Frankfurt a. M.* Gelnhausen, 1933.

Lerner, Franz, *Beiträge zur Geschichte des Frankfurter Patrizier-Geschlechtes von Holzhausen*. Frankfurt, 1953.

————, *Die Frankfurter Patriziergesellschaft Alten-Limpurg und ihre Stiftungen*. Frankfurt, 1952.

————, *Geschichte des Frankfurter Metzger-Handwerks*. Frankfurt, 1959.

————, *Gestalten aus der Geschichte des Frankfurter Patrizier-Geschlechtes von Holzhausen*. Frankfurt, 1953.

Lüttecke, Wilhelm, *Das Benderhandwerk zu Frankfurt a. Main bis zur Einführung der Gewerbefreiheit*. Borne-Leipzig, 1927.

Meinert, Hermann, "Das Stadtarchiv Frankfurt am Main im zweiten Weltkriege," *AFGK* 5. Folge 1 (1948), 35–41.

Moritz, Johann Anton, *Versuch einer Einleitung in die Staatsverfassung derer oberrheinischen Reichsstädte*. Erster Theil: *Reichsstadt Frankfurt*. Frankfurt, 1785. Zweiter Theil: *Reichsstadt Frankfurt*. Frankfurt, 1786.

Nathusius-Neinstedt, Heinrich v., "Die Frankfurter Kirchenbuchführung," *AFGK* 3. Folge 6 (1899), 161–186.

Quarck, Max, *Soziale Kämpfe in Frankfurt am Main vom Mittelalter bis an die Schwelle der grossen Revolution*. Frankfurt, 1911.

Richel, Arthur, "Verzeichnis der seit 1914 neu erschienenen Frankfurter Literatur," *AFGK* 4. Folge 2 (1929), 220–256.

Römer-Büchner, B[enedict] J[acob], *Die Entwicklung der Stadtverfassung und die Bürgervereine der Stadt Frankfurt am Main*. Frankfurt, 1855.

Ruppersberg, Otto, "Frankfurt a. M. und das Reichskammergericht," *AFGK* 4. Folge 4 (1933), 81–106.

Scharff, Friedrich, "Die Niederländischen und die Französische Gemeinde in Frankfurt a. M.," *AFGK* Neue (2.) Folge 2 (1862), 245–317.

Schnapper-Arndt, Gottlieb, *Beiträge zur Frankfurter Finanzgeschichte*, ed. Karl Bräuer. Frankfurt, 1910. Originally *AFGK* 3. Folge 10 (1910), 29–76.

————, *Studien zur Geschichte der Lebenshaltung in Frankfurt a. M. während des 17. und 18. Jahrhunderts*, ed. Karl Bräuer. 2v. Frankfurt, 1915.

Spaett, Georg, *Das Frankfurter Fischereigewerbe als Beitrag zur Zunft-geschichte*. Grünberg i. H., 1927.

Speyer, Otto, *Eine unblutige Revolution: Der Frankfurter Verfassungs-kampf im XVIII. Jahrhundert*. Offprint from the *Frankfurter Zeitung* (December, 1897).

"Theuere Erinnerungen aus der Vorzeit," *Frankfurter Jahrbücher* 11 (1838), 251–253.

Unna, Joseph, *Statistik der Frankfurter Juden bis zum Jahre 1866*. Frankfurt, 1931.

Voelcker, Heinrich, ed., *Die Stadt Goethes: Frankfurt am Main im XVIII. Jahrhundert*. Frankfurt, 1932.

Witzel, Georg, "Gewerbegeschichtliche Studien zur niederländischen Einwanderung in Deutschland im 16. Jahrhundert," *Westdeutsche Zeitschrift für Geschichte und Kunst* 29 (1910), 117–182, 419–451. The promised concluding section of this highly valuable article has, to my knowledge, never been published.

Wolff, Emil, *Zur Geschichte des Bierbrauergewerbes in Frankfurt a. M. vom Jahre 1288 bis 1904*. Nürnberg, 1904.

IV. Related Secondary Works

Albrecht, Hans, "Das Lübecker Braugewerbe bis zur Aufhebung der Brauerzunft 1865," *Zeitschrift des Vereins für Lübeckische Geschichte und Altertumskunde* 17 (1915), 63–117, 205–266.

Asch, Jürgen, *Rat und Bürgerschaft in Lübeck 1598–1669: Die verfassungsrechtlichen Auseinandersetzungen im 17. Jahrhundert und ihre sozialen Hintergründe*. Lübeck, 1961.

Barber, Bernard, and Seymour M. Lipset, contributions to "Social Stratification," *International Encyclopedia of the Social Sciences* (New York, 1968), XV, 288–316.

Barkhausen, Max, "Der Aufstieg der rheinischen Industrie im 18. Jahrhundert und die Entstehung eines industriellen Grossbürgertums," *Rheinische Vierteljahrsblätter* 19 (1954), 135–177.

Bátori, Ingrid, *Die Reichsstadt Augsburg im 18. Jahrhundert: Verfassung, Finanzen und Reformversuche*. Göttingen, 1969.

Borst, Otto, "Die Kulturbedeutung der oberdeutschen Reichsstadt am

Ende des alten Reiches," *Blätter für deutsche Landesgeschichte* 100 (1964), 159–246.

————, "Zur Verfassung und Staatlichkeit oberdeutscher Reichsstädte am Ende des alten Reiches," *Esslinger Studien* 10 (1964), 106–194.

Brunner, Otto, "Souveränitätsproblem und Sozialstruktur in den deutschen Reichsstädten der früheren Neuzeit," *VSWG* 50 (1963), 329–360. Now included in his *Neue Wege der Verfassungs- und Sozialgeschichte* (Göttingen, 1968), 294–321.

Coser, Lewis, *The Functions of Social Conflict*. New York, 1956.

Domarus, Max, *Rudolf Franz Erwein v. Schönborn*. Wiesentheid, 1954.

————, *Würzburger Kirchenfürsten aus dem Hause Schönborn*. Wiesentheid, 1951.

Eisenbart, Lieselotte C., *Kleiderordnungen der deutschen Städte zwischen 1350 und 1700*. Göttingen, 1962.

Ewald, Martin, *Der hamburgische Senatssyndicus*. Hamburg, 1954.

Feine, Hans Erich, "Einwirkungen des absoluten Staatsgedankens auf das deutsche Kaisertum im 17. und 18. Jahrhundert, insbesondere bei der Besetzung der Reichsbistümer," *ZRG GA* 42 (1921), 474–481.

————, "Zur Verfassungsentwicklung des Heil. Röm. Reiches seit dem Westfälischen Frieden," *ZRG GA* 52 (1932), 65–133.

Fischer, Georg, "Absolutistische Handwerkerpolitik und Friedrich Karl von Schönborn," *Jahrbuch für fränkische Landesforschung* 29 (1969), 19–38.

Fischer, Wolfram, *Handwerksrecht und Handwerkswirtschaft um 1800*. Berlin, 1955.

Ford, Franklin L., *Strasbourg in Transition 1648–1789*. Cambridge, Mass., 1958.

Franz, Günther, *Der Dreissigjährige Krieg und das deutsche Volk*. 3rd ed.; Stuttgart, 1961.

Hantsch, Hugo, *Reichsvizekanzler Friedrich Karl Graf von Schönborn, 1674–1746: Einige Kapitel zur politischen Geschichte Kaiser Josefs I. und Karls VI*. Augsburg, 1929.

Hiesel, Rudolf, *Die staatsrechtliche und soziologische Stellung des Stadtadels im deutschen Mittelalter, hauptsächlich in den oberdeutschen Städten*. Dissertation; University of Mainz, 1952.

Hofmann, Hanns Hubert, "Nobiles Norimbergenses: Beobachtungen zur Struktur der reichsstädtischen Oberschicht," *Untersuchungen zur gesellschaftlichen Struktur der mittelalterlichen Städte in Europa*, ed. Theodor Mayer (Konstanz, 1966), 53–92.

Hoskins, William George, "English Provincial Towns in the Early Sixteenth Century," *Provincial England* (London, 1963), 68–85.

Hoyer, Karl, "Das Bremer Brauereigewerbe," *Hansische Geschichtsblätter* 19 (1913), 193–232.

Keller, Siegmund, "Der Adelstand des süddeutschen Patriziates," *Festschrift Otto Gierke* (Weimar, 1911), 741–758.

Keyser, Erich, ed., *Hessisches Städtebuch*. Volume IV, i, of *Deutsches Städtebuch: Handbuch städtischer Geschichte*, ed. Erich Keyser. Stuttgart, 1957.

Maschke, Erich, "Verfassung und soziale Kräfte in der deutschen Stadt des späten Mittelalters, vornehmlich in Oberdeutschland," *VSWG* 46 (1959), 289–349, 433–476.

Mauersberg, Hans, *Wirtschafts- und Sozialgeschichte zentraleuropäischer Städte in neuerer Zeit: Dargestellt an den Beispielen von Basel, Frankfurt a. M., Hamburg, Hannover und München*. Göttingen, 1960.

Mols, Roger, *Introduction à la démographie historique des villes d'Europe du XIVᵉ au XVIIIᵉ siècle*. 3v. Louvain, 1954–1956.

Mousnier, Roland, "Problèmes de methode dans l'étude des structures sociales des seizième, dix-septième, dix-huitième siècles," *Spiegel der Geschichte: Festgabe für Max Braubach zum 10. April 1964*, ed. K. Repgen and S. Skalweit (Münster, 1964), 550–564. Now available in his *La plume, la faucille et le marteau* (Paris, 1970), 12–26.

———, *Problèmes de stratification sociale: Actes du colloque international (1966)*. Paris, 1968.

———, *Problèmes de stratification sociale: Deux cahiers de la noblesse pour les états généraux de 1649–1651*. Paris, 1965.

Ossowski, Stanislaw, *Class Structure in the Social Consciousness*. New York, 1963.

Prange, Ruth, *Die bremische Kaufmannschaft des 16. und 17. Jahrhunderts in sozialgeschichtlicher Betrachtung*. Bremen, 1963.

Riedenauer, Erwin, "Kaiser und Patriziat: Struktur und Funktion des reichsstädtischen Patriziats im Blickpunkt kaiserlicher Adelspolitik von Karl V. bis Karl VI.," *Zeitschrift für bayerische Landesgeschichte* 30 (1967), 526–653.

Rössler, Hellmuth, ed., *Deutsches Patriziat 1430–1740.* Limburg/Lahn, 1968.

Weber, Max, "Class, Status, Party," *From Max Weber: Essays in Sociology*, tr. and ed. H. H. Gerth and C. Wright Mills (New York, 1946), 180–195.

Wiest, Ekkehard, *Die Entwicklung des Nürnberger Gewerbes zwischen 1648 und 1806.* Stuttgart, 1968.

Wild, Karl, *Lothar Franz von Schönborn: Bischof von Bamberg und Erzbischof von Mainz 1693–1729.* Heidelberg, 1904.

Index